CONTAINMENT IN
THE COMMUNITY

CONTAINMENT IN THE COMMUNITY

Supportive Frameworks for Thinking About Antisocial Behaviour and Mental Health

edited by
Alla Rubitel and David Reiss

Routledge
Taylor & Francis Group

LONDON AND NEW YORK

First published 2011 by Karnac Books Ltd

Published 2018 by Routledge
2 Park Square, Milton Park, Abingdon, Oxon OX14 4RN
711 Third Avenue, New York, NY 10017, USA

Routledge is an imprint of the Taylor & Francis Group, an informa business

Copyright © 2011 to Alla Rubitel and David Reiss for the edited collection,
and to the individual authors for their contributions.

The rights of the contributors to be identified as the authors of this work
have been asserted in accordance with §§ 77 and 78 of the Copyright
Design and Patents Act 1988.

British Library Cataloguing in Publication Data

A C.I.P. for this book is available from the British Library

ISBN 978 1 85575 848 3 (pbk)

Edited, designed and produced by The Studio Publishing Services Ltd
www.publishingservicesuk.co.uk
e-mail: studio@publishingservicesuk.co.uk

CONTENTS

ACKNOWLEDGEMENTS

First, and most vitally, we thank all the contributors of chapters to this volume for taking valuable time out of their busy lives and schedules to share their thoughts, emotional experiences, and knowledge. We also express our deep gratitude to all the organizations and teams, as well as the individuals within them and their clients, which have inspired us to undertake the endeavour of editing this text and provided the essential human and clinical material on which it is based.

We would like to particularly express our debt to Philip Stokoe for his generous support and thoughtfulness, as well as for providing the "Supervision of supervision workshop", which he facilitated for many years at the Tavistock Clinic. Of course, this workshop could not have taken place without the participation of all the other members, and we acknowledge their vital contribution as well.

AR gives special thanks to Valerie Charles for her help with the editing of her chapter. AR is also grateful to David Armstrong and Dorothy Lloyd Owen for their encouragement to engage with emotions that are, apparently, very difficult to stay with but, when understood, often lead to powerful insights.

We are very grateful to the exceptionally talented artist Aude Van Ryn, who produced the book's cover.

Finally, we would like to express our heartfelt appreciation of the hard work that Stanley Ruszczynski and David Morgan, the Portman Papers series editors, have put into this project, both for giving us the opportunity to contribute the second book in the series, as well as for their support and assistance during the commissioning and editing process.

Alla Rubitel and David Reiss
London
January 2011

ABOUT THE EDITORS AND CONTRIBUTORS

John Adlam is consultant adult psychotherapist in reflective practice and team development with South London and Maudsley Foundation NHS Trust; principal adult psychotherapist and lead for group psychotherapies with the St George's Adult Eating Disorders Service at Springfield Hospital, Tooting, and was formerly principal adult psychotherapist with the Henderson Hospital. He trained in psychoanalytical group psychotherapy at the Tavistock Clinic, and in forensic psychotherapeutic studies at the Portman Clinic. He is a visiting lecturer in forensic mental health at St George's, University of London, and was formerly vice-president of the International Association for Forensic Psychotherapy. He worked for many years in voluntary sector supported housing projects for mentally disordered offenders, and now trains and consults to a range of services working with homelessness, severe personality disorder, and chronic social exclusion.

Jina Barrett is a psychoanalytic psychotherapist and organizational consultant. She holds two National Health Service (NHS) posts: at the Adult Directorate of the Tavistock Clinic, where she trained, she is lead for consultation to organisations and manager of a training and consultation service for front-line health and social care staff aimed at the developing worker and organizational health; at Camden and Islington NHS Foundation Trust, from 2005–2009, she developed and co-ordinated a consultation and training service for voluntary organizations working with people with personality disorder, a post created as part of the National Personality Disorder Development Programme in 2004. She was a member of the team responsible for developing the National Personality Disorder Knowledge and Understanding Framework (PD KUF) for the Department of Health 2007–2009.

Nick Benefield is currently senior policy advisor and head of the Department of Health Personality Disorder Programme. In this role he is responsible for policy oversight covering the Emerging PD, Mainstream Mental Health PD, and Dangerous and Severe PD pilot programmes as well as development of training and education initiatives in personality disorder. He is also joint head of the Department of Health (DH)/National Offender Management Service (NOMS) Offender Personality Disorder Policy Programme responsible for strategy and policy implementation of the forthcoming Offender PD Strategy. His background is in social work, analytic psychotherapy and service commissioning working in the health, social care and voluntary sectors.

Ruth Berkowitz, PhD, is a senior member of the British Association of Psychotherapists (BAP) as well as a BAP trainer. She is a consultant adult psychotherapist at the Portman Clinic, and also works in private practice in London.

William Crouch is a clinical psychologist in psychoanalytic psychotherapy in the Adolescent Department, Tavistock and Portman NHS Foundation Trust. Before this, he set up and ran a mental health service in an inner-city Youth Offending Team (YOT). As well as working as a clinician, he has taught and conducted research in many areas of child development. He has a particular interest in offending and self-harm by young people. He is joint editor (with Steve Briggs and Alessandra Lemma) of *Relating to Self-harm and Suicide* (Routledge, 2008).

Oliver Dale, MB, BS, MRCPsych, a consultant adult psychiatrist at Charing Cross Hospital, London, is the responsible clinician for a recovery ward and leads the development of services for those with personality disorder in Hammersmith and Fulham. He is training as a Jungian analyst at the British Association of Psychotherapists. He is interested in personality disorder and the manifestation of personality difficulties in those with major mental illness.

Rob Hale has been a consultant psychotherapist and psychoanalyst at the Portman clinic since 1980. His clinical interest has been in the area of sexual perversions, particularly paedophilia. Over the past fifteen years, he has developed a number of consultations with medium and high secure hospitals. These focus on the clinical problems posed by the patients, and their impact on both the individual staff member and on the institution as a whole. He was formerly the director of the Portman Clinic and the postgraduate dean of the Tavistock and Portman Trust.

Gabriel Kirtchuk is a consultant psychiatrist in psychotherapy and psychoanalyst. He has worked in forensic settings for many years, and has established a department of forensic psychotherapy in a medium secure unit in London. He is also lead clinician of the National Forensic Psychotherapy Training and Development Strategy and an honorary clinical senior lecturer at Imperial College London. His areas of interest include the development of psychotherapeutic approaches within forensic mental health, as well as training and educational programmes in this field.

David Morgan is a clinical psychologist and consultant adult psychotherapist at the Portman Clinic. He is a fellow of the British Psychoanalytic Society, a training analyst and supervisor for the British Psychoanalytic Association, and works in private practice. He has authored a number of journal articles and book chapters.

David Reiss, MA MPhil DFP FRCPsych, is consultant forensic psychiatrist and deputy medical director (Medical Education) at West London Mental Health NHS Trust, and an honorary clinical senior lecturer at Imperial College London. His research interests examine the interface between clinical forensic psychiatry and public policy, including work on personality disorder, recidivism, homicide inquiries, and educational issues. His clinical and educational work focuses on enabling the multi-disciplinary team to gain an enhanced understanding of patients, thereby improving care and reducing risk.

Rosemary Richards, MRCPsych, is the clinical director and associate medical director for the Child and Adolescent Mental Health Service at 2gether NHS Foundation Trust for Gloucestershire. She completed her forensic psychotherapeutic studies at the Portman Clinic.

Alla Rubitel, MD MRCPsych, is a locum consultant psychiatrist in general and forensic psychotherapy. She works at both the Gordon Hospital, Central and North West London NHS Foundation Trust, and the Portman Clinic. Her interests include psychoanalytic approaches to understanding and treating patients suffering from violence, delinquency, and perversions; as well as supervision and teaching of medical and non-medical staff. She has contributed to research in the Adult Attachment Interview and forensic personality disordered patients. She is also an analyst with a private practice.

Christopher Scanlon is consultant psychotherapist and lead for group psychotherapy, reflective practice, and team development in the Department of Psychotherapy, St Thomas' Hospital, South London and Maudsley Foundation NHS Trust. He was formerly consultant psychotherapist and lead for training and consultation, Henderson Hospital Services. He is a training group analyst at The Institute of Group Analysis (London); senior visiting research fellow, Centre for Psychosocial Studies, University of the West of England, visiting lecturer in forensic psychotherapy, St George's University of London, has acted as a professional adviser to the Social Inclusion Unit at the Department for Communities and Local Government, and was a member of the Department of Health's Severe Personality Disorder Expert Advisory Group. He was a trustee of the Zito Trust, a mental health charity which campaigned for improved services for mentally disordered offenders and their victims.

Mike Solomon, BA (Cantab) MSc MA DClinPsy, CPsychol, member of the British Psychological Society, is a consultant clinical psychologist. He works in both the Child & Family Directorate at the Tavistock Clinic, and the London Borough of Camden's Secondary Behaviour Support Service. His clinical work is with young people excluded from school, their families, and professionals working with them. He also offers training and consultancy to individuals and teams working with young people, particularly those in education.

Philip Stokoe BSc, MSc, CQSW, FInstPsychoanal, is the clinical director of the Adult Department of the Tavistock & Portman NHS Foundation Trust, a psychoanalyst in private practice working with adults and couples, and an organizational consultant, providing consultation to a wide range of organizations. His interests include the application of psychoanalysis to all sorts of settings: supervision, leadership, groups, organizations, ethics and couple relationships. He is also visiting honorary professor, City University, member of the APP, and member of OPUS.

Richard Taylor, Bs, DFP, MRCPsych, trained at the Maudsley Hospital and Institute of Psychiatry. He has been consultant forensic psychiatrist at the North London Forensic Service since 2000. He was a visiting consultant forensic psychiatrist at HMP Holloway between 2001 and 2006, and has been involved in service developments for female mentally disordered offenders in the NHS and the private sector. Dr Taylor was consultant for the Camden Forensic Outreach Service based at the Royal Free Hospital, where he provided consultation liaison service to local adult mental health services. He is the medical member of the London Strategic Management Board for Multiagency Public Protection Arrangements (MAPPA) and he is a member of the Special Committee on Human Rights of the Royal College of Psychiatrists. Research interests include: the ethics of confidentiality and public protection, fraud, terrorism, and women who are mentally disordered offenders

Jessica Yakeley, MB, BChir, MRCP, MRCPsych, is consultant psychiatrist in forensic psychotherapy at the Portman Clinic and director of medical education and associate medical director, Tavistock and Portman NHS Foundation Trust. She is also a fellow of the British Psychoanalytic Society, and has a small private practice in London. She has a longstanding interest in medical education, and has published papers on risk assessment, MAPPA, prison health, antisocial personality disorder, and a recent book on psychodynamic approaches to violence. Current research includes a trial of mentalization-based treatment for men with antisocial personality disorder.

PREFACE

Alla Rubitel and David Reiss

We developed the concept of this book when we were both work-ing together at a medium secure psychiatric unit as a senior trainee (specialist registrar) in forensic psychotherapy (AR) and a consul-tant forensic psychiatrist (DR). Our work included the provision of outreach support and links to a variety of mental health and crim-inal justice system community settings. In all these environments, we were struck by the complexity of the psychopathology of the patients, as well as their high level of clinical and social need. We experienced at first hand how working with this population has powerful effects on all involved in frontline care and management. While there are a variety of existing structures designed to support professionals in their attempts to process these forces, both their provision and uptake is patchy. We noticed that many of these insti-tutions, instead of providing space for thought and reflection, have various risk policies. Although these documents may contribute to a helpful framework of care, if used in isolation they can create a superficial illusion that safety and security is being attended to effectively, where this is actually deficient.

We have been particularly interested to observe and try to understand how a combination of mental illness and offending behaviour has an impact not only on our patients, but also the staff looking after them. The latter, when faced with the patients' difficulties in a relatively close relationship, which is intended to be therapeutic, often develop strong defences. Experienced and well-trained staff in apparently well-supported high and medium security inpatient settings may experience "burn out", which can result in difficulties such as extended sick leave, or an apparent "blind and deaf" response to the risks that patients present.

The high walls of secure institutions are only able to contain temporarily the anxiety about reoffending risk carried by both the community and mentally disturbed individuals themselves. Moving on from hospital into less secure community settings, both staff and patients leave behind the real physical barriers which served psychologically to lock anxieties out, protecting the patients from their unconscious fears that they will reoffend, as well as damping down the more conscious fears of the public. The latter have been at least partially addressed in England and Wales through the Multi-Agency Public Protection Arrangements, described in this volume by Jessica Yakeley and Richard Taylor, designed to increase co-operation between various community agencies dealing with offenders, including those with mental disorder.

Staff resources and skills to support the task of rehabilitation appear scarce outside the walls in comparison to within high and medium security hospital units. Yet, the individual forensic patient's needs are still very high: they require intense rehabilitation, as well as pharmacological treatment to prevent a relapse if they are mentally ill. Professionals commonly experience anxiety and tension when delivering this complex task, an issue explored by Alla Rubitel, who describes how staff members manage to work with chronically mentally ill offender patients in a forensic hostel. The provision of support to such settings is also discussed in the chapter by Jina Barrett. Caring staff in such institutions not infrequently experience potentially very risky situations, which have to be dealt with in a much less structured and supported environment than pertains in secure hospital units. There may also be less expertise available in such settings, except in highly specialized services, which can lead to difficulties with teamwork, with problems such as excessive anxiety and splitting, as reflected in Rosemary Richard's essay about how a homicidal adolescent was managed in the community.

Although many general psychiatric teams are willing and able to look after complex, risky patients, some services express concern about their capacity to assess and manage them. As a consequence, the latter teams may be reluctant to engage with mentally ill offender patients, perhaps frightened of the consequences if things go wrong. They might believe that they are unable to deal with such cases in the absence of sufficient back-up, for example by forensic colleagues, or because they perceive they might lack appropriate internal resources. Richard Taylor explores the area of the interface between general and forensic psychiatric services.

Some individuals in the community have antisocial and borderline personality disorder traits, but their level of perceived dangerousness is not high enough, and offences committed already are not grave enough, to be deemed to require the routine attention of forensic psychiatrists. At different stages of their lives, they may be perceived as too risky, not sufficiently psychotic, and too difficult to engage by general psychiatrists and/or therapeutic communities. However, they may pose a significant and continuing threat with regard to potential violent acting out behaviour that may well warrant care by the multi-disciplinary team. Some mental healthcare teams may not consider these individuals to be their patients at all; others may view them as priority patients, or they may be seen as patients that nobody can deal with. They might be picked up by forensic teams as a gesture of goodwill without community resources available to look after them, or general psychiatrists may attempt to provide a cohesive treatment plan to individuals who apparently do not want to be patients. These risky and vulnerable individuals crop up in different statutory and non-statutory services at various times, often falling into the cracks between fragmented services. They may be accepted and discharged again just after or before they create another episode of disturbance. Rob Hale looks at these issues in his chapter on personality disordered offenders, highlighting the diagnostic value of the staff's emotional responses. There is clearly something amiss for these service users to act the way they do: attention and understanding is needed to find meaning in what may appear to be meaningless acts.

Mentally ill adults and adolescents who behave in antisocial ways, and those with abnormal personality traits, become well known to services through the amount of action, frequently not allowing much space for thought, that develops around them. Professional carers in community settings need to find ways of understanding and engaging with these individuals, which should involve responding appropriately rather than knee-jerk reacting to the disturbance. They may be seen as projecting their inner chaos outside themselves in the unconscious hope that they will be free of it, yet, in the process, generating a new external disturbance. Society and its community facilities may attempt to get rid of the unwanted problem in a similar fashion by expelling these difficult individuals and the disorder they stand for into more secure places. Will Crouch and Mike Solomon, respectively, consider these issues, and illustrate them with vignettes. John Adlam and Chris Scanlon reflect on how, to be able to be effective with the antisocial and marginalized, the teams involved have to be able to think about not only who and what they are dealing with, but also their own responses to antisocial individuals or those who are at risk of becoming them.

Psychoanalytical thinking can help us understand these issues, starting from the concept of the unconscious, contributed by Freud. Melanie Klein subsequently elaborated theories of projective identification and unconscious fantasy. Bion subsequently developed our understanding of the container–contained concept, as well as group processes. These ideas were expanded and applied to institutional dynamics by Isobel Menzies Lyth, Tom Main, R. D. Hinshelwood, and many important others. They described defensive manoeuvres which deal with unbearable anxieties about change in organizations as well as staff contact with patients. However, it is not the remit of this book to focus on the history of these developments, although we acknowledge them.

The contributors to this volume make reference to the psychoanalytical literature throughout, yet we have asked them to refrain from using complex language wherever possible, in the interest of bringing these ideas to a broad readership. We hope that you will fully understand the psychoanalytical concepts as illustrated by the case examples given, without the use of unnecessary jargon. Most of our contributors are either psychoanalysts, psychoanalytical psychotherapists, or they have been exposed to psychoanalytic concepts and use them. We found that in the work they are presenting here it has been valuable to apply psychoanalytical thinking, as well as some concepts from other modalities, such as systemic and attachment theories, as long as these can be adjusted to various settings and the differing needs of staff. David Morgan has attempted to examine these issues through a number of empathic patient vignettes, and Oliver Dale, David Reiss, and Gabriel Kirtchuk address the issue of how to turn complex theory into useful teamwork, outlining the practicality of their framework of interpersonal dynamics.

We have aimed in this volume to bring together and share a variety of accounts from different professionals of their experiences of working in community settings with complex patients and clients; for example, as described by Ruth Berkowitz in her chapter on reflective practice. The reader may find some of the themes run through a number of the chapters, written by different authors. We do not view these as repetitions, but, rather, patterns of experiences and interpersonal dynamics, which have been observed in various settings and are described in first hand accounts: for example, those by Jina Barrett, who writes in her chapter about how to foster a "team mind", and Phil Stokoe who describes how a "healthy institution" might be achieved. To preserve confidentiality, the contributors have developed fictitious cases, based on those that they have discussed, assessed, and treated over a prolonged period of time and in different institutions.

This book is intended to support the wide range of professionals working in healthcare and criminal justice settings in the community, both qualified and unqualified, including social workers, probation officers, psychologists, nurses, hostel support workers, and managers. The chapters illustrate, using vignettes, how understanding of teams' anxieties is facilitated by psychodynamic and systemic ways of thinking, providing insights that can improve functioning, safe practice, and care delivery. The shared experiences and supportive framework models, described in various community settings, provide a blueprint for improved interagency co-operation and should also assist service mangers and budget holders to build such support into the core structure of future services.

The National Health Service is currently being target driven from the top downwards. This potentially supports the creation of defensive structures and polices devoid of meaning, as clinicians may be taken further away from the patients, lacking encouragement to think in a meaningful way about how to deliver quality services. It is very easy to forget that some policies originally had an aim and a reason, perhaps resulting from an inquiry into an adverse event. This top-down culture should not subvert the principle of case work. Actual understanding is difficult to measure, but we hope that researchers will further develop work in this area. Staff working in teams must develop thinking spaces and frameworks that will support their practice. Our volume describes how such structures can be used in a variety of ways to explore anxieties about tasks and to more effectively engage with clients/patients/service users. As professionals, we are not alone in our conundrum; we may hear about a difficult problem experienced many times before by others and still not have a clear answer to it. We should think out solutions to such complex issues, rather than allow a reflex response to happen by default.

We have, therefore, not designed this book to be prescriptive, but to encourage reflection, thoughtfulness, and understanding. We believe that your teams can get together to think about your patients/clients rather than feel persecuted by being forced to tick yet another box on an apparently meaningless form. We hope that the words of our colleagues and ourselves can help achieve this aim.

This book aims to promote excellence in professional practice with individuals at high risk of antisocial and violent behaviour in the community. We invite you to use it to help reflect on how you work and how your team functions. We hope it will provide you with guidance as to how to work more effectively with these individuals, wherever you are in this complex network of support, such as on the front line, leading a team, or commissioning future services.

R. D. Hinshelwood

If you work with disturbed people, it is not improbable you will feel disturbed. Complacently we assume that a professional training immunizes you against anxiety and emotional stress, but it does not. And, moreover, it should not. There is something immeasurably valuable about remaining human when confronted with those people in most pain and conflict. But the emotional labour of care is neither really expected not properly appreciated. Though much can be gained by formal risk management procedures, the actual *emotional* risks to caring professionals get lost in the *mêlée* of everyday work. Then each individual takes his survival into his own hands, often becoming disengaged from the personal encounter that patients and, indeed, most staff seek, and the whole work culture can become corrupted—as did the old mental hospitals.

However what goes wrong is often more illuminating than what goes right, and this book is about turning full circle to take the time and space to consider all these emotional processes, in tandem with the technical ones. This work is about the debilitating processes, about the need for a different kind of awareness, about a psychology of caring, and about the kinds of reflective interventions that are seriously needed to complement the formal measures and policies.

Centred in the work of the Portman Clinic, and in other therapeutic settings working with forensic and personality disordered
patients and offenders, the writers of these chapters have enormous
experience in a wide range of teams and services. They make an
extended study of the needs of those who toil to make a difference
to the lives of the most difficult of clients and patients. Despite
being a tribute to this work, the book is, at its core, a thoughtful collection of essays on managing the emotional impact *on the professionals* who are in contact with the despair and distress of offenders
of all ages, and in all forms of service, including youth offending
teams, forensic hostels, secure units, prison blocks, and therapeutic
communities. The plea is to keep to the fore the quirks of relationships, meanings, impulses, and those intangible human characteristics which cannot always be "managed" but have to be contained.
Without such reflection, there are unassessed risks arising from an
unseen neglect. This book is a triumph in keeping sight of those
unseen dynamics from which the dangerousness of the most dangerous people stems. It balances the formal needs and the strident
impulses of tearaway children, and adults, and helps us think about
the equilibrium points that are more easily dislodged than gained.

Introduction

Nick Benefield

The primary focus of this volume is to support practice by individuals and teams that deal directly either with individuals diagnosed with mental disorder or with those whose presentation causes the same dilemmas for practitioners. The following chapters draw on experience gained across a wide spectrum of settings: within the NHS, the National Offender Management Services (NOMS), and the wider criminal justice services, as well as various services for children, young people, and their families.

The subject matter of this text covers antisocial, offending, and challenging behaviours: in particular, behaviours that create unusual levels of anxiety in practitioners or the public. Valuable insights are offered, with examples, into ways of thinking about these problems and practical guidance is offered on the way professional teams and the individuals within them can develop and maintain effective work. While not explicitly focused on those identified as having a personality disorder, I suggest that the material concerns individuals with psychological difficulties that are pervasive, enduring, and which have a particularly intrusive impact on caring staff members working with them.

In 2007, I jointly edited (with my colleague Dr Rex Haigh) an issue of the *Mental Health Review Journal* on new services for those with personality disorder in England. We suggested a life pathway strategy towards individual disorder that has a number of implications that have an impact on the approach taken to preventative or treatment interventions:

- the epigenetic and developmental nature of such disorders;
- early environmental disruption or failure may appear as later symptom across a range of settings and services;
- the effects of such disorders at an emotional and inter relational level are complex;
- dependency on a diagnostic classification can be problematic;
- the often severe internal states that develop in the individuals themselves, and the impact this has on the relationships they have with others in their world(s), can be transient or long term;
- there is a deep resonance between internal failure and the failure of services to respond with psychologically informed understanding at the right time in the right way.

If we accept these hypotheses, it is our challenge to determine which conceptual framework will enable us to make best use of current knowledge and meet the following three objectives, phrased as questions looking at our still developing knowledge of what works and why.

- What will provide members of staff at all levels and in all settings, where those with these difficulties present, with a basic way of thinking about the problems presented in order to maintain their ability to work in a reflective and enabling way?
- How can we provide specialist practitioners and managers with a deeper level of understanding that will inform the development of more focused interventions based on analytic practice models?
- How can we sustain work with those individuals with complex, entrenched, and resistant behaviours, which can have a debilitating effect on even the most robust and competent practitioners, with the means to stay "alive" and available when this requires a high level of emotional literacy and careful attention to the impact on both practitioner and client?

The numbers of those in need of more informed and consistent intervention is, of course, very significant for the development of health, social care, and criminal justice strategies. In addition to a general population prevalence for personality disorder of between 5–13% (Department of Health, 2003), the Prisoner Cohort Study (Ministry of Justice, 2007) has shown that 73% of prisoners sentenced for sexual or violent offences have one. With the number of Indeterminate Public Protection (IPP) sentences currently surpassing 7500, there is an urgent requirement both to find effective ways of reducing risk behaviours and to provide offenders with improved community case management.

The consensus view is that mainstream psychiatric services have not been able to deliver the necessary models of practice to tackle the demands of some of the more complex psychological disorders. We need to undertake a new and radical rethinking of our approach with these populations to meet both governmental policy objectives and what patients/offenders say they need. We must recognize that complex needs often mean a more complex response, often involving support to multi-professional work, and use this as a critical starting point to how services might be improved. This requires a fresh openness to determine the way that established expertise, such as that explored in this book, will support this project.

The emergent relationship between genetics, personality development, and behaviour represents the foundation of a new vision for mental health policy and service modernization.

Current government policy on mental health, including personality disorder, seeks to support this approach and achieve three objectives:

- to improve health and social outcomes;
- reduce social exclusion;
- improve public protection.

No single model or conceptual framework can answer the different meanings, significance, or context surrounding the presentation of each individual. There is developing empirical evidence for a direction of travel, but more than anything there is a need to develop and maintain the capacity to think about our ways of working with those who present challenging behaviours.

Future development of services for those with complex needs does not lie in a traditional mental health treatment model, but in sophisticated cross-agency work that takes in the experience and expertise from various sectors, including health, social services, offender management, housing, social security, and the voluntary sector. It also involves new forms of partnership with service users themselves—where they can be active agents in their own recovery, rather than the passive recipients of technical expertise.

Evidence of effectiveness is such that research and experimental initiatives will be required for some years to come. Government policy and implementation programmes expect to identify the organizational structures and design, the workforce capability, and the research questions that will facilitate the next phase of development in the field. What is essential is a consistent framework for psychological formulation that can provide the foundation for different models of intervention and guide practice. In order that services improve, are sustainable, and promote further learning, it is vital that we build staff capability through supervision and support. This book is a valuable contribution to service improvement and provides essential support for our ability to provide effective intervention and a more capable workforce to assist those with complex and often challenging needs.

References

Haigh, R., & Benefield, N. (2007). Editorial. *Mental Health Review Journal*, *12*(4): 2.

Department of Health (2003). *Personality Disorder: No Longer a Diagnosis of Exclusion*. London: Department of Health.

Ministry of Justice (2007). *Predicting and Understanding Risk of Re-offending: Prisoner Cohort Study*. London: Ministry of Justice.

CHAPTER ONE

Working with hard-to-reach patients in difficult places: a democratic therapeutic community approach to consultation

John Adlam and Christopher Scanlon

"An eye for an eye makes the whole world blind."
(Quote attributed to Gandhi)

Introduction

The difficult relationship between the forensic patient and the system of care is characterized by the giving and taking of offence. The capacity of the individual to act out violently an offended state of mind is what has resulted in his entry into the forensic system, rather than any more conscious motivation for treatment or recovery. In relation to the offender, the wider social systems in turn, for the most part, cannot help but be offended. Those who offend and those who are offended then enter into a reciprocal relationship in which violence and offence of different sorts are transacted in both directions (Scanlon & Adlam, 2009). In this chapter we attempt to examine the quality of hostile dependency that lies at the heart of this relationship, most obviously in the case of recidivist offenders and chronically disturbed and excluded personality disordered individuals.

The very public nature of this relationship is inherent in the very term "forensic", which derives from the Roman idea of the forum as a public space. There is necessarily something very public about the way that each party to the long and fraught relationship prosecutes and defends the publication of their grievances with each other. The index offence, where there is one (the criminal record), can be understood as both a cryptic and a straightforward expression or publication of the patient's distress, disturbance, or disaffection (Cordess & Cox, 1996; Morgan & Ruszczynski, 2007; Welldon & Van Velsen, 1997). The sentence meted out is an equivalent public expression of the extent to which the judgement of the courts has taken offence on behalf of the wider community. In cases where the community has taken greatest offence, the offending individual is not only deprived of his liberty or "freedom to act", but is then often further punished through degrading and inhumane treatment under the cover of correction or rehabilitation (see, e.g., Department of Health, 1992). These are the outward, psychosocial manifestations of the difficulties which follow from the problematic relationship between the offender and the offended. As in any problematic long-term relationship, below the surface there are many less obvious, but no less destructive, behaviours and responses which often make it difficult to distinguish victim and perpetrator or initiator and responder.

In this chapter, we want to examine and explore this complicated relationship. We are thinking about men and women with forensic histories and criminal records who have been caught and sentenced, or who have hurt others but have not been caught, or who have done violence to themselves and to the minds of others but have not been considered to have committed any crime (Motz, 2008; Scanlon & Adlam, 2009b). What we are addressing in all these instances is a reciprocal problem of the antisocial position and the societal response (Norton & Dolan, 1995; Scanlon & Adlam, 2008a). Borrowing a term from Bion (1961), we will consider both the antisocial position and the societal response as expressions of disturbances of "groupishness", a concept we elaborate upon below. We explore the question of who is or was responding to whom by means of the giving and taking of offence. We suggest that the judgement of the forensic system of care, enforced on behalf of the wider community, might often be itself antisocial and actively offensive to some of the most vulnerable members of our society.

To counter this tendency, we suggest that the primary task is one of engagement between the system of care and the chronically excluded. We go on to describe some of the obstacles to engagement between offenders and the offended. We illustrate our argument by making metaphorical use of what we have called the Diogenes Paradigm, within which we explore the fabled encounter between Diogenes of Sinope and Alexander the Great and its possible implications for the relationship between the offender and the forensic system of care. We illustrate some of the practical difficulties in this relationship using composite clinical material assembled from our own experience. We conclude with an exploration of a model of outreach (to the offender in the wider community) and inreach (to the offender in custody), a model that is derived from our experience in democratic therapeutic communities, and of the ways in which this model can be helpfully applied to other services working with the excluded forensic client.

Assessment and engagement

At the point of contact with a given service, the antisocial individual generally expects to be surveyed, judged, and found wanting. This is so partly because the familial, educational, and social systems he grew up in usually generated this expectation by means of their own punishment structures and the intrusion into the child of their own disappointments and disillusionments. It is also so because it is often precisely his experience of desperate wanting that has driven him to act in the first place, and because, in this state of mind, he cannot easily or reasonably expect to be a reasoned judge himself. Once inside the forensic arena, this judgemental surveillance becomes formalized in terms of the assessment: most particularly in relation to the perception of his risk to self and others (Blumenthal & Lavender, 2000; Doctor, 2003). This assessment often becomes particularly contested because his supposed riskiness is not so much a part of his own experience as it is a function of other people's experiences of him. This is problematic because, in the judgemental relationship, within which others may perceive him as dangerous, he simultaneously experiences himself as having become endangered and, thus, really dangerous. He may also be aware that he is being asked to give up, or give away, the very dangerousness which he may feel has helped to hold him together. He also feels that he may need to preserve his secret access to his dangerousness in order to survive this examination.

At the same time as feeling endangered, he may also be aware of a painfully contrasting longing for acceptance and inclusion: to be brought inside. The oscillation between these internal states of mind finds its echo in a duality inherent in the nature of the assessment, which presents him with both carrot and stick. The carrot is an implicit invitation that, if he engages with the assessor on the assessor's own terms, he can "come in from the cold". The stick is an implicit threat that if he cannot or will not do this, he must stay out in the cold and remain dangerous and endangered. Of course, he also knows that the invitation is heavily conditional and that there will be certain parts of his experience of himself that may not be allowed through the door, such as the sense of himself and of the offence as having been justified and justifiable, reasoned and reasonable.

The antisocial patient is all the more vulnerable to becoming alienated in this kind of assessment because, as is well documented (Tyrer & Stein, 1993), the prevalent normative model of personality disorder is one that collects groupings of "symptoms" without necessarily prioritizing an understanding of the distress, disturbance, or disaffection in relation to which the symptoms are produced. Both diagnosis and treatment can become infused with hostility, both individually and systemically (Adshead & Jacob, 2009; Declerk, 2006; Department of Health, 2003; Hinshelwood, 1999; Johnson & Webb, 1995; Kelly & May, 1982; Lewis & Appleby, 1988; Stockwell, 1974). There can be little room to consider the ways in which these symptoms may display an offended reaction to offence, or a sane reaction to an insane world (Foucault, 1961; Laing, 1960). The filling in of the diagnostic interview and the administering and application of risk assessment tools tend to fuel the illusion that there is the possibility of a conversation. In reality the two parties to the transaction inevitably become interrogator and interrogated: 'us and them'. There is little scope for the interpersonal encounter, for conversation and interaction, or for any shared questioning of the meaning of the process.

The patient, perhaps in particular the "revolving doors" patient or recidivist offender, who may be the veteran of many such assessments, will do extremely well to allow himself to be emotionally available during the encounter, even if to withdraw is to relinquish a longed-for experience of engagement and inclusion. Many such patients tend to launch into their "history", scripted and sculpted in the studio of so many previous encounters. Clinicians can show a parallel tendency to go through the (risk) assessment almost as if the patient was not there, ticking boxes in order defensively and safely to conclude that he is indeed a threat to self or others— whether or not this is probably the case (Blumenthal & Lavender, 2000). There is often a palpable sense of shared relief as both patient and clinician veer away from the stormy seas of the possibility of making and sustaining contact with each other into the familiar backwaters of, for example, a *pro forma* family history or a conventional substance misuse assessment. The potential for a more empathic understanding of the wanting that emerges from this potentially dangerous liaison does not survive the assaults upon it inherent in such an encounter. Instead, the potential for a real meeting is replaced with reciprocal disinterest, detachment, and disaffection.

The Diogenes paradigm

In previous papers (Adlam & Scanlon, 2005; Scanlon & Adlam, 2008b), we have explored encounters between systems of care and "offensive" persons using the legendary encounter between Diogenes, the Cynic philosopher, and Alexander the Great. We have suggested a framework for imagining this encounter as a kind of paradigm for the problematic relationship as it is played out between the antisocial individual and the system of care in our own times. Diogenes' index offence was that of debasing the currency of Sinope, the city where he lived. If this offence was "merely" a white-collar crime, it certainly caused sufficient offence that he had to flee his home to escape retribution. He made his way to Athens, where he established himself in a barrel in the main square or forum. Diogenes' ongoing offensiveness, his Cynicism, was to refuse accommodation from societal systems that he regarded as fundamentally untruthful. He would also express something perhaps of the shamefulness inherent in the poverty of his unhoused state by masturbating in his barrel. When challenged, he is supposed to have said that "he wished it were as easy to relieve hunger by rubbing an empty stomach".

Diogenes seemed to understand, if people were offended by him, that this was not his problem: but that, if he was offended by what he saw in the world around him, this then *was* his problem, one that he needed to manage as best he could. He took up the only position in relation to the world that was open to him, a position that was both criminal and *liminal*. His was a threshold, borderline existence that was neither in nor out. His Cynical position was necessarily an antisocial one, but he also maintained a questioning and challenging stance. His protest took the form of a kind of running commentary, through both words and deeds, on the corruption inherent in the power relationships between people and how they were played out in the world around him.

This powerful combination of social challenging and Cynical enquiry comes into focus in Diogenes' encounter with Alexander the Great. Alexander is supposed to have sought out Diogenes in his barrel when Diogenes (dangerously) *refused* an *invitation* to join Alexander at a public function. According to legend Alexander greeted him saying, "I am Alexander the great king", and Diogenes answered, "And I am Diogenes the Dog", explaining that "I brown-nose those who give me alms, I yelp at those who refuse, and I set my teeth on those who are rascals" (Navia, 2005). Alexander found himself so impressed, both by Diogenes' insights and also by the parlous state of his living conditions, that he asked if there was anything he could do for Diogenes. The latter replied from his barrel, in terms familiar to any clinician seeking to offer "help" to the difficult-to-reach patient, that, yes, there was something he could do: Alexander was blocking Diogenes' light, and would he please step out of the way?

Part of Alexander's own response to Diogenes is supposed to have been to declare that if he were not Alexander, he would be Diogenes, thereby recognizing how much they were a part of each other, how close they were as well as how far apart. Each expresses something of his disturbance of groupishness: each is, in Bion's words, "a group animal at war, not simply with the group, but with himself for being a group animal and with those aspects of his personality that constitute his groupishness" (Bion, 1961). In the same way, a forensic worker may work in a secure unit by way of managing something of his own antisocial tendency or aggression (Bray, 1999; Scanlon & Adlam, 2009a), or a support worker in a housing project may identify herself with the outsider culture of the clients she serves in order to manage something of her own unhousedness (Adlam & Scanlon, 2005; Scanlon & Adlam, 2006).

The difficulty here is that this position is, in itself, as dangerous as it is humane. It is humane in recognizing a truth, that "there but for the grace of God go I". It is dangerous because, in so doing, it runs the risk of ignoring or minimizing another reality: that the most dangerous difference between "us" and "them" may lie in the vexed and vexatious concept of "role" and the potentially humiliating power differential that goes with it (Gilligan, 1996; Žižek, 2008). Foucault (1975) makes the point that the brutality of punishment in the Middle Ages reflected the conception of a crime as an offence against the person of the King and of the punishment inflicted upon the offender's body as a very public reassertion of royal omnipotence; he argues that all that has changed is the method and object of punishment (now directed against the mind of the offender rather than his body), not the power differentials. From this perspective, it is not clear who is the more dangerous, except that Alexander's expression of his dangerousness is socially sanctioned (perhaps especially by those populations that he conquered) whereas the antisocial position of our latter day Diogenes rarely is.

This, then, is our paradigm for the problem of *refusal* that is both clinical and societal. Diogenes stands for the socially excluded: the homeless, the truant, the antisocial, the borderline, and all others who, in their "unhoused" states of mind, literally and metaphorically, cannot be accommodated either in the formal structures of the social world or in the minds of its members. Standing in relation to these latter-day Diogenes, Alexander comes to represent both the might and the impotence of the system of care and of those who choose or otherwise find themselves working within it. What, then, becomes of us as clinicians, or, for that matter, as citizens, when our authority is disregarded? If we stand in Alexander's shoes, do we follow one impulse, to force Diogenes to emerge from his barrel and deal with the dangerousness of the "real world", and to deal with it on our terms, not his? Alternatively, do we wash our hands of him, pass by on the other side, mindful only of our own personal safety? Do we forcibly exclude, include, or seclude?

In the next section, we wish to address these questions by seeking to describe what we might call an "in- and out-reaching" approach, which, whether in-reaching into prison or other secure settings or out-reaching into the community, asks of clinicians that we develop the capacity to be able to move in-and-out; to step aside and out of the light when Diogenes demands it of us, but not to vanish; to plant a seed, to try to make contact and to build a relationship; to signal an availability.

Consulting to the relationship: a democratic therapeutic community approach

In the democratic therapeutic community (DTC) model, pioneered at Henderson Hospital and developed in a wide range of other forensic and non-forensic treatment settings, the clients, patients, prisoners, or residents actively collaborate with staff in the planning, design, and delivery of treatment and, as such, the staff team have limited control over admission and discharge, such decisions being taken by majority vote of the community as a whole. Even within secure settings, there is at least some degree of voluntary opt-in to treatment. Constraints on conscious freedom of choice, such as imposed conditions of treatment, residence, curfews, or sections of the mental health act are reduced in some such settings and in others are not admissible at all. There are variations on this model both inside and outside custodial settings (Adlam & Scanlon, 2009; Jones, 2008; Kennard, 1983; Morris, 2004; Norton, 1996, 2006; Parker, 2007). Some such units have separate in- or outreach teams (Morant, Dolan, Fainman, & Hilton, 1999; Wrench & Menzies, 2005).

Our purpose here is not to examine the work of such units, but to consider how the DTC model might open up a way of thinking about these problems of engagement that has applicability across the range of community-based forensic services. We focus on two interlinked aspects of the DTC model: patient influence on, or control of, admission; and the DTC considered as the provider of treatment (the "community as doctor"). We discuss the application of the model of in- and outreaching work with both patient and referrer. To illustrate this approach, we now offer a composite vignette evoking a category of difficult-to-reach patients living in the community, and we show how these principles deriving from the DTC model might aid clinicians in thinking about the task of engagement.

Vignette

Our modern-day "Diogenes", whom we shall call Mr D, is a white male in his early forties. He lives alone in unsupported social housing in a small town. He is on income support and he has come back to the attention of local services after he told his GP that he had come close to a serious physical assault upon a Benefits Agency worker whom he felt had queried his continuing unfitness for work. He was seen in his local Community Mental Health Team by a care co-ordinator and a locum registrar, neither of whom are still working for that team. They felt he had an emotionally unstable personality disorder with antisocial traits and referred him to local forensic outpatient service for assessment after he told the registrar that he habitually carried a weapon when he ventured out of his flat. The forensic service said, in so many words, that he was too dangerous (to his therapist and to himself) for outpatient psychotherapy and not dangerous enough (to others) for treatment in a secure setting. There is a recently established local day hospital for patients with severe personality disorder, but they have had a recent serious untoward incident and also feel that he is "too forensic".

Mr D had a severely deprived childhood as the unwanted child of alcoholic parents. He was exposed to scenes of explosive domestic violence until his father left home when he was eight years old. His mother was unable to manage him and he was taken into local authority care in his early teens, where he was sexually and physically abused by a member of staff. He left school without any qualifications and has not worked since his early twenties. He became an alcoholic himself, but has maintained himself in abstinence for the last nine years, initially with the help of regular Alcoholics Anonymous groups but latterly by isolating himself from the world around him, remaining "holed up" in his flat and never venturing further than the corner shop except when dealings with the system of care require it.

He has convictions for assaulting police officers and minor affray, and a number of petty acquisitive offences on his criminal record, but his most serious offence was an act of extreme violence against an acquaintance of his when he was drunk, for which offence Mr D served five years in prison. He lives in fear of his own capacity for violence, although he has not been convicted of any offence since being released from that custodial sentence and maintaining abstinence from alcohol. However, he lives in a "violent state of mind" and sustains himself by means of running revenge fantasies. When in acute distress, he bangs his head repeatedly against the wall of his bedroom. When seen by the outreach service of the DTC, he had not been told his diagnosis and he is wondering who he has to hurt before someone will offer him someone to talk to about his problems.

Engaging with Diogenes: the outreaching consultation

The first point to make is that the voluntary nature of possible admission by consent of the community as a whole allows the outreaching clinician to have no agenda as to whether Mr D should take up the potential offer of treatment. Although it would be a job well done if Mr D, through the outreaching consultation, finds his own way to emerge from his "barrel" and into treatment, it might equally be a job well done if the outcome of a consultation is to help him to decide *for himself* that treatment is not the best option for him at that time. Some of the constraints noted above that connect to the internal and external pressures to *assess* are, therefore, lifted. The greater part of the assessment can be undertaken at the inner gateway of the admission procedure, through a peer-led process, such as the selection group model developed by the Henderson and its sister DTCs (and also in an ongoing way during the period of treatment, by means that include self-assessment instruments and peer feedback). Instead, the primary task at the outer gateway of the consultation can be understood as one of offering *consultation to the relationship* between Mr D and the therapeutic community itself. This clinical consultation has a psycho-educational aspect to it, including explaining and describing the actualities of the structure and function of this treatment, and involves current and former service users in group consultations, this involvement being part of the current service users' therapy. The outreaching clinician is a third party to this relationship: the democratic selection process is beyond his power and his remit to influence or control. Rather than running the risk, either of assuming the authority to exclude the would-be/won't-be patient from treatment, or of seeking to persuade him of the wisdom (for whose wisdom would it be?) of entering into treatment, the focus of the consultation can be to engage with Diogenes' free-associative and Cynical questioning of the premises on which the encounter is predicated.

What, then, might be the form and content of the fantasies that each party (Mr D and the treatment service) has about the other? How productive, or how dangerous, might it be for these parties actually to meet? How close, or how far apart, do the protagonists need to position themselves before the relationship feels safe? Mr D may feel more *at home* in his "barrel" than he would be if resettled, but not necessarily *housed*, in the empty conformity that may be what is being offered to him by the system of care. This is the case whether he be Mr D in his bedsit, the homeless man in his bash, the dangerous prisoner ostensibly detained in solitary confinement for the protection of others, the sex offender ostensibly held in segregation for his own protection, or a young man quietly cutting himself in the emptiness of his own bedroom. The refusal may be a "not ever" or it may be a "not yet". Why *would* our contemporary Diogenes want to emerge from his barrel into what is so clearly such a dangerous and endangered world? *Does he need to be "rehoused", or is it primarily a function of our own need of him not to be so dangerously "unhoused"?*

The *in-* or *outeaching* response is to consult to these questions in an open—even Cynical—manner. The endeavour is to consult to the relationship as it is experienced by Mr D and his counterparts: to *consult the patient*. In this context, clinicians must somehow *obtain and retain a clear enough and safe enough sense of their own security to* "think their own thoughts" (Gabbard & Wilkinson, 1994) *and feel confident enough to believe that no lasting harm will be done as a result of what they say and do, or don't say and don't do.* The clinician is freed to work in this way only if it is conceptualized as an acceptable possible outcome that Mr D might, in the end, feel empowered to decide that treatment is *not* what he wants, that the distance that exists between him and the DTC, as surrogate for the wider social community, is, for the time being at least, just about right. An understanding and recognition of why the barrel has become his refuge must be the starting point for any subsequent consideration of whether it might be safe to emerge.

Mr D looks out from his barrel at the possible offer of treatment and, very understandably, concludes that the world is insane. Why cannot his conflicted need both for isolation, confinement, segregation *and* for total care be understood, he wants to know? The system of care seems to expect of him that he bare his soul to strangers' groups when his full-time preoccupation is to avoid social situations of any kind for fear of exploding into violence. Small wonder that he keeps us at bay in the encounter. We must then try to take up a Cynical questioning of everyone's assumptions about what *should* be happening. We need to understand, and to signal that we understand to Mr D, wherever we may encounter him, that we may be every bit as dangerous to him as he may be to us. The outcome of consulting to the relationship between the individual and the system of care may "simply" be that something in the *quality* of that relationship shifts, in a way that the individual and, perhaps, also the referring team experiences as *liberating*. That shift has the nature of an unknown quantity, the unpredictable outcome of a risk taken and shared in the encounter. All parties to the dynamic may share a fear of such change.

The referral as a symptom of the disturbance of the referrer?

Having described the model of consultation to the relationship in these terms, we trust it is apparent that the same process must also apply to considering the position of the referring team and, indeed, the wider system of care. We have previously described some of the processes whereby teams charged with addressing the antisocial position in their work may, through an incapacity to manage the traumatic impact of the work, come to identify themselves with the offender and to take up arms on his behalf against the system of care, joining with him in his grievance and in his denial of grief (Adlam & Scanlon, 2005; Scanlon & Adlam, 2009a; *see also* Hopper, 2003). The flattening of the hierarchy and the culture of enquiry of the DTC model, particularly with regard to patient-led admission procedures, facilitates a thoughtful questioning of the referrer's motivation for treatment as much as for that of Mr D, who is unlikely to be offered admission if it is felt that the referrer is trying to "muscle in", either to evict Mr D from their service, or to push the DTC to "accept" their view of why Mr D *should* be helped (whether he or the DTC like it or not).

Whether in response to a direct referral or to a specific request for consultation to the team, the task of consulting to the relationship between the team and Mr D, or his counterpart, remains the same. The exploration of possible mutual identifications may be an important aspect of this process, particularly in the area of severe personality disorder, when it is not uncommon for there to be what Main (1957) called "special patients" who can often be understood as part representations of the referrers' wish to come into treatment themselves. On the other hand, we find those patients, perhaps like our Mr D, who are hated and vilified both because of what they have done and also because of their refusal to be helped. However, in both cases, it is equally important to attend to what it is that this *unconscious* identification with Diogenes (on the part of the referrer) defends against, which is frequently the dis-ease that comes from an awareness of actually occupying Alexander's position in the relationship, that is, one of great power and potentially of great frustration and the risk of retaliatory violence.

Gilligan (1996) offers the concept of "structural violence", locating individual, behavioural violence in the context of the harm that comes from the way that we organize ourselves societally, with structural oppression imposed and reinforced by hierarchical organizations and systems. These are the deaths and illnesses and exclusions generated by our own collective disturbances of groupishness. Žižek (2001, 2008) applies the term "systemic violence" to describe the same societal structures and processes in terms of "the often catastrophic consequences of the smooth functioning of our economic and political systems" (Žižek, 2008, p. 1). Simply to suggest the idea of a relationship between the individual and the system of care is to generate an enquiry into the ways in which these dynamics are re-created and played out in the referring team's relationship with Mr D. Any discussion of the structural power differential between referrer and patient then requires that, while continuing to deploy a conscious adoption of Diogenes' Cynical questioning, the in- or outreaching clinicians can also allow themselves to be both kindly and actively *helpful* to these significant others, without losing the focus on consulting to the relationship between them and the (not-yet-a-)patient.

It is a truism of forensic work that the team, or family for that matter, which is unconscious of the shaming potential of the power differentials between them and the individual in their care, is more likely to enact them by means of violence and humiliation. In order to be made aware of this, as empathically as is possible, it is necessary to facilitate and support a culture of enquiry within these systems (Main, 1983). Mr D's referral is arguably typical of a category of referrals that are often made of individual patients who are directly and actively aggrieved with their teams, some having assaulted or stalked mental health professionals and others having been excluded from all clinical services within their catchments for threatening apocalyptic revenge. Such responses are often precipitated by these services' often unwitting pursuance of formal or informal policies of zero tolerance and the imposition of unilateral treatment contracts on to people who are already deeply disturbed by analogous conditional relating during their early lives. In so doing, a renewed exclusion from meaningful participation in decisions about their own lives is re-created.

The task here is, therefore, to help members of these groupings and systems to see the ways in which they may themselves be contributing to the problems that they purport to be trying to solve, and to recognize the ways in which systemic disturbance has become located in the patient in ways that he cannot accommodate (Hinshelwood, 2002; Norton & Dolan, 1995). Often, the negotiation of this more triangular relationship is resisted far more by the "significant other", the referrer, than by the patient himself, because it endangers their cherished belief that the problem is located in the "patient" and that they are part only of the would-be solution. It is important to ensure that the focus remains on consulting to the relationship *between* the parties rather than interpreting the internal worlds of individual stakeholders themselves. Service users considered to be experts by experience can play an active role in this aspect of the consultation, acting as colleagues alongside the clinicians in particular situations such as psycho-educational workshops for referrers and keyworkers as well as more conventional teaching and training opportunities. In the DTC model, peer service users are typically present alongside staff at care planning meetings, thus again actively intervening in the relationship between the patient and his local services. These experts by experience can represent the experience of being in treatment far better than clinicians, who are mostly *merely* experts by training. The approach is trans-theoretical in that does not set out to teach or promote a stance, a set of techniques or skills, but, rather, to confront reality collectively in a permissive, democratic way (Rapoport, 1960). The process also has to address the fears and fantasies about these forms of organization, and all that it represents, in the minds of the patient, as well as his family, friends, advocates, and referrers (Armstrong, 2005). A central part of this process is to seek to engage the dangerous and endangered parts of the minds of this group of stakeholder participants as they emerge in the conversations.

Remoralizing and revitalizing the culture of enquiry

Diogenes' Cynical questioning and challenging of the terms and conditions of membership presented to him by society has a strong echo down through the ages in Main's definition of the essence of therapeutic community practice as a "culture of enquiry . . . into personal and interpersonal and intersystem problems, and the study of impulses, defences and relations as these are expressed and arranged socially" (1983, p. 141). The outreaching and inreaching work of DTCs has directly addressed the difficulties of working with dangerous and disordered patients who are actively seeking help. It has also involved an attempt to be with and alongside those patients who refuse, avoid, or attack the help that is offered, and to aspire to enable their "significant others", including referrers, to maintain an humane and moral attitude towards them.

There is an important question to be addressed as to how this model can extend, beyond the DTCs that generated it in the first place, to inform the work of services of often very different kinds. Residential DTCs in community settings exist, where they do survive, under constant threat of closure, and in secure settings, under constant threat of losing such democratic aspects of their functioning as they have been able to develop. Yet, their learning from experience cannot be so casually discarded; Diogenes' predicament, as represented in our vignette, and the intensely problematic nature of the relationship between the antisocial individual and the system of care, are issues that will not go away.

To illustrate this point, we would like to return to the vignette of Mr D and to imagine what might have become of him following the consultation. On the face of it, his prospects are bleak and so also, in relation to him at least, are those of the referring service. The relationship of reciprocal violence between Mr D and those parts of the system of care that he has been in contact with has become rigid and entrenched. In his unhoused and dis-membered state he presents the twin problems of chronicity and refusal and has good reason to feel that such are the characteristics of the societal response to his predicament: a dynamic of reciprocal violence and exclusion similar to that painfully demonstrated in Masters' (2006) remarkable biographical portrayal of the early adulthood of his anti-hero, Stuart. As with Stuart, we could envision many situations and encounters that could lead eventually to Mr D resorting to violence, against the referring team or against himself, with tragic consequences for one party or the other. Even in the absence of overt violence between them, the tensions inherent in these violent states of mind are, in any case, seriously debilitating, and potentially damaging, for both parties to the relationship.

But might we also dare to hope for a different kind of outcome? An outcome which depends upon our Diogenes having an experience of finding a different place to stand, of feeling understood in his particular predicament in relation to the system of care? Might Mr D come to find that his dilemma in relation to the immediate perils of treatment—his exposure to the madness of the "housed" (Foster & Roberts, 1998; Scanlon & Adlam, 2008a)—is appreciated and respected? Perhaps the in- or outreaching clinicians are prepared to sit with him in that shared dilemma and not rush to judgement. The idea that they are not inveigling him, or otherwise "twisting his arm", into managing *their* anxiety by coming into treatment starts to make the possibility that he might enter into treatment *for his own sake* seem to him at least thinkable. One possible outcome of this reciprocal repositioning is that the relationship between Mr D and his referrers starts to become less entrenched. The referrers are helped to understand that their threat that they will discharge Mr D from their service if he refuses to engage with the outreaching team is self-defeating. As a consequence, Mr D comes to the discovery that engagement and co-operation with this team represents much less of a loss of face than he had previously imagined possible. He starts to feel that each step taken towards entering into treatment is more informed, more consensual, and so more meaningfully his own. These shifts in the quality and the morality of the relationship do not necessarily follow a smooth and consistent trajectory. There is considerable residual hurt and grievance on all sides, and the outreaching clinicians must respect how painful it might be for each party in the triad to move closer to each other.

If treatment is finally entered into, it proves to be no magical solution. Mr D may "drop out" and the referrers and funders may well ask questions about whether this represents a treatment failure, a waste of money, rather than think with us that it was a testament to a protracted and difficult process that Mr D was able to be engaged in treatment at all. But, more optimistically, it might be that Mr D's engagement might be timely and skilfully negotiated and he may enter into treatment. This treatment might even be enough to effect clinically and statistically significant changes in his level of functioning in the world (Chiesa & Fonagy, 2000, 2003; Chiesa, Fonagy, & Holmes, 2003; Dolan, Warren, & Norton, 1997; Lees, Manning, Menzies, & Morant, 2004). Or it might be enough that our Mr D has ventured some way in from the cold and that he feels sufficiently helped to have understood something important about how far "in" he could wish to be, and how far "out" he needs to remain in order to feel safe. Perhaps he is never far from his "barrel"— but perhaps he can venture further than the corner shop and not need to feel he must go out armed into the world, and perhaps the world might feel a little more accommodating of his predicament than before. Perhaps, as a consequence, all parties to the encounter might end up feeling just a little safer.

When Rapoport (1960) studied the Henderson Hospital in the late 1950s, he identified four key components of its functioning as a therapeutic community: democratization, communalism, permissiveness, and reality confrontation, combined within a culture of enquiry that enables problematic interaction to be explored and new ways of relating to be experimented with. We do not believe that these approaches should be available only to those who are, at any given time, sufficiently "help seeking" to get themselves through the "inner gateway" of the admission process. Rather, we believe that this approach has much to contribute to our shared obligation to seek to engage those people, like our Mr D, who are presenting as refusing help. Any services working with clients such as Mr D can make some use of this approach to outreaching (to community settings) and inreaching (to secure settings) without needing to change their basic structures in ways that would likely be both impractical and inappropriate.

We have outlined a triadic model of consultation that aspires to accept the patient in both his predicament and his potential to be an active participant in, and authority on, his own life, but which seeks to address the *intervention* to the relationship with the system of care itself. Rapoport's observations provide a template for the desired outcome of such an intervention, in which significant others within the system of care can be helped to think about and relate to those who are, at any given time, refusing such offers of help. His notions of permissiveness and communalism entail neither judging nor even "helping", but, instead, embrace the power and the potentiality of living with and being with rather than "doing unto". A model whereby patients are not only consulted but are enabled to consult with each other, not so much in *treatment* as in community, is a participatory model and an approach to communal living that we consider to have relevance and implications for us all.

Acknowledgements

We would like to acknowledge the contribution of the former outpatients, residents, and staff members of Henderson Hospital and of the many students, workshop participants, and conference delegates who have, in their different ways, helped us to develop the ideas being put forward in this chapter.

References

Adlam, J., & Scanlon, C. (2005). Personality disorder and homelessness: membership and "unhoused minds" in forensic settings. *Group Analysis, 38*(3) (Special Issue: Group Analysis in Forensic Settings): 452–466.

Adlam, J., & Scanlon, C. (2009). Disturbances of "groupishness"? Structural violence, refusal and the therapeutic community response to severe personality disorder. *International Forum of Psychoanalysis*, *18*(1): 23–29.

Adshead, G., & Jacob, C. (Eds.) (2009). *Personality Disorder: The Definitive Reader*. London: Jessica Kingsley.

Armstrong, D. (2005). *Organization in the Mind: Psychoanalysis, Group Relations and Organizational Consultancy*. London: Karnac.

Bion, W. R. (1961). *Experiences in Groups*. London: Routledge.

Blumenthal, S., & Lavender, T. (Eds.) (2000). *Violence and Mental Disorder: A Critical Guide to the Assessment and Management of Risk*. London: Zito Trust.

Bray, J. (1999). Psychiatric nursing and the myth of altruism. In: P. Barker & B. Davidson (Eds.), *Psychiatric Nursing. Ethical Strife* (Chapter 8). London: Arnold.

Chiesa, M., & Fonagy, P. (2000). Cassel personality disorder study: methodology and treatment effects. *British Journal of Psychiatry, 176*: 485–491.

Chiesa, M., & Fonagy, P. (2003). Psychosocial treatment for severe personality disorder: 36-month follow-up. *British Journal of Psychiatry, 183*: 356–362.

Chiesa, M., Fonagy, P., & Holmes, J. (2003). When less is more: an exploration of psychoanalytically oriented hospital-based treatment for severe personality disorder. *International Journal of Psychoanalysis, 84*: 637–650.

Cordess, C., & Cox, M. (1996). *Forensic Psychotherapy: Crime, Psychodynamics and the Offender Patient*. London: Jessica Kingsley.

Declerk, P. (2006). On the necessary suffering of the homeless. In: R. Scholar (Ed.), *Divided Cities: The Oxford Amnesty Lectures 2003* (pp. 161–175). Oxford: Oxford University Press.

Department of Health (1992). *Report of the Committee of Inquiry into Complaint about Ashworth Hospital*. London: HMSO.

Department of Health (2003). *Personality Disorder: No Longer a Diagnosis of Exclusion. Policy Implementation Guidance for the Development of Services for People with Personality Disorder*. London: National Institute for Mental Health for England. www.nimhe.org.uk, accessed 28 February 2008.

Doctor, R. M. (2003). *Dangerous Patients: a Psychodynamic Approach to Risk Assessment and Management*. London: Karnac.

Dolan, B., Warren, F., & Norton, K. (1997). Change in borderline symptoms one year after therapeutic community treatment for severe personality disorder. *British Journal of Psychiatry, 171*: 274–279.

Foster, A., & Roberts, V. Z. (1998). "Not in my back yard": the psychosocial reality of community care. In: A. Foster & V. Z. Roberts (Eds.), *Managing Mental Health in the Community: Chaos and Containment* (pp. 27–37). London: Routledge.

Foucault, M. (1961). *Madness and Civilization*. London: Routledge Classics, 2007.

Foucault, M. (1975). *Discipline and Punish: The Birth of the Prison*. London: Penguin, 1991.

Gabbard, G., & Wilkinson, S. (1994). *Management of Counter-transference with Borderline Patients*. Washington, DC: American Psychiatric Press.

Gilligan, J. (1996). *Violence: Reflections on our Deadliest Epidemic*. London: Jessica Kingsley.

Hinshelwood, R. D. (1999). The difficult patient. *British Journal of Psychiatry, 174*: 187–190.

Hinshelwood, R. D. (2002). Abusive help—helping abuse: the dynamic impact of severe personality disorder on institutions. *Criminal Behaviour and Mental Health, 12*: 20–30.

Hopper, E. (2003). *Traumatic Experience in the Unconscious Life of Groups: The Fourth Basic Assumption: Incohesion: Aggregation/Massification or (ba) I:A/M*. London: Jessica Kingsley.

Johnson, M., & Webb, C. (1995). Rediscovering unpopular patients: the concept of social judgement. *Journal of Advanced Nursing, 21*(3): 466–475.

Jones, D. (2008). *Understanding Criminal Behaviour: Psychosocial Approaches to Criminality*. Cullompton: William Press.

Kelly, M. P., & May, D. (1982). Good and bad patients: a review of the literature and a theoretical critique. *Journal of Advanced Nursing, 7*: 147–156.

Kennard, D. (1983). *An Introduction to Therapeutic Communities*. London: Routledge.

Laing, R. D. (1960). *The Divided Self: A Study of Sanity and Madness*. London: Quadrangle Books.

Lees, J., Manning, N., Menzies, D., & Morant, N. (2004). *A Culture of Enquiry: Research Evidence and the Therapeutic Community*. London: Jessica Kingsley.

Lewis, G., & Appleby, L. (1988). Personality disorder: the patients psychiatrists dislike. *British Journal of Psychiatry, 143*: 44–49.

Main, T. (1957). The ailment. *Journal of Medical Psychology, 30*: 129–145.

Main, T. (1983). The concept of the therapeutic community: variations and vicissitudes. In: T. Main (Ed.), *The Ailment and Other Psychoanalytic Essays* (pp. 123–141). London: Free Association Books.

Masters, A. (2006). *Stuart: A Life Told Backwards*. London: Delacorte Press.

Morant, N., Dolan, B., Fainman, D., & Hilton, M. (1999). An innovative outreach service for people with severe personality disorders: patient characteristics and clinical activities. *Journal of Forensic Psychiatry, 10*(1): 84–97.

Morgan, D., & Ruszczynski, S. (2007). *Lectures on Violence, Perversion and Delinquency*. London: Karnac.

Morris, M. (2004). *Dangerous and Severe: Process, Programme, and Person: Grendon's Work*. London: Jessica Kingsley.

Motz, A. (2008). *The Psychology of Female Violence* (2nd edn.). London: Routledge.

Navia, L. (2005). *Diogenes the Cynic*. New York: Humanity Books.

Norton, K. (1996). Management of difficult personality disorder patients. *Advances in Psychiatric Treatment, 2*: 202–210.

Norton, K. (2006). *Setting Up New Services in the NHS: Just Add Water*. London: Jessica Kingsley.

Norton, K., & Dolan, B. (1995). Acting out and the institutional response. *Journal of Forensic Psychiatry, 6*: 317–332.

Parker, M. (2007) *Dynamic Security: The Democratic Therapeutic Community in Prison*. London: Jessica Kingsley.

Rapoport, R. N. (1960). *Community as Doctor: New Perspectives on a Therapeutic Community*. London: Tavistock.

Scanlon, C., & Adlam, J. (2006). Housing "unhoused minds"—interpersonality disorder in the organisation? *Journal of Housing, Care and Support, 9*(3): 9–14.

Scanlon, C., & Adlam, J. (2008a). Homelessness and disorder: the challenge of the antisocial and the societal response. In: C. Kaye & M. Howlett (Eds.), *Mental Health Services Today and Tomorrow: Part 1 Experiences of Providing and Receiving Care* (pp. 27–38). Oxford: Radcliffe.

Scanlon, C., & Adlam, J. (2008b). Refusal, social exclusion and the cycle of rejection: a *Cynical* analysis? *Critical Social Policy, 28*(4): 529–549.

Scanlon, C., & Adlam, J. (2009a). Nursing dangerousness, dangerous nursing and the spaces in between: learning to live with uncertainties. In: A. Aiyegbusi & J. Clarke (Eds.), *Relationships with Offenders: An Introduction to the Psychodynamics of Forensic Mental Health Nursing* (pp. 127–142). London: Jessica Kingsley.

Scanlon, C., & Adlam, J. (2009b). "Why do you treat me this way?": reciprocal violence and the mythology of "deliberate self harm". In: A. Motz (Ed.), *Managing Self Harm: Psychological Perspectives* (pp. 55–81). London: Taylor and Francis.

Stockwell, E. (1974). *The Unpopular Patient*. London: Royal College of Nursing.

Tyrer, P., & Stein, G. (1993). *Personality Disorder Reviewed*. London: Gaskell.

Welldon, E. V. and Van Velsen, C. (Eds.) (1997). *A Practical Guide to Forensic Psychotherapy*. London: Jessica Kingsley.

Wrench, M., & Menzies, D. (2005). Henderson Outreach Service Team: offshoot or graft? *Therapeutic Communities, 26*(2): 174–185.

Žižek, S. (2001). *The Fragile Absolute: Or Why is the Christian Legacy Worth Fighting For*. New York: Verso Books.

Žižek, S. (2008). *Violence*. London: Profile Books.

CHAPTER TWO

The lived experience of rehabilitation work with forensic patients in the community

A work discussion group with staff at a forensic hostel for residents with mental illness

Alla Rubitel

In this chapter, I would like to share what I have learnt from my experience of facilitating a work discussion group in a forensic hostel. Through talking with colleagues, I became aware that my experience in this endeavour has been shared by numerous professionals working with this group of patients in similar settings. I anticipate that many of you will relate to this thought-provoking material.

A hostel team faces a challenging task: to help their residents, who have been discharged from secure forensic settings, with their transition towards independent living in the community. I shall focus on some of the anxieties and difficulties encountered by hostel staff in their work with chronically mentally ill residents who have been convicted of crimes, as well as the way these difficulties are managed. I will describe my own experience of being exposed to these anxieties, together with the impact they had on me, using the resources of my training and clinical work.

My two-year period of work with the hostel staff and residents are illustrated with vignettes, which use the composite "staff" and "residents" to protect confidentiality, yet still preserve the dynamics of actual cases as reported by the caring team.

Setting

This independent sector hostel caters for chronically mentally ill patients who have committed acts of violence. It provides intensive rehabilitation support in the community for an approximate two-year period to patients who have been transferred from regional secure units in order to prepare them for independent life. Forensic psychiatry locality teams provide clinical input, holding regular meetings in order to review the residents' needs and treatment plans.

Residents

Most have committed violent offences, such as sexual assault, attempted murder, or robbery. All suffer from varying degrees of psychotic illness, many from chronic and enduring schizophrenia. Some are "restricted patients", which means that they are subject to statutory supervision in accordance with section 41 of the English Mental Health Act. These patients are liable to be recalled to a psychiatric hospital if, for example, they show signs of mental health deterioration, or breach their supervision conditions in the community. The majority of the residents have complex needs, coming from very deprived and traumatized backgrounds.

The team

This consists of staff members, who are varied and mixed in their training and experience, ranging from those who have worked as prison officers, substance misuse and mental health support workers, to the less experienced, who are interested to know about this work, such as university graduates who are considering a career in mental health and want to gain some exposure to this complex group of patients.

The team's task is to prepare residents for independent living by encouraging their engagement in various educational and / or social activities at the hostel and / or in the community to enable them to move towards independent life. The staff take residents on trips and teach them everyday tasks, such as cooking and handling their finances.

My task

I was commissioned by the hostel management to provide "clinical supervision" to the staff. My predecessor had facilitated this in the form of a forum where the staff had space to reflect on their work using systemic and psychodynamic concepts. I called this a "work discussion group".

Anxiety

When I first met with the team manager to introduce myself and to discuss our contract, he diplomatically warned me that the staff would not like anything "psychoanalytic" as it "makes them anxious, and they want to discuss the residents rather than themselves and their feelings. They do not want to feel exposed." I pointed out that it might actually be helpful for the staff to consider the way they felt in relation to the residents, who would inevitably have had an impact on them, together with how this affected the way they worked. It would, therefore, be very useful to take into account actual feelings evoked by working with their residents. The manager expressed the view that it would be better if he were not present at the meetings, as this would enable the staff "to feel more free to discuss their issues". I perceived some inconsistency in his request, and I sensed his anxiety at the thought that the staff might wish not only to discuss the patients, but also how they felt about themselves and their work, at the same time being afraid that I would see him and his staff as patients in need of group therapy. This made me wonder whether part of my task was to witness something understood by the manager to be a threat and from which he wanted to exclude himself. Was there a sense of suspicion and mistrust circulating in a complex system of care where I had become a new potential irritant?

I had initially believed I was entering a situation where there was an existing contract between the commissioning organization running the hostel and the organization that I represented. However, it emerged that this contract was ambivalent and unclear to the staff. I needed to determine how they viewed it, and who was anxious about what.

In our first meeting, there was a sense in the room that the staff either felt under pressure to do something unfamiliar and/or fear-provoking, or they were anxious about the effect I might have on them. My suggestion that we should develop a rota to present the patients was ignored. When we discussed how the staff reacted to the residents, I was given standard responses. There were those who claimed they were not affected by the patients or felt "nothing", and those who believed that as professionals it was inappropriate to disclose their personal reactions. This made me see myself as the only person in the room with feelings that I *could* reveal and try to understand. However, I was also aware of a part of myself telling me I should not do this. I surmised, therefore, that I was having the same experience as the staff, that is, if they were to talk about their feelings they would expose themselves to criticism. It also became apparent that a way to understand the manager's anxiety in telling me that the staff did not want my psychoanalytic capacity was that if we were to become aware of their personal responses, it would be experienced as a threat to the status quo. They would then have to be confronted with their reluctance to review their position because of their anxiety that they would have to change.

A further example of resistance to seeing something disturbing was when a female member of staff presented the case of Mr A, a resident sex offender, who was notorious for flirting with women. She stated that she was confident that she was not affected by this, as she knew Mr A so well. I raised the concern that this was the patient's way of disengaging her from appropriate vigilance with regard to his potential dangerousness. She replied as if I had done something terrible to her: "You are making me feel worried now. Aren't you supposed to help us with our paranoid anxiety? Instead you are making me more anxious!" I remarked that it seemed to me as if the staff were unsure whether I had come to soothe their anxieties or to stir them up, but stressed that it was only if their anxieties were made evident that we could address them.

A need for excitement

In my first few meetings with the staff, I sensed an unvoiced uncertainty among them about the purpose of my being there. I was made to feel unwanted and redundant even before I started. The team members said that they knew their residents well, and that the majority of them had repetitive patterns of behaviour that were often discussed, even though nothing ever changed. Therefore, they proposed that I should come back in a month rather than in a fortnight, as there was nothing more to talk about. They knew that some of their residents would never be able to live independently, and it was apparent that they felt uneasy about this. I sensed that in order to defend themselves from this painful knowledge, both the residents and the staff withdrew from each other into a "comfort zone", where none of the participants was truly engaged in the rehabilitation process, but just passed the time with nothing apparently happening. I felt I was expected to follow suit and return in a month rather than engage in any exploratory process. Although I found it difficult to be there, I did not want simply to give up and leave. I noticed a dead atmosphere in the room. I wondered if this was the effect of chronic psychosis which, along with psychotropic medication, can dull the emotional engagement of the residents, which, in turn, has an impact on the staff in such a way that they withdraw to protect their own minds from fragmentation. Despite having told me that they had not learnt anything from my predecessor, the staff admitted that he had been very helpful when things did go wrong: that is, when there was a crisis in the hostel. Then they became more animated, and I sensed they wished to break away from the frustration of the repetitiveness and flatness of their experience into something more lively and stimulating. Was this an invitation for me to introduce some excitement into our meetings?

I was aware of a split: staff either tended to view the residents as so well that they required little intervention, or else so ill that the staff had a major, dramatic problem on their hands. When I shared this thought with the team, it seemed to spark a degree of interest and hope. A few asked, apparently in surprise, if I really *was* there to help them engage with difficult patients, and some proposed that I teach them more about psychiatry. My response, that we would learn "psychiatry" from the residents, was met with disappointment. This made me wonder whether, in disappointing them by not bringing the drama they were looking for, I might become yet another repetition in the life of the hostel by "replicating" my predecessor, in whom the staff had expressed disappointment. They themselves would "replicate" their complex patients in their disengagement from me.

"Selective amnesia" and "déjà vu"

At first, when I visited the hostel, each time I arrived the staff seemed surprised to see me. In spite of clear advance notice of the meeting for that day, I was made to feel unexpected. After six months of working together, when I thought some progress had been made in this regard, once again I found the staff surprised and annoyed when I arrived. I shared these observations with them. They claimed they did not know I was coming and that they did not know whose responsibility it was to remind them of this. I picked up a lot of frustration and confusion in the room, as if nobody knew what was going on.

When we eventually got down to discussing that day's difficult-to-engage patient, Mr B, who denied his index offence, nobody could remember his past history, despite their initial claims that they knew him well. I sensed the staff's reluctance to consult his file, as if to do so would be both humiliating and, by implication, a criticism. I thought that the team probably was unaware of an underlying anxiety that their residents may, at times, appear charming like Mr A, or, like Mr B, guarded and/or avoidant in their repetitive presentation, and so might be unconsciously masking what was really going inside their minds. The staff and I were confronted by the question of how to remain inquisitive about the risk posed by the residents, without getting overwhelmed by anxiety about their potential for violent acting out. The staff might have felt it was too dangerous to admit that there were things they did not know about their patients. If faced with forgotten and unsavoury aspects of themselves, the residents would be forced to acknowledge the dangerous and, at the same time, vulnerable parts of themselves. By the same token, their index offences, like a residual memory trace, could be momentarily recovered as a kind of *déjà vu*, only to be "forgotten" again by both carers and residents.

Was this selective amnesia and *déjà vu* an unsafe but convenient refuge from the anxieties described above that otherwise would interfere with the capacity of the staff and residents to get through the day?

Prizing knowledge over experience

Some members of the hostel team claimed they knew everything they needed to know about the patients: they wanted me to teach them something new and different through lectures. Others said that they wanted to keep to our usual format, as I made them think "really deeply" about their residents. One member of staff commented to another, "If you aren't prepared to talk about the residents, it's not surprising you can't learn anything new." I felt we were going over the same old ground and that I was contributing all the effort, although the staff were complaining about having to do all the work. Once again, I was left feeling that I had become an unwelcome visitor, an extension of senior managers who asked the carers difficult questions and made them do extra work for which they were not paid. One member of staff actually asked if these sessions were for *their* benefit, or simply to boost the managers' targets.

I had learnt in one of the meetings that the hostel was going through a lengthy consultation process with regard to how it should move forward in order to survive financially. The staff felt pessimistic, as they had heard that their salaries were to be cut to help rescue the organization, which was facing the threat of closure. I wondered whether the prospect of further change was adding to their anxiety. Were they giving me the experience of being closed down, shut down, and cut off?

There also appeared to be a hidden anxiety among the staff that the residents, who apparently did not gain insight into their mental illness and offending, would not improve, and that the team would be held responsible for this failure by their senior managers. I deduced that the team wanted to escape this anxiety by inviting me to tell them new, exciting things, or transmit my knowledge to them by "magical" means. This would distance them from their sense that nothing in the hostel ever changed. If I did not succeed, I, too, would be criticized or dismissed by them, just as they felt their managers were criticizing or dismissing them. Through this flight into academic interest, they avoided knowing about their patients' "stuckness".

After all this to-ing and fro-ing, one of the team members took it upon herself to give me an ultimatum which, in a nutshell, meant that unless I was prepared to compromise and include didactic teaching in our "clinical supervision", we would not get anywhere. I resisted the temptation to either withdraw into a defensive pseudo-psychoanalytical stance in order to rescue myself from this annihilating experience, or to retaliate. I reminded myself that it was my task to look beyond her ultimatum, and so fell back on my analysis of what was going on. After some consideration, I agreed to have a review meeting with the team manager present to discuss the purpose of the "clinical supervision" again. After this discussion, I was left wondering whether there was a resistance to learning from experience, or whether the team was genuinely requesting help appropriate to their needs, and it was for me to pitch my contribution differently.

Ignorance

To be able to learn we have first to accept that we do not know something, as well as to be prepared to show our ignorance. In doing so, I felt that it was probably easier for the staff to admit that they did not know enough about the *theory* behind running the hostel, rather than admit to ignorance about both their residents and about themselves. When trying to process this, I asked myself why there was such resistance to learning about the patients from experience. Why was there so much mistrust of me? Why did some residents make the team reluctant to know how they felt about them? I wondered how some patients managed to affect the hostel team to the degree that the workers felt all the effort to bring about change with these patients was futile, and the best way to deal with this frustration was to shut their eyes or turn away to something more interesting or exciting. Thus, I realized that there was an unconscious collusion on the part of both staff and patients to block further exploration of the latter's difficulties. What the patients knew about themselves at some level was not allowed to be explored further, and both they and the team were expected to give up on any such enquiry. This unconscious painful communication to the staff by the patients, I think, had created in the former a sense of omniscience and consequently of boredom, claustrophobia, and irritation. At the same time, their sense of impotence was projected on to me, the expert, who should have the answers but did not, who was expected to produce instant magical solutions but was failing. Why, then, was I asking what they thought about their residents? This allowed the staff to feel justified in being bored and deprived. The "omnipotent" solution was, therefore, one of greed for new interesting theories ("lectures") and practices in order to avoid facing pain and frustration caused by what they were actually dealing with.

Lack of gratitude

I sensed a lack of appreciation on the part of both managers and patients towards the carers, and that the managers themselves felt unappreciated by the staff. The hostel team felt it was unprofessional to complain about this. Instead, a large part of this unspoken experience was being transferred to me. The staff felt "wasted"; so did I. Despite years of training, I felt I was on trial, reduced to nothing. Apparently, the carers needed me to understand their predicament. However, they did not want to consider how they unconsciously projected this unwanted feeling into me so that they momentarily felt relieved from their burden. I perceived a tremendous pressure to retaliate or become defensive. However, I believe it made a difference that I was able to listen to them without actually being crushed. They seemed to be fearful that I would retaliate and damage *them*, just as some of their residents did, and the fact that I did not, but remained interested, was a turning point in our work together. Their lost sense of self-value was partially recovered by this experience. (I later learnt that the staff had felt marginalized in the pecking order of forensic mental health care, and that they had been landed with an extremely difficult task which they were ill equipped to deal with.) By our next session, the staff had produced a list of topics for the "lectures", although we never needed to consult it again. Somehow, we always had a case to discuss after that, and the staff were much more active and engaged during our meetings. I did not change my methods much, apart from introducing some explanations about psychopathology when I thought appropriate.

Omnipotence

As noted above, I discovered that the whole organization faced a huge financial deficit with consequent proposed cuts to staff salaries. This affected the team members adversely, making them feel used and undervalued by management. Staff believed that while NHS hostels could select new residents for admission, independent sector organizations did not have this advantage. Hence, there was always anxiety that the hostel would not be able to survive in the face of fierce competition without a continuous stream of new patients, despite the lack of adequate resources and training to manage some of them. Pressure was also apparently passed from the managers of secure units looking for beds down to the hostel managers, who were compelled to accept the new residents.

I learnt that, on a couple of occasions, the staff carried out assessments and decided against the transfer of unsuitable patients, but the managers ignored their recommendations. The staff were left feeling belittled, as their opinions were not valued, while at the same time they were led to consider that they were in charge. This was an echo of my earlier experience, when I was made to understand that I was dealing with a team who believed, and wanted me to believe, that they knew everything, could manage anything, and did not need me. Similarly, there was an unconscious expectation on the part of the patients for the staff to be parent, nurse, and rehabilitation worker all in one, on top of the manager's demand to deliver high quality work. I was given an example of how there were often only two staff during night shift, supervising more then fifteen residents, rather like a "parental couple" expected to look after a large, needy family. Unable to cope, they, in turn, left the residents to deal with their difficulties on their own: "cheap care", as the team manager called it.

The pressure to provide hasty solutions was brought into focus in one of our sessions. There was a lot of frustration and concern among the staff over Mr C, who was supposed to be moving towards the end of his hostel rehabilitation period, but completely lacked insight into his index offence and mental illness, claiming that he was God. I addressed the team's anxiety about the unworkable expectation of putting things right in too brief a period of time. I told the staff members that although they could not cure Mr C, they could help him agree to a compromise, even though this would inevitably challenge his deluded omnipotence. The task would be to enable him to collaborate in such a way that the God part of him would be able to tolerate a potentially humiliating experience. I looked at how the staff might unconsciously feel pressured, or tempted, either to put things right, or to be an ideal parent to very deprived patients like Mr C. Alternatively, they could give up and withdraw into a depressive functional mode: a parent/support worker, just going through the motions, feeling defeated, impotent, and, therefore, unable to engage with the disturbed aspects of Mr C's mind. However, by doing so, the staff would fail to attend to the less deluded part of Mr C, thus depriving him of the potential support which could lead to his growth and development. Drawing on my own experience of working with these very complex patients, where I had to recognize that even the smallest change is important, I was able to point out that it was more realistic to move the goalposts from the expectation of a full cure to a position where the professional constantly seeks to *understand* these patients with their complex pathologies and infantile longings for all their needs to be met. This repeated attempt at understanding might, in itself, bring about some improvement in their condition and quality of life. If the staff could not put everything right, this did not mean they should give up and lose interest in their residents or devalue their work.

At times, the staff complained to me that they felt bored with some residents. When we took a closer look at these experiences, we could figure out what was behind this boredom, and how this feeling was set up in the staff by the residents' unconscious communication, which created a corresponding response in staff, killing off their interest. Through my interest in the team's state of mind, I attempted to restore their capacity to be interested in the patients. By the end of our discussions, the staff members were consistently visibly engaged in the thinking process, reflected in detailed and lively descriptions of episodes from interactions with residents that revealed something very personal and emotional about both groups. This was a recurrent experience in our sessions.

Zest for learning

After we had addressed the wish of the hostel team for an omnipotent solution to internal and external pressures, we were able to talk more openly about work difficulties. The carers became able to accept some responsibility for their apparently passive role. On the one hand, they claimed they were powerless and unimportant in relation to the decision making process in the hostel. On the other hand, they inadvertently undermined the authority of the mangers, represented by me, when they tried to turn me into someone who was there to deplete them, rather than allowing me to provide an opportunity for thinking and support.

"Selective amnesia" for the cases presented at the meetings changed to a painful memory of frustration that our previous discussion was just an attempt to understand a resident rather than produce a recipe for fixing the team's difficulties in managing him. The staff saw this as my failure to provide complete answers, and they resented having to discuss the same resident again in our next meeting. This was in contrast to my perception that we had, in fact, done a lot of work together. Was this disillusionment a result of their expectation that I should provide the "magic"? Or was it an attack on the discovery of their own capacity to think and feel disappointed if they did not always find the answers, which was projected on to me.

Normalization: "If only he had a girlfriend"

Mr D, a young resident with a history of early deprivation, mental breakdown, drug use, and violence, was not responding to the rehabilitation programme as well as the staff had hoped. As Mr D was likeable, the staff found it difficult to see him as mentally ill, sharing his frustration at not being able find a stable girlfriend and so "move on". However, as soon as girls knew he was ill, they left him. After some consideration in our work discussion session, the staff were able to understand their own unconscious feelings of guilt and sadness in relation to this young man. It was painful to see how his chances for a better life were compromised by both his mental illness and propensity to violence. Their wish to give him everything he needed, above all the normal life he believed he should have, was clear. We thought about an idealized recovery model, where a split between the healthy and the ill part of Mr D might be encouraged. I proposed that his mental illness was being dismissed by the staff due to their sense of guilt at having a better and a healthier life themselves. In addition, both patient and staff were unconsciously minimizing his illness to compensate for his lack of a normal life. The staff had to carry this painful knowledge on behalf of the patient, who did not have the psychic resources to do so himself. At the same time, at the other extreme of this attitude to his mental illness, there was a medical model in which the patient was seen as a heavily medicated chronically mentally ill person, a harsh alternative that both Mr D and staff tried to avoid.

I pointed out the need for mental illness to be recognized in its own right. If it is not, the patient experiences the staff as not taking his situation seriously and he then becomes abandoned as a patient by his carers, who do not want to know about his mental illness, just as he had been deserted by his girlfriends.

A missing thought: a missing patient

The team were concerned that they might have "failed" one of their residents, Mr E, who had not been seen for two days. He turned up eventually, but by then, according to the hostel's protocol, the staff had reported him to the police and the clinical team as a missing person, with the consequence that he was recalled to a secure hospital.

Mr E, a young man from a war-torn country, had suffered an early separation from his mother during the hostilities, and had witnessed a lot of violence. He had immigrated to the UK in his early teens, initially being looked after by his strict father, who worked as a security guard. He became involved in drugs and street crime, was diagnosed with paranoid schizophrenia, and subsequently treated in a medium secure unit for a few years. He had been transferred to the hostel a few months prior to his disappearance. Mr E initially claimed that he could not understand the importance of being on time or sticking to the hostel rules, but, with the help of the staff, was, in time, able to adapt to the restrictions and show some signs of improvement. He started to attend a college and his streetwise appearance changed to that of a regular student. However, his college attendance soon became erratic, and he dropped out as he could not concentrate or keep up with the demands of his studies, his primary interest being in acquiring expensive items of clothing and pampering his body. He had also applied to join a body-building course, but was unable to do so as it was fully booked. Concern was expressed that the patient had started "losing structure" after dropping out of college. One member of staff commented that Mr E was "a bit naïve" and "in too much of a hurry ... If you go against his views, he gets angry. He needs trust and time." He was also described as "just a vulnerable guy" who could not take a joke and was in need of affection, "but not the sort we can provide". He was used to being looked after by older girlfriends as if he was a young boy who needed his mother's attention. The staff felt that their trust was betrayed by the patient's non-adherence to his treatment contract when he breached the hostel's rules and did not turn up at the expected times.

We explored the nature of Mr E's experience of care, his perception of freedom in the secure unit from where he had been transferred, and his expectations of care in the hostel. The staff became aware of the contrast between their patients' treatment in medium secure units with rigid security rules and the system of trust in the hostel. We thought about the overwhelming and confusing effect this may have on some of them, including Mr E. While he already had a compromised internal psychic structure due to his early trauma and mental illness, he was expected to adapt from the hospital to the very different hostel setting, without getting "drunk on freedom". This might have such an effect on the patient's mind that he would experience the staff as omniscient, that is, magically knowing where he was at any given moment, and there would consequently be no need to report prolonged absences to the staff. Thus, the staff colluded with resident's sense of omnipotence when he believed that he was free and capable of managing his space and time boundaries without having to be accountable for his behaviour to anyone.

On the flip side of the coin, the patient freed himself from thinking that the staff would be capable of holding him in mind, and might notice or be bothered by his absence.

Fear of contact: safety vs. intrusion

On further discussion, it transpired that there was some confusion as to whether Mr E had been seen at all by the staff during the two days prior to his disappearance, as if he had somehow slipped out of their minds. There was a bedside light and television left on in his room, creating the impression that he was still in the hostel. Anxiety that Mr E was absent was passed from the day shift to the night shift, together with the hope that he would come back any moment from his college or his girlfriend, with a repetition of this anxious cycle on the following day.

As we advanced in our thinking, the staff expressed unrest about the system of checking residents' rooms. They had initially provided a familiarly dismissive statement about not being there "to police" the patients or to intrude on their private space without invitation, which soon changed to voicing anxiety about what one might find in the residents' rooms. This was an unconscious reference to Mr F, another patient, who had been found dead in his bedroom many years before. It was apparent that the staff had been anxious about making contact with Mr E, as if in checking his room they would be checking what was going on inside his mind. They described an anxious psychiatrist from the care team who, while having left the staff to manage Mr E within the hostel in the absence of any extra backup, requested a reinforced police unit to escort him to hospital on the day of his return to the hostel. This shows a split in the doctor's mind between over-concern on the one hand, and an apparent disregard of any risk on the other. Fearing a re-enactment of Mr E's early childhood trauma of being taken away from his mother/the staff, a violent response was anticipated.

Apparently, the police traced him and informed him about his recall to the secure hospital. This sent him into a panic and he resorted to antisocial acting-out behaviour. The staff commented that the police wanted to "wash their hands and have nothing to do with him". Mr E was eventually apprehended while driving a stolen motorcycle above the speed limit, having returned to what he knew best, a life of street crime.

Discussion of Mr E led us to consider how difficult it was for the team to maintain a safe balance in their work without being either too punitive and controlling or over-permissive.

This tension pertains to the question of how we should engage patients in making contact with the risky parts of themselves that they want to forget. In our subsequent meetings, as we struggled together, we developed the notion that it might be helpful for staff to, metaphorically speaking, stand alongside residents, using stories with narratives of comparable situations and characters to illustrate the behaviour that put the residents at risk. To start with, the patients see these stories as separate from themselves, which allows the staff member to highlight the risk and later to connect it with the patient's own experience.

As we developed this idea, it became evident that the staff felt that a fleeting but meaningful contact with the residents had become possible, through which the residents could experience staff as less punitive and controlling, but concerned and supportive. By the staff acknowledging the psychological defences in this way, the residents might themselves become able to develop and tolerate benign enquiring, and, as a consequence, become less frightened of think-ing about the terrifying aspects of their minds. The residents might eventually experience the staff as holding them in mind rather then intruding and "breaking into" their minds, mirroring the team's own experience of me standing alongside and thinking with them about their complex cases. However, the staff, on some occasions, told me that if they were to engage a resident and he opened up, they would not be equipped for what might emerge.

Emotional age of the patients: "I am not his father"

On one occasion, I had to wait fifteen minutes for the staff to finish an urgent meeting with Mr G, who had not returned on time, making the staff worried about him. He said he did not know that there were rules, that he was ill, and, after all, it was not his responsibility to be well. He told the staff, "It is your task to keep me well and out of hospital." Our discussion revolved around whether the patient had displayed passive irresponsibility, or a real need to be parented, bearing in mind that both patient and staff members find it painful to acknowledge the latter. Mr G's responsibility was completely disowned and delegated to the hostel team, so that when they confronted him with a reminder of *his* responsibilities, he perceived this as persecution, and turned it back on the team with great force, thus feeding into a cycle of dependency. In a case such as this, the staff felt that they had limited choices in how to relate to the patient: either to collude, or to retaliate and return the patient's responsibility to him. At the root of this difficulty lay parental failure to meet the patient's early developmental needs. This resulted in his unconscious wish for compensation and a sense of entitlement for his needs to be instantly magically gratified, which the staff knew they would never be able to do. Working with patients with histories of deprivation, in some cases compounded by mild learning disabilities, brings about infantile longings in the residents and parental responses in the staff. On an unconscious level, the support workers' own adverse childhood experiences may be revived, taking the form of a wish to put things right. The staff might find themselves feeling confused between their own roles as project workers and a demand to be parents to these infantile patients who refuse, or are unable, to grow.

"Depersonalization"

On another occasion, I walked in on a scene where Mr H was shouting abuse at a member of staff. The latter was responding in a professional and polite way, inviting Mr H to reciprocate, but the resident said that he would report the staff member for raising his voice. In our meeting, we considered whether Mr H was a vulnerable patient or a violent offender. The carer involved said he was not prepared to take the abuse, as Mr H had his own responsibility for following the rules. Somebody else noted that Mr H was vulnerable due to the nature of his mental illness and his level of violence risk. He needed to be spoken to when he was not aroused, so as not to increase his potential for violence. The first support worker then argued that Mr H would not make progress if he behaved in such way: "If he is at an overcrowded bus station and gets annoyed with somebody, he could be arrested if he becomes abusive." It seemed that Mr H was treating the hostel as his temporary accommodation, where the staff were just an inconvenient presence reminding him that he was a mentally ill offender-resident. I picked up that the staff felt inadequate in trying to question him, as if doing their job properly was a wrong thing to do. Their concern was experienced by Mr H and, subsequently, by the staff themselves, as interference. The staff, therefore, feared encountering his hostile responses, while the resident felt it was his right to tell the staff off. As a result, the staff became self-doubting, hesitant, and a few even avoided questioning Mr H altogether. They appeared to have lost the core sense of their task as well as their professional role, while Mr H was being denied his identity as a patient and offender. This is an example of how "depersonalization" (different aspects of this phenomenon are described in other chapters of this book) takes place. Both staff and patient become vulnerable parties at this point, which increases the risk of residents acting out.

Conclusion

It has been a challenge to write this chapter without running the risk of appearing critical of the patients, staff, mangers, or myself. I have described the process of engaging with staff, which, from the very beginning, was difficult. When I arrived at the hostel I was presented with a collection of staff anxieties and patients' complex needs. My observation was that the origin of the carers' anxieties was mostly to do with the nature of the task they were entrusted with. There is a tension between the workers' wish to do the best they can, and an unconscious, unrealistic expectation by society of what this task might entail. Dorothy Lloyd-Owen, who worked for many years with forensic staff and patients wrote: "The situation becomes further compounded by the public nature and expectations of the worker's role: the legislative system and public opinion accord an omnipotent role to the agency and hence to its workers" (Lloyd-Owen, 1997, p. 89). The staff are expected to be almost everything for this very complex patient group of mentally ill offenders, often with histories of early deprivation and trauma. Hence, it is easy to see how the former might be expected to view themselves as almighty support workers in the face of this Herculean task, rather than risk collapse into impotence or walk away disillusioned. Omnipotence is a solution to the anxiety of being under-resourced in the face of an impossible task. Another way of dealing with this pressure is to view the task in the context of reality, setting a limit to what can be expected and achieved. The question is what gets in the way of the limit-setting process?

In such settings, the staff are well aware that some of their residents give the appearance of engagement with treatment and rehabilitation. However, their unconscious aim is to keep themselves hidden from those who care for them, first in the secure ward and then in the hostel. The residents fear that what their support workers might see inside them is unbearable, and therefore they develop unconscious psychological defences to protect themselves by retreating from their carers. This results in the residents stripping themselves of any knowledge of their offences, as well as often refusing to see themselves as mentally ill patients who are expected to engage with the process of rehabilitation. It is important for the team to recognize these defences and to understand that, at an unconscious level, the patients are worried that the staff might not be able to hold them in mind. Like the patients themselves, the carers forget the extent of the patients' mental illness as well as the risks they pose. In addition to having to carry their own workload, the staff are the recipients of the patients' projected anxieties and those of the institution.

Through our meetings, I identified the carers' fear of new learning in the face of paralysing anxiety about engaging with their residents and what the staff felt about this. I put it to them that it was possible for us to tackle these anxieties, in order to regain their interest in their work and to facilitate new learning. As I addressed this, I was able to develop the notion that I was an external source of vision for the staff. Initially, they feared that I could either see that they were incompetent, or reveal that they had "dangerous" emotions that they felt they could not deal with. Thus, I threatened to expose them to the awareness of this unconscious experience. To acknowledge their ignorance of this would expose their fear of fail-ure. It is in this way that an organization can unconsciously create defensive responses and structures which aim at disabling, or even eliminating, both an external observer/expert and the team's exper-tise projected in the observer, which was exactly how I felt at times. The positive effect of this was that it gave me an idea of how the staff might feel in their day-to-day work, and how they had to divorce their capacity to learn from their need to survive. The pursuit of knowledge is natural, and this desire to learn can be rekindled when paralysing anxiety, which inhibits learning, is iden-tified and addressed by an interested and containing professional representing the caring aspects of an organization.

Afterword

After two years of working with the team, a shift in attitude was apparent. It became possible for senior managers to recruit fresh, often less experienced but more enthusiastic staff, while some of the more entrenched members of the team reached the stage where they felt able to move on. A new team manager made a point of attending clinical supervision, and this encouraged the team's deci-sion-making. It was evident that staff members were learning from their experience of being with their patients. They were able to recognize the full extent of the damage in their mentally ill resi-dents, which facilitated working together towards more realistic goals. The carers became aware of their need to have clinical super-vision more often so that we could focus on old, "stuck" cases and look at them again in closer detail. I found myself bringing in rele-vant articles and papers for the staff to read. I was also able to attend out loud to the unconscious group process, which had become less feared and more welcome. This has now truly become a clinical discussion group, what Bion (1961) describes as a "work group", engaged with the difficulties of its primary task, the care of the residents, rather than evading discussing the task's problem because it is too painful or causes psychological conflict within or between the staff group members.

References

Bion, W. R. (1961). The work group. In: *Experiences in Groups and Other Papers* (pp. 135–136). London: Tavistock.

Lloyd-Owen, D. (1997). From action to thought: supervising mental health workers with forensic patients. In: B. Martindale (Ed.), *Supervision and its Vicissitudes* (pp. 87–100). London: Karnac.

CHAPTER THREE

Sustainable organizations in health and social care: developing a "team mind"

Jina Barrett

Introduction

There are significant challenges involved in providing care, support, treatment, and custody for people who are adjudged antisocial or self-harming, disturbed, or experiencing chronic exclusion.

One area of challenge, apparent to any observer of how such services function, is that the business of staying on task seems often to be affected by teams and their individual members taking on or replicating service user coping strategies, such as: "getting rid" of problems; relying on reaction rather than using reflection to inform action; rejecting help while insisting upon the need for it; and "forgetting" important information like histories of abuse, index crimes or the fact of suicide.

Given that knowing, and working to, agreed tasks is linked to organizational survival, sustainability then becomes a key problem, whether it refers to sustaining contact with service users in the service of promoting "recovery", wellbeing or change, or sustaining service provision when workers cannot continue to do effective work together. In some of these kinds of settings, the task will include simply sustaining life against insidious destructive forces.

One of the ways in which organizations support staff in such work settings involves the provision of reflective practice groups, or staff support meetings. Establishing and integrating such forums is a challenge in itself, and is increasingly so in a world dominated by requirements to achieve measurable outcomes for clients in performance-managed systems. The challenge lies not so much in the actual demands of measure-ability or manage-ability (these demands can promote development of useful frameworks), but in the existence of a state of mind which *only* measures or manages and, thus, excludes thinking about human realities of service provision. It is the promotion of an either/or approach that undermines quality of services.

This chapter argues that the provision of "supportive frameworks" for staff (such as reflective practice groups, or forums which attempt to establish shared thinking about the work) is likely to be ineffective unless explicitly designed to explore practice in relation to management processes (organizational tasks, systems, and structures), which, in turn, are used to promote and sustain active reflexive interagency structures, or "care pathways". The repeated difficult realities that emerge in well-functioning reflective practice forums can leave workers feeling exposed and vulnerable unless the information processed therein can be actively used to make practice decisions in organizationally transparent ways. When staff and their managers cannot *see* the links between the *thinking* developed in reflective practice spaces and the everyday *doing* of the work, thinking can come to feel like a useless activity, which exists only to make staff feel bad and emphasize their apparent failures.

So-called "staff support" structures in these circumstances come to be feared and avoided, properly in my view, given that they add to the experience staff often have of feeling responsible for the difficulties of their clients or patients. The problem is that such arrangements are abandoned as malignant more often than investigated benignly for what has gone awry. The unexplored catastrophe of an abandoned staff support arrangement can often be found in teams who profess a hatred of something they contemptuously call "psychodynamic" or "therapeutic" groups or meetings. The apparent impossibility of exploring these experiences undermines sustainability, and can lead to quite mechanical, and sometimes dehumanized, working practices.

It is also true that these kinds of difficulties are caused by clinicians who embark on providing reflective practice forums armed only with a therapeutic or counselling training, in the belief that self-disclosure or the revelation of personal feelings will help workers, while ignoring workplace systems of task, role, and function. Such importation of distorted reality on the part of professionals also undermines sustainability. Working with the effects of disturbed and perverse behaviour in teams requires robust capacities for facing, naming, digesting, and surviving difficulties which often seem to be in the team as well as in the clients, within an explicit framework of managed service delivery and development.

The heart of the solution (like all the best solutions) is in the problem: in technical terms, the process of "taking on", or replication of, the service's users' characteristic coping strategies, or "becoming like" service users, can be thought of as a form of identification with those one is seeking to help. The purpose of this chapter is to show that this is not an intentional "act", but, rather, appears to be an inevitable consequence of work in this area. Further, the process of replication can be "read" by experientially or emotionally literate teams as a communication about the work. The core of the chapter is about how this often unrecognized feature of the work can provide its most sustaining food for thought, and for decision making, and, therefore, promotes organizational sustainability.

The chapter looks briefly at the recent history of a specific area of social policy that has direct implications for health and criminal justice policy and, ultimately, for the communities we live in. Two organizational case studies then present the very real difficulties experienced in providing help to vulnerable and disturbed people, followed by an attempt to use the problems presented by these difficulties to develop a way forward. Identifying features of services described in the case studies have been changed.

Recent policy context

There are high numbers of people in vulnerable social groupings, the funding of support for whom is delegated to housing-related services that function separately from mainstream mental health, justice or penal, and social care services. This is a sector from whence individuals arrive into hospital or custody settings and is the place to where they return, even if to a different location or service. This is also often the sector where individuals in receipt of secondary and tertiary care and treatment live, although far too often, as has been the case for people who may be diagnosable with personality disorder, it is the sector which has no access to care or treatment: it is the world of supported accommodation.

The funding for such services is allocated by local authorities, using central government grants framed by the Supporting People programme, the concept of which began in 1996 when a judicial review decided that Housing Benefit was being misused and should only be paying for bricks and mortar rent, and not support services.

> The aim of the programme is to enable people to remain in a more independent living situation, avoiding institutional care such as hospitals or, at the extreme, prison or a life on the street. Equally it aims to help people in such institutional care to move to more independent and stable homes in the community. [ODPM, 2004]

One of the impacts of this attempt to manage the economics of social care has been an artificial divide between "care" and "support" that, along with an insistence on "move on" (to "independence"), has fragmented the frontline social care systems and, therefore, the lives of thousands of vulnerable members of society in this decade.

When Foster and Roberts published their book *Managing Mental Health in the Community* in 1998, the community care "revolution", which saw many patients moved out of large institutions, or asylums, into "homes" in the community, was already well under way. Foster noted then that

> if we ignore the experience of mental health professionals and appoint too many untrained staff to key positions in community care, we are in danger of neglecting the [service] users through creating systems of care that are unable to address their dependency needs . . . [Foster, 1998, p. 69]

Now, ten years later, it is possible to see that this advice has been ignored on a scale that will contribute to even more serious problems in the decade to come. The "homes" which were created to provide care in communities are services now becoming subject to Supporting People funding requirements and quality assurance frameworks, which insist on provision of "support" only, and "move on", in many cases after only two years. The resulting economies of scale particularly affect staffing, training for whom tends to be limited to being competency based. The experience of Foster's "mental health professionals" has not only been ignored, but severed, leaving often very good, even if untrained, staff floundering, overwhelmed by uncontained need and distress, and disaffected in turn. High levels of staff turnover characterize this sector, which undermines the most useful aspect of any human service, its human relatedness.

This wholesale political effort to deny individual dependency needs has disrupted and continues to disrupt the lives of people who were moved out of those traditional care settings (who were promised "a home for life") and of those who rely on the help of the state (the rest of us) to maintain anything resembling a "home". There is a distorted reality at the heart of social policy which requires services to move people on to ever more independent settings because policy makers (those who work on behalf of all of us as citizens in our present society) cannot face or understand the problems that are presented by individuals, whether in need, at risk, or a risk to themselves or others. As with all defensive manoeuvres, these policies then fail to address real difficulties, and, in some cases, sabotage local attempts to reduce inpatient care with integrated health and social care initiatives.

The fact that relative independence of service users and reasonable standards of self care require dependable services, and sometimes extended periods of actual care by such services, seems to have been "forgotten" in policy development.

Characterizing services as providers of "support only" represents a disavowal of the need for dependability. Policies that insist that people learn independence skills for "move on" through cognitive methods, when the very source of their difficulty rests on the impossibility of learning from experience, can only result in short term gains, and leaves core psychological and social functioning difficulties unaddressed.

The exclusion or excision of the individual histories and diffi-culties—a recognized dynamic in working with offenders—has become an established feature of frameworks or approaches to care and support: these frameworks emphasize competence and capa-bility rather than recognizing incapability or disturbance, either in the worker or the service user. This means the ordinary (as in ever-present feature of social functioning) societal projection of distur-bance into service users is hidden by twin forces of denial of real difficulty *and* the insidious pressure to move service users on after limited periods of support. The mind's eye of the staff team is drawn to movement, to action, rather than being allowed to stop and think, to reflect on individual need with the individuals involved. This imperative for "move on" in housing and other sup-port settings is actually contributing to the continuation of home-lessness in society, through implicit avoidance of the significant social and psychological problems which underlie the condition of being unable to sustain a "home", at whatever point in an individ-ual's life-cycle this might occur.

Workers in these settings frequently baulk at the idea of move on for clients because they know the reality of their clients capacities, and also how disturbing and stressful moving house/home is for any individual: it does not make sense to them, so they have to dis-avow their awareness of the acutely disturbing aspects of the impact of the move. This can result in dehumanized, cut-off, and, some-times, violent acts of expulsion, with the inevitable consequence of breakdown, and, for some, hospitalization, because the individual's coping capacity as linked to the support setting is sundered. The eco-nomic as well as humanitarian risk at the heart of current policy is hidden by the artificial divide between care and support. It is to be hoped that before current funding arrangements are changed yet again, commissioners notice that the apparent difficulty in reducing acute admissions is concomitant with the contracting out of "sup-port" to services cut off, or acting separately, from mainstream health and social care organizations.

"Anti-reflective" practice: when thinking is dangerous

Acres of Stone was an organization providing accommodation and housing support services for homeless people, where I was asked to provide a consultation event for a hostel team. The aim of the inter-vention was to identify staff support needs in the lead-up to a planned closure of the service. The date and location for the event were speedily agreed because the commissioning manager was just about to take three months' leave and seemed under pressure to give the staff group something before he left. Under some pressure myself to provide services, I missed the warning implicit in this sidestep-ping of pressure and in the manager's departure, but also in the report that a recent Away Day for the staff group had led to serious complaints from staff about the parent organization, and that they hoped the consultation event would provide a place to "recover".

Training and consultation, even when provided on site, is likely to be of short-lived use (or even ineffective) unless transparent account is taken of the "structure, culture and mode of functioning" (Menzies Lyth, 1988) of the organizational setting where the inter-vention is taking place. When I am asked for consultation or train-ing, I will sometimes use a Diagnostic Event—a consultation structure I designed to provide both the team and myself with an assessment of the current state of the organization. This involves using Stokoe's model for a healthy organization as a template for a day-long team event (see Chapter Thirteen), starting with an exer-cise to capture the experience of the workers at that moment in the existence of their service, then establishing structural requisites—whether a shared view exists of the primary task, the structure of roles and responsibilities, and the basic operational principles underpinning the work, and finally exploring what best supports workers in carrying out their daily work. In this way, teams can begin to identify gaps in the organizational framework of the service, and make plans to address these in other forums, as well as making plans for training and support needs.

Experience of the work at the hostel

In the opening exercise of the Event, staff members were eager to describe their experience of the work in the hostel setting. They did this through creating individual pictures, which they then presented to their colleagues. The overall picture of the hostel that emerged was of a dark, grim, and dangerous world, which had a prison-like quality. There were no windows from which to view the outside

world or through which to look inwards, and working there frequently provoked the sense of being in a whirlpool or vortex.

Service users were described as "residents", but were represented as existing in a world of their own, not linked to other
people or to ordinary workaday or social life, but, paradoxically,
not completely excluded because of a marked feature of belonging
to a group or "gang" culture, by virtue of sharing the same kind of
life. This existence was repeatedly pictured as a loop from which
the only exit appeared to be a grave; as a world where time stands
still or is obliterated, and where smell or body odours are used to
keep people away.

Residents were portrayed as people who cannot trust anyone,
who would try anything to get what they want, and seem to care
about nothing. The idea of consequences or responsibility was
absent. The rule of law and the ordinary caring authority of an
accommodation provider remained unrecognized, and leadership
or management roles, where acknowledged, were felt to be abusive.

Pictures showed residents as walking wounded, with weeping
abscesses and missing limbs. One drawing showed a figure eating,
vomiting, and then consuming the vomit. Another picture showed
a man unconscious in a communal area of the hostel with a needle
in his groin: this was a scene a worker had come across a few weeks
earlier and could not get out of her head. Hands appeared in a
number of pictures as a representation of a hostel worker's motto:
"If you cannot see your hands, you are dead". Needle-stick injuries
are a constant risk.

Another worker described the hostel as a pinball machine,
where staff follow residents to make contact. Contact with residents
is dominated by demands for entry to their rooms, as they
constantly lose their own keys. Overall, the sense was of a battle-
ground not far under the surface, with an outbreak of war waiting
to be triggered by a wrong move on the part of a worker.

Organizational structure for the work at the hostel

In the second session of the event, the group was divided into three
sub-groups to discuss and describe the organizational structure for
the work in response to three questions:

- what is the primary task of the service?
- what is the system (or hierarchy) of roles and responsibilities in place to achieve the task?
- what are the basic principles informing how the task is achieved?

There was consistency across two sub-groups about a primary task of providing accommodation and support to access a more settled life; the third sub-group described the task in terms of taking people off the streets and reducing rough sleeping, as if they believed themselves to be agents of a government directive.

There was consistency across all three groups about what is involved in achieving the task, but roles and operational structures (the "who" and the "how") were collapsed into each other and jumbled. Where roles were clarified, the hierarchy appeared flattened. The choice appeared to be between a dehumanized or depersonalized approach to the task in this interchangeability of "who" and "how", and an apparently "undependant", isolated self-sufficiency.

There were tangibly different perspectives of the work hinted at in attempts to address the question of operating principles, but these differences remained unacknowledged, so that a spurious sense of sameness was maintained. One stated operational feature was that if one worker could not achieve something, such as making contact with a resident, then someone else would pick up the baton. This produced a sense of a shadow of the gang or group which apparently operated together in an undifferentiated way, again producing this sense of depersonalization. This "if I can't do it, someone else will" approach meant that no one could see what they *cannot* do.

At midday, as people dispersed for lunch, I had begun to feel that this work was of no consequence, in contrast to the usual experience I have at this point of the event when substantial group energy for the task has been generated by acknowledging realities of work.

Support systems at the hostel

In the third session of the event, three different groupings addressed the question about what best supports workers in carrying out the work of the service. Much of the support listed was structural, and contributions developed a somewhat concrete quality, as people described changes to the building (such as the installation of windows), organizational structures, and resources which would help. The communication forums sought were ordinary, such as team meetings, supervision sessions, appraisals, but had rather idealized qualities. Support was sought in the form of peer supervision or team building from within: there was no sense of help from higher up or outside being either useful or available. Workers wanted to be consulted, or at least communicated with, they said, by senior managers who were portrayed as "blind" to the existence of workers. Resources such as onsite medical staff were also seen as essential to the work.

When the whole group came together to discuss the identified support needs, an argument broke out between a member of the cleaning team and the other workers. I thought this was the "war" breaking out, triggered by the cleaner's "wrong" move: describing reality. He wanted to make the point that the residents did not care about or respect the work of the staff, because, if they did, they would not put shit all over the showers, basins, and bathroom floors after he had cleaned. Some workers tried to silence him, and successfully inveigled the manager into leading the attempt, by telling him he did not understand the residents, that they are damaged people, and, therefore, expectations had to be lowered. Others took offence at the idea of "damaged people", and thought a "there but for the grace of God go I" approach saved them from feeling more disturbed by the work. The sense of guilt about being unable to help inherent in both attitudes was tangible.

I talked to them about how they had graphically demonstrated how difficult their work was, mentioning some of the horrors they have to deal with and their sense of isolation, despite portraying themselves as a working group. The specialist drugs worker interjected that he and his colleagues were more like the street gang of the homeless in that sense, and that it probably was not a helpful way to work. I noticed with them that attempting to think about their own support needs very quickly re-created the kinds of interaction between them that they experienced every day with the anti-social and disordered aspects of their clients. I thought this made them concerned that they might be like the residents, and noticed how difficult it was to get enough space to think together and toler- ate facing the very real problems such as that described by their colleague the cleaner. The responses varied from agreement to downright dismissal of these ideas.

Despite an apparent return to the work of the end of the day, as the event closed I was left with the feeling that *I* had done some- thing "wrong", but could not identify the source of this experience, apart from it being something to do with not being able to help, or helping in the "wrong" way.

Review of the Diagnostic Event

At a review of the event a week later with the commissioning manager and the acting manager appointed to replace him, I was told in no uncertain terms that the staff group (as one, no dissent- ing voices) thought the first two sessions of the event (workplace experience and structure) were "good", but that they did not see the point of generating a wish-list of support structures as nothing was going to change anyway, and that I should not have allowed or encouraged the cleaner to speak, because he was always complain- ing and "taking over" their meetings. The new acting manager said he felt I had suggested they (the staff) "had personality disorders". The "commissioning" manager, having arrived an hour late for the review meeting, told me he thought I was going to "give them something" on the day: I reminded him of our planning discussions and referred to the programme we had agreed; the acting manager behaved as if shocked to see this, having not, same as all the other workers, been given a copy by the commissioning manager before the day.

Neither he nor his colleague engaged with my feedback about the difficulty of their work and the potential usefulness of some basic mental health training, or of a case discussion forum to address individual residents' needs in detail. They thought nothing I had offered could be accommodated in their schedule, and told me that unless I could "open doors" for their residents, I was of no use. In other words, *their* door was slammed in *my* face.

In this way, a feeling of profound uselessness was effectively lodged in me and I was sent on my way, left alone to contemplate the way the shit had been smeared across the instruments of psychological hygiene I had had the temerity to offer. When I recovered, I realized that in such a setting, thinking is dangerous, because it opens one up to being used (or ab-used) as a receptacle for evacuation of truly unbearable experiences: the constant pinball-like movement of the pursuit of the (euphemistically named) "residents" effectively dodges any attempt to face reality. From this point of view, thinking, as an activity that might enable the conversion of raw experience into thoughts, which could, in turn, enable reality to be faced and development to take place, is difficult precisely because it is reality that has to be killed off or repudiated.

Reflecting their experience to them as "being like" the characteristics of their client group was tantamount, to their ears, of telling them they were "the same as" the client group. This evidence of a compromised capacity to symbolize or to use metaphor, in this setting, suggests that the work traumatizes the workers and, thus, hinders the capacity to achieve the necessary psychological distance to reflect. I have come to think of the "managing system" in such services as depending on anti-reflective practice, because the realities of engaging in the work have the potential to be profoundly dehumanizing.

Subsequent exploration through trial and error experiments with the parent organization in this instance has benefited from this experience. It is important not to face these workers with what they *cannot* know "in-side" themselves until they have a very safe, dependable setting for facing what they can know "out-side" themselves, that is, about the clients. This is generally better achieved by providing straightforward, non-jargon information about their clients and strategies for managing individual behaviours. The prerequisite for such input is robust leadership with a capacity for insight, in order to build safe reflection opportunities over time.

Be afraid, be very afraid . . .

When I worked in Child Protection services many years ago, my manager had a screen saver on her computer which flashed into being each morning when she switched it on, with the words "Be afraid, be very afraid . . .", and again, later on in the day, disturbingly, as a response to being allowed to "fall" into sleep mode. I have found it helpful to hold that screen saver in my mind when I am engaged in consulting to organizations working with disturbance and perversion, like a default setting: when it disappears from my consciousness, it is inevitably a sign of appropriate anxiety being removed from view and heralds a defensive operation which militates against the proper activity of work: finding and engaging with reality in the service of development.

Fear and anxiety are experiences that are often squeezed out when reality is too difficult and too complicated to face, and yet are key indicators of the potential for risk. For example, in a pre-suicide state, service users can convey a sense that all is well and there are no reasons to be concerned, yet it is the very fact of the absence of the feeling of worry which ought to alert us to a crucial change in a previously troubled, suicidal person's state.

In a voluntary sector supported housing service for women making the transition back into the community from prisons or special hospitals, called Sunrise, where I provided a version of the Short Course Intervention (for a description, see Chapter Thirteen, by Stokoe) adapted for the setting, I encountered a difficulty with managing fear and anxiety which provided an insight into the special challenges of that setting. At the time of the Intervention, the numbers of service users at the project were low. Some staff members were being redeployed to other parts of the parent organization to save money, and the service manager was preoccupied with finding new referrals.

As the course started, a worker described being taken through a disciplinary procedure by the parent organization (still ongoing at the time), following an incident where she had spoken sharply to a client. She felt misunderstood, frightened, angry, and ill-treated, as she struggled to understand what she had done wrong. She had been working for twenty-four hours continuously when the encounter which led to her speaking sharply took place: she had had to work a day shift on the back of a night shift when a colleague failed to turn up for work. She admitted to feeling tired and short-tempered, and when a client complained about not being helped in response to the worker's refusal to do something practical for her, suggesting she was able to manage the task in question herself, she told the client sharply, "I am not your servant". Her managers took this as evidence of ill-treatment of the client when they received the complaint, and no attempt was made to understand the situation; instead, disciplinary procedures were instigated against her. When the worker spoke of these events in the group context of the course, there was a marked lack of engagement on the part of her colleagues, which contributed to a sense of the worker being isolated and, it seemed, "criminalized".

Some time later, in a discussion of teaching about human development, the service manager objected to the idea that, in early development, an infant might feel bad in response to the absence of his mother, which might lead to him having an experience of a "bad" mother. She asserted in a concrete fashion that there is no such thing as "a bad mother", and seemed unable to countenance the idea that the infant's experience of absence of his carer was the thing that led him to feel bad. The service manager replicated the conversion of a feeling into a fact: she thought that I must be wrong (i.e., a bad person) for talking about such ideas. Her "feeling" of dislike or discomfort about the idea I introduced became a "fact" in her mind, which quickly became an "act" in saying I was wrong.

In the work discussion which followed, it emerged that one of their service users, soon due for discharge into an independent flat in the community after the requisite two-year preparation phase, had murdered her infant son. There was some competition to present the client as having "not known" she had killed the child, so could not possibly be responsible (this is in a setting post-conviction and imprisonment for the crime). In other words, the staff group wanted to get rid of this woman's history by distorting the reality of her actions, converting "bad" into "not knowing", and, thence, into "not responsible". At that moment in time, they could not face the actual reality that this woman had killed her own child.

In the dynamic between managers and staff, the misguided political correctness of instituting disciplinary proceedings against someone for stating the obvious, albeit tersely delivered, appeared to indicate difficulties in managing everyday encounters, while indications of the existence of homicidal aggression seemed to be being denied. Staff members seemed under pressure to demonstrate superficial good behaviour and blind positivity, and to not respond to clients in real, ordinary, and human ways. This created the sense of an autocratic regime designed to replicate the institution of prison, while allowing staff to behave as if they had no idea why their clients had been imprisoned in the first place. This is where there is "no such thing as a bad mother": engagement with only the victim part of the client means engagement with only the abused child part, not the part with the capacity to be a violent parent.

In this distorted reality, the staff member was left worrying and frightened about whether she would be dismissed from her job, not knowing what her real crime was. Denigrating the staff member for being ordinary and human and telling a kind of everyday truth hints at the perversion of real work. This was reflected in the invitation I experienced to feel as if I was a bad person for describing an ordinary, if complicated, feature of human development.

In both teams described, there is something that seems to have disabled particular functions of staff members. Attitudes, ways of thinking about people, difficulties with facing reality, denying existing information, efforts to be rid of anxiety and fear, feelings being turned into facts: these functions are evidence of the human mind working in different ways. Given that such functions appear to be shared by individuals in their organizational groupings or teams, it poses the question of whether a team can be considered to have a mind.

What is a "team mind"?

To begin to explore the idea of a team mind, it is useful to ask what "mind" means: simply put, it is the function or "place" in humans where thinking happens. Thinking is an activity which converts feelings and experiences into thoughts, and, in turn, into words, through a process of trying to make sense of these experiences using what is already known, in the form of an internal conversation (Stokoe, see Chapter Thirteen). Another way of describing "mind" is as the place in individuals where mental operations (Garland, 2000) are carried out—mentalizing, imagining, recognizing, remembering, connecting, and putting words to experiences felt through senses and emotions—before deciding to act or behave in a particular way.

To describe a team as having a mind, then, is to describe a team engaged in mental operations, or thinking and, therefore, converting experiences into information to inform decisions about actions. As Stokoe puts it in answer to the question, "what does thinking in a team look like?", whereas thinking for the individual is like having an internal conversation, thinking in a team looks like a team having an actual conversation (Stokoe, see Chapter Thirteen). In settings where the team is unable, for whatever reason, to have "conversations" about experiences in the workplace, the question arises as to whether the team can think.

> When people come to their business enterprises each day—be it a commercial company, a hospital, a university—"they have to think to know what they are supposed to be doing—if they all forgot this the company would collapse and would cease to exist" [Bohm & Edwards, 1991, quoted in Lawrence, 1999, p. 41]

However, in the helping services, there is an extra level of experience to take into account: what happens if the work the people come to work to do affects their capacity to think about what they are supposed to be doing?

In the case of Acres of Stone, the "team mind" could manage activities of describing and putting the experience of the work into words, and members could say what the work of the team consisted in, including different perspectives. However, in the state it was in at the time of the Diagnostic Event, the mind of the team struggled to differentiate roles and operational activity, who and how, such that people became the thing they did (support work became "doing" support to residents through mechanical, rote-like interactions which enabled workers to report something had been done or not done at handover). Workers who are consistently treated as being the thing they do in concrete terms do tend to give up having a mind with which to think about what they do.

The idea that the team might be able to ask for help or support in their work seemed to disturb them: in fact, the idea that they could be helped appeared to provoke aggression. The way in which the team mind then managed conflict was to establish right and wrong, and to battle for dominance of "right" while getting rid of the "wrong" (on that day, pushing this into both the cleaner and myself). This seemed to create a perverse moral system: however, it felt defensive, as if designed to avoid (or, more accurately, to actively seek to be rid of) reality, and, specifically, any notion of being in need of help or support.

This avoidance was also reflected in the recourse to "pinball" operations of staff in pursuit of residents, and in the persistent losing of keys through which residents locked themselves out of their rooms. However, the true perversion of the idea of help lay in the fact that workers were constantly being forced to witness extreme methods of killing off psychic reality, whether through self-medication or self-mutilation: "watch and suffer while I do not". It ought not to be surprising that in such circumstances, the team "mind" becomes instrumentalist and its relations become depersonalized: the interactions they are called upon to engage in are, literally, *de-thinking*, that is, designed to remove or annihilate thinking, or to remove oneself from being "in mind". If the survival of staff depends upon giving up having a mind with which to think, then it is likely there will be difficulties with task and role performance.

At Sunrise, at the particular point in time described above, the "team mind" had developed a positivistic and politically correct approach to the work, a kind of prison outside prison walls where judgements about right and wrong held sway over any attempts to understand experiences. This extension of the custodial system state of mind into the community setting clearly provided some psychological safety (the certainty of rules) for staff and service users alike, but effectively risked being used to pervert the real and very complicated task of preparing the service users for returning to live in the community (the same "community" of society which had required incarceration for their crimes).

This task might be described as enabling service users to face enough of the reality of their crimes, which, in turn, ought to help them to use ongoing support to survive these realities, and enable community organizations to manage the inherent risk into the future. This task, at Sunrise, was hindered by the struggle that the mind of the staff team encountered in thinking about and facing the reality of the criminal actions of a service user on this occasion, particularly where the murder of a child by a mother was concerned. The absence of a "team mind" in this instance, which could be used to make sense of experience, having instead a "managing" system which distorted the reality of the service user's history and actions, undermined the possibility of real help. This "managing system" turned the task of rehabilitation into one of rescuing the denigrated client (from conviction and imprisonment) and restoring the idealization (particularly of motherhood) which avoided reality.

What begins to emerge, then, in thinking about these teams and their capacities of mind, is that their ways of being, relating, and behaving appear to replicate the ways of coping or managing which characterize their service users.

Coping system vs. mind: why do teams appear to replicate service user characteristics?

Whatever views we hold about why we choose the kinds of work we do, it might help to be curious about why there is such a tendency not only to operate in ways that are fundamentally anti-task, but, in the very nature of being so, to appear to replicate key characteristics of the functioning of service users in their work setting.

At Acres of Stone, if we consider that the team, by inviting him to the Event knowing what he would do, put the cleaner in the position of describing the appalling reality of the way in which the everyday work of attempting to create a decent environment is attacked and destroyed, we might also notice that the soon-to-depart manager succumbed to pressure to lead the posse to silence him. We could hypothesize that this represents a central characteristic of a hostel "resident", *viz.* a never-ending and virulent internal battle between the wish for a home (represented by paying some state benefits to live at the hostel rather than on the street) and a simultaneous attack on that wish intensified by the attempt to silence it. The evidence to support the idea of an attack on an ordinary need for a home is sobering: smearing, injecting drugs, continuous alcohol consumption, losing keys, avoiding contact, putting others at risk by not disposing of needles safely, turning workers into things rather than accepting them (and making appropriate use of them) as potentially helpful human beings. We might further hypothesize, therefore, that the idea of a home must be so intolerable that even death is preferable: home, in these circumstances, must be dangerous. (It is also possible that death is another kind of home from which one is excluded and consigned to a tortuous marginal existence.) My own experience, then, of having the door slammed in my face, and having crippling, dehumanizing feelings of "uselessness" lodged in me for suggesting it is possible to think about the work, for seeking to put into words what it is like to work at the hostel, is paradoxically, even if painfully, useful. It tells me that curiousity and thinking are unwelcome activities, and are likely to have been turned away previously. It tells me that such activity, given that it involves facing reality, may even be dangerous.

If the nature of my exclusion by the workers mirrored the exclusion of the workers by the residents, as such it is likely that the residents had extensive damaging experience of exclusion—in the form of having curiousity and concern turned away, of being denied access to the mind of another. The actions of the managers and team, whether they know it or not, replicate the actions of their service users, and, in doing so, "describe" important aspects of the functioning.

At Sunrise, the "parent" organization put the transgressing worker in a position of feeling persecuted and being frightened that she would be dismissed for doing something wrong. The service user parent, in order to be cut off enough from the effects of her actions in killing her baby, would have had to split off her awareness of the reality of what she was doing. Drawing on what we know about infanticide (Motz, 2008), what she was probably doing was managing an overwhelmed and frightening state of persecution. By putting all her bad self experience (feelings) at that moment into the child and believing (conversion to a fact) that he was the bad part of her, so getting rid of him (the act) would get rid of the bad part of her.

The managers and staff at Sunrise would be appalled to think they were acting in any way like a service user in a homicidal frame of mind at that time, yet their actions are a form of replication. Feeling persecuted by low numbers and frightened about survival, workers sought to put all their fears of being a "bad service" into one worker, who, if successfully proved to be the "bad worker", would mean they could get rid of appearing to be a bad service by getting rid of the worker, without ever acknowledging their aware-ness of the effects of their actions. (In addition, living with service users constantly struggling to manage to live in a world that has convicted them of the "badness" they fear and have tried to evacu-ate can affect staff, making it particularly difficult to be helpful, except by excising parts of reality.)

If such behaviours of service users as those described (seeking and simultaneously rejecting help or "housing"; splitting the world into extremes of "good" this and "bad" that and trying to get rid of the "bad"; preferencing action over reflection) can broadly be considered to represent psychological coping systems; these could perhaps be seen to be designed to "de-think". These coping or managing systems demonstrate either the destruction of thinking, or, in developmental terms, a severely compromised ability to think. In some cases, the coping system exists because of the absence of the development of a mind that could cope with anxiety in the first place.

With this evidence of impaired thinking capacity, it becomes possi-ble to hypothesize that teams replicate service user functioning in certain settings because service users in these settings need the mind of an "other" (worker, team) to take in, digest and make sense of their experience, because this is a capacity unavailable in their own psychological functioning at that time. The difficulty, however, is that part of the "taking in" involves ingesting an impaired think-ing capacity, which can imprison workers in non-thinking states.

Staff members need colleagues who recognize the signs of think-ing-gone-missing, to help with the recovery. However, because whole teams can be affected, managers need to be aware of, and responsive to, the straying from task and role that can result. The exploration and interpretation of the *experience* of undertaking the work of the setting becomes a significant managerial function, whether performed by managers or delegated to an organizational consultant, because of the information available therein, but also because of the recognition that the continuity of workers' capacity to work is at stake, with consequences for the ability of the organi-zation to do its work. That job performance in human service systems will be always be affected by the experience of the work ought to point to the need for systems designed to help recover thinking.

Where whole teams are disabled by "de-thinking", or by attacks on thinking capacity, the kind of help that is required involves a capacity for the dual position of participant–observer, someone who can both see and feel, who can encounter *and* describe the state of mind of the team to the team. This, in turn, helps to return their own professional mind to them, through an enquiry about task, roles, and principles.

Recovering thinking: using the team mind to sustain work

Put in another way, key information about the functioning of service users can be found in the way team members interact with each other and with the adjacent world. It is helpful to recognize this replication, or *identification with* service users, as a necessary communication of characteristic ways of operating or coping in relation to the setting and, therefore, to the workers, which can be "read" or understood. When this "reading" and attempting to understand takes place in the context of a group meeting which has been deliberately constituted to study such communications, it becomes possible to then translate the resulting understanding into decisions designed to help the people using the service, and has the benefit of developing the staff.

This is an extra dimension: teams that work in this way come to learn that such understanding (which is hard won and easily slips away again, hence the need for continuous exploration) over time reveals that clients can only function through provoking particular identifications. In turn, the identification, or the "being like", reveals the circumstances, or disturbance, of development, which has led to the fact of being a user of the service. This results in a greater and more realistic understanding of individual service users' difficulties. Team members are also instinctively affected by the force of this kind of communication from the service users, but are often appalled to find they are "being like" their client group in their responses. The truth is, of course, that they "are like" because of being human, but also "not like" because different, not least because of being in a work role, and it is this very difference which is important to the quality of the work done with the service user. The service user provokes a "being like", and the worker has to recognize the dimensions of the "being like" at the same time as "not behaving like" in order to be of most use to the client. Teams that work in this way have access to complex layers of insight into human functioning, and are often more consistently helpful to the users of their services. However, to achieve an ongoing capacity for metabolizing the "effect" of the work in this way, a principle is required that teams relinquish both the tendency to want to claim as their own the feelings the work produces in their members and the equivalent tendency to ascribe the feelings to someone else. In other words, feelings that occur in role in the workplace are likely to be the result of taking up that role in that workplace (Stokoe, see Chapter Thirteen).

Looked at in this way, the deliberately constructed "team mind" (regular authorized meeting for thinking about the work as it is expressed in the experience of the workers) in the workplace—with a clear task, roles, basic operational principles, policies, procedures, and appropriate buildings, as Stokoe describes—is made available to the service user (Stokoe, see Chapter Thirteen). The use he or she makes of this "mind" provides the most real information about individual functioning, being as it is the use of the *relationship* to another, and provides the most appropriate basis for decisions about care and support.

Working in teams is the only way to manage work with fragmented or damaged human minds: when teams work together with some awareness of the effect on thinking capacity, and can stand this damage repeatedly, their ability to draw back together and reintegrate different parts of their experience of the work supports both themselves and, ultimately, the service users. The key to sustainability in human service organizations lies in the recovery of a functional team mind through having a space to think, where the damaged link with the reality of workplace task, role, and function can be restored, over and over again.

There are settings, or, more accurately, moments in the life of all settings, when the "team mind" has to tolerate repeated discovery of the impossibility of being of use to the people who are in receipt of the service, sometimes having to endure evidence of literally unbearable states of mind in their clients (as at Acres of Stone). Hinshelwood (2008) describes the way in which teams whose psychological work on their clients' behalf will never be accepted continue to work to understand in order to survive the knowledge of these clients' lives. This insight underscores another feature of reflection on practice: that of staff care. The workers at services such as Acres of Stone and at Sunrise are constantly working with extremes of destructiveness, and are at the margins of systems of care with little or no psychological training; they will be affected and they can recover. The damage to such staff groups is not from the clients, but from the economically-driven social policies which require them to work without provision of time, structures, and resources to recover thinking in the service of their clients.

References

Foster, A. (1998). Psychotic processes and community care. In: A. Foster & V. Zagier Roberts (Eds.), *Managing Mental Health in the Community: Chaos and Containment* (pp. 61–70). London: Routledge.

Garland, C. (2000). From troubled families to corrupt institutional care: the long term outcome for the child. Text for a Public Lecture for the Australian Psychotherapy Assocation, Sydney, 13 April 2000.

Hinshelwood, R. D. (2008). Foreword. In: J. Gordon & G. Kirtchuk (Eds.), *Psychic Assaults and Frightened Clinicians: Countertransference in Forensic Settings* (p. xxiii). London: Karnac.

Lawrence, W. G. (1999). A mind for business. In: R. French & R. Vince (Eds.), *Group Relations, Management, and Organization* (pp. 40–53). Oxford: Oxford University Press.

Menzies Lyth, I. (1988). The functioning of social systems as a defence against anxiety: a report on a study of the nursing service of a general hospital. In: *Containing Anxiety in Institutions: Selected Essays, Volume 1*. London: Free Association Books.

Motz, A. (2008). Maternal physical abuse. In: *The Psychology of Female Violence: Crimes Against the Body* (2nd edn) (pp. 52–79). Hove: Routledge.

Office of the Deputy Prime Minister (ODPM) (2004). Working Group on Local Government Financial Statistics WGLGFS(04).

CHAPTER FOUR

Bearing and not bearing unbearable realities: the limits of understanding

David Morgan

Afamous dictum of Freud's was that bad men do what good men dream. The difficulty for staff working with forensic and psychotic patients is that they are working with patients who confront them with their own worst anxieties. They are being asked to manage the most extreme form of concrete thinking—murder and violence to the self, as in some psychotic patients, or murder and violence toward others, as in forensic work. Even in specialist services such as medium secure units, staff on inpatient wards are often not equipped to manage the extremely difficult task of understanding patients' concrete behaviours in symbolic terms. This is not a criticism of the staff, but an acknowledgement of the nature of the patients they work with. Constant exposure to the patients' very concrete modes of thinking inevitably erodes the staff's own capacity to reflect, often leading to "mindless", institutionalized responses that may recreate the patients' very early deprived relationships.

In this chapter, I describe my experience of applying a psychoanalytic perspective to such patients, seen in both institutional settings and in my private practice, and how such an approach might begin to translate patients' concrete enactment to often painful and terrifying thinking. The unbearable thinking, which is deeply resisted, is often to do with the nature of early attachments, or, more specifically, the lack of secure attachments and, even worse, to do with the confusion and even reversal of the "who's caring for whom" relationship.

For myself, a very early experience of this was working on a ward that treated psychotic patients in which the staff had ceased to relate to the patients as individuals. The bizarre behaviour of the patients had led staff to behave in ways that were equally strange. The names of patients had been forgotten and there was no regular space for reflection, even the euphemistically named practice of staff groups for reflective thinking had been obviated. Not surprisingly, patients on this ward were acting in severely regressed and disturbing ways, confirming the staff's belief that they were unreachable. A consultative staff group was introduced which encouraged staff members to think about patients' communications. In addition, each patient on the ward was to be seen by a key worker at least twice a week at exactly the same time each week. This created a regular space within which to listen to the service user. This was subsequently written up and taken to a supervision group, where the meaning or apparent meaningless of the patients' communications were explored with myself and another colleague. This model of trying to listen and to think resulted in the team regaining an interest in patients' material, and this led to a more thoughtful atmosphere on the ward. One consequence of this was a gradual reduction in patient enactment.

The staff on this ward had become identified with projected aspects of the patient, particularly those that represent early infantile experience of breakdowns in attachment. The painful aspects of these communications are easier for staff members to identify with and replicate than think about.

In similar ways, a consultant is often brought in to deal with very complex problems, and is required to demonstrate a capacity for reflection, which might enable a shift to take place in the clinical staff's capacity for thinking symbolically and away from concrete identification with their patients' minds. This is a particularly difficult task for the consultant on wards containing very disturbed patients, as there will be a great deal of resistance in the organization as a whole, which often has as much resistance to thinking as the patients in their care. Paradoxically, however, it has to be recognized that some of the most painful psychic experiences are unbearable and it is omnipotent to imagine that anyone can encompass them successfully through thought.

This is beautifully described by Hinshelwood (1993) writing about when he provided a consultation to a prison. The splitting required to work in such a setting defied thinking: staff, like the inmates they were working with, saw any therapeutic intervention as soft and, as such, a threat to the equilibrium required to manage the often cruel and violent setting. This resulted in the cult of the hard man dominating the environment, all therapeutic intervention was seen as part of a soft culture and, therefore, suspect.

The problem around thinking about psychotic and forensic patients has been exacerbated by the limited number of settings that offer a therapeutic milieu for the severely mentally ill or personality disordered. This means that psychotic and forensic patients are treated on wards that have little or no serious therapeutic function. Often, concrete thinking patients are met by staff who are not equipped with either time or space to consider the meaning of patients' communications.

One of my first experiences of consulting to an organization brought this home to me. It was a hostel for the homeless. For my first three meetings with the staff, there was literally no room to meet: our first meeting was held in a garden shed. It was clear how the staff were unconsciously demonstrating their own difficulties in accommodating thinking about their clients by placing both me and themselves in a position of homelessness. I was able to explore the meaning of this communication through exploration of their thoughts about what it was I was being asked to experience when I turned up for planned meetings that had been forgotten about, or literally wiped off the timetable. Despite this exploration, it took several weeks before I was a properly acknowledged part of the schedule with a room set aside for our meetings. One way of dealing with this experience at the time could have been to insist on my right to a room. Another way was to accept that the experience of homelessness that these staff were being asked to manage by their clients had first to be projected into me; that is, I had to feel it. I then had to find ways of processing this experience and then to communicate it to the staff in a manner that they could accept.

The major exploration in these situations is an investigation of the mind of the consultant: do you have the equipment to manage to bear what we do? I remember feeling quite anxious about arriving for my appointments at this establishment, as I wondered each week whether I would be remembered, or have to experience psychological dismemberment with all its painful consequences. The link between homelessness and a sense of potential loss of identity could not have been brought home to me more forcibly.

Such concrete forms of communication are quite familiar to the psychoanalyst in the consulting room. For instance, a patient tells me how she has come to analysis because she and her boyfriend decided to have an abortion following her accidentally becoming pregnant by him. The boyfriend then disappeared and became incommunicado. She was left abandoned and alone to make a decision about whether she should have this baby or not. The patient was shocked to discover that she had unwittingly enacted her own early life experience. Her father impregnated her mother and then abandoned her; ironically, to go abroad to work with families requiring repatriation. She never saw him until she reached twelve years of age.

This concrete enactment of her own earliest experiences is, at one level, an unconscious attempt to gain mastery over the experience, with the unborn foetus being used as an unwilling container. The patient creates a new life redolent with all her own problems. In this scenario, she becomes the mother and the abandoning father is played by the boyfriend. It was a feature of this patient's early analytic work that she spent a great deal of time arguing that she should leave the therapy she had started with me so that she could go abroad to do work with disadvantaged children. This powerful need to re-enact eventually gave way to a series of dreams in which the question of whether or not a couple could start something and take care of it became something we could begin to think about. The analysis had survived early pressure to re-enact her formative experience.

The experience of consultancy to the homeless hostel and the analysis of the patient who aborts her foetus are similar. The main communication by both is at first evacuative, an attempt to gain mastery over unbearable experiences by placing them in the minds and bodies of others. The patient, however, is able to assist the analyst by dreaming, bringing their own unconscious meaning to bear on the work. However, this function of proto-thought is not available to the consultant to an organization. For example, it would be difficult for Hinshelwood (1993) in the prison environment to ask staff about their dreams.

Freud (1911b) stated that action makes thinking possible and that some psychic elements of certain patients can only become recognizable through actions that later become thoughts. Acting out, therefore, can be seen as a dramatized dream acted during wakefulness, a dream that could not be dreamed that is often replayed over and over again in staff reactions to patients but is unlikely to be elucidated or understood.

I have been interested in the development of an approach to patient symptomatology provided by the recent innovation of Early Intervention into Psychosis Teams. My experience of this potentially useful model of early intervention is of often very young, enthusiastic staff becoming gradually burnt out and disillusioned through exposure to apparently relentless psychotic behaviour with all its attendant anxiety. Very little thought is given to the meaning of these communications, which are often extremely complex enactments at a very concrete level. Staff often fall back on models of "help" that involve befriending the patient or they become disillusioned, hopeless, and end up leaving the service for less arduous work. Having a model of the mind and how it functions helps staff to try to think about their patients' behaviour.

Every infant needs to project their anxieties into someone, a container, who can process them and return them to the infant in a more digestible form, so lessening anxiety. Failure in this, particularly around separation and death, means that the infant can be left with intolerable anxieties. The failure in containment is experienced as if the infant is intruded upon by his or her anxieties and, as a result, is likely to evacuate rather than reflect. This can often have a transgenerational quality, where successive traumas have been transmitted, often ending up with a patient who is adrift in a psychotic enactment, the meaning of which has been lost and can only be regained through analysis.

A patient, Dr L (all clinical material has been used with the consent of the patient and disguised to protect their identity), was a young woman with a history of hospital admissions that began as a result of working on an obstetrics placement, where she had had to be involved in an abortion. She developed, apparently without precedent, a hallucination of her mother's voice telling her that she should kill herself for this mortal sin. (This patient's treatment has been written about elsewhere (Jackson & Williams, 1994.) She tried to kill herself on successive occasions, which involved cutting, lying down in front of an ambulance, and overdoses. Staff on the in-patient ward she was admitted to were sophisticated and able to understand the nature of this patient's proto-communications as a terror of loss, a reversal of difficult experience so that it was the ward staff who were constantly threatened with an experience of loss of someone that they were attached to. The fact that this patient was a health worker herself made this a powerful piece of projective identification for staff to process. This was the first time that this patient's communications had been thought about. It was the staff members who had to think and reflect on what the patient's communications might mean.

It emerged, after a great deal of work in the inpatient unit, then later in psychotherapy, that Dr L's own mother had been a survivor of six older children who had died in childbirth due to blood group complications. Dr L was her first surviving child. In individual therapy, it was eventually possible to discern this traumatized mother, who, like the staff, the therapist, and her daughter, the patient, felt unable to face the awful experience and the possibility of dead babies. She felt she was left alone in the world and accused of a crime of infanticide. Dr L's own feeling of culpability was a projection into her mother, who, probably due to her own pain and unprocessed guilt, was unable to deal with her child's aggressive impulses and returned them in a persecutory way. In enacting the abortion, she was presumably enacting her mother's feelings: "you are a bad murderous person who kills off other children and you deserve to die for your attacks on life".

The onset of dreaming during the analysis of psychotic patients can represent the beginnings of symbolic functioning and a move away from acting out of unconscious phantasy. Dr L's first dreams in her inpatient treatment tended to be about bombing and terrorism, where there was little evidence of survival. A turning point came with a dream in which

The whole of London had been bombed, she had lost her cats, and her hands had been burnt. She was able to locate her husband's office in the city, which had been reduced to rubble. Despite the pain in her hands, she began to dig for him in the rubble because she knew he was still alive.

As we can see, the evacuative nature of the dreams, if contained in the minds of staff exposed to her thinking, begins to give way to something more elaborative and the beginnings of some painful work involving herself and the recovery of lost objects. When she was seen in outpatients in more formal analytic sessions, she had a dream that seemed at least to suggest that murderous feelings could be explored. In it there is

> An unknown doctor on a ward full of patients. All the patients are dying of a strange illness caused by someone shooting arrows up the patient's bottoms and some poison removing all the nourishment from inside of them.

While psychotic patients attack their own minds, the forensic patient enacts their unprocessed thoughts on the minds and bodies of others. For instance, a destructive attack on a young woman, in front of her small baby, by a man who clearly has murderous intentions towards her, once again fills our newspapers. In the absence of a more thinking response from society, it is often the next generation that is used as a receptacle. The man who attacks a young woman with a young child present could be seen to be reversing his own experiences of abuse and violence by unconsciously creating a situation where the child experiencing the abuse and violence towards their own mother by a murderous man is somebody else. The perpetrator, through a process of reversal, relieves himself of his own violent experience by evacuating it into the mind of the other.

Another example would be the apparently motiveless murder of Jamie Bulger by two young boys. A child who is abducted and killed a long way from anyone who could possibly intervene and save him is a chilling communication, albeit an unconscious one, forcing itself into the mind of society. A child dying where no help is available is surely also the story of the two killers, whose psychic death in cruel, negative environments led to this enactment. It is a dreadful irony that the two boys who perpetrated this crime have probably received better help and education than they would have done had they been left in their respective homes and environments. "I write my story on the minds and bodies of my victims", as one young man I saw so eloquently put it.

These cases demonstrate how, after years of neglect, the acted-on child, adolescent, and adult eventually enacts their own abuse and neglect by abusing and neglecting another. This reversal and projective identification of their own experience is an attempt to evacuate into others unbearable experiences that they have felt evacuated into them.

The capacity to feel deeply with another human being and for this feeling to be reciprocated is one of the most profound experiences any of us can expect.

As we know, this capacity for deep involvement with significant others depends on our earliest experiences. How I experience you, and within that experience the emotional relationship we have, affects how I feel about myself. My knowledge of myself reflects how I feel known by the other.

One of the things we might get to know about ourselves if we are fortunate is that all of us have a capacity for destruction. No one is without this pleasure in destruction. It is only our capacity for getting help to bear this aspect of ourselves, and realistically valuing the achievement of loving intercourse, that can modify it. It is generally agreed that the excess of pleasure in human destructiveness may be in direct proportion to the weakness of love of human commitment.

But what about those for whom there has been little exposure to the power of a loving relationship—those who have been exposed to violence and corruption at the hands of their care-takers, violent couples and parental figures who appear to use their children, from the foetus onwards, as receptacles for their own psychosis? What hope is there for them, and those that work to help them to modify their behaviour in some way, when the basic requirement for parental containment has been reversed so that, in one generation after another, infants become receptacles for their parents?

Over the years, working at the Portman Clinic, I have come up against silent, deadly, self-destructive forces in some of the patients I see and hear about which are antithetical to any change or help.

These are patients in whom it seems the pleasure of physical or emotional annihilation takes over from fear of death. As we know, the sense of right and wrong, good and bad, develops very early on, laying the foundations for subsequent, more elaborate judgements of good and evil, rightness and guilt. Clinical experience has helped me to understand the dichotomy of good and evil, so that the problem of guilt as a consequence of innate destructiveness tends to assume a strongly expiatory significance, that is, healing comes to be seen as substantially coinciding with reparation for the damage done to the object.

The assumption here, however, is that the love object can be placed in a position of ideal goodness. This perspective appears to disregard the offences emanating from the object and tends to undervalue defensive, life-giving, vital hate. Hate is a way of keeping something alive. This has exercised me somewhat over the years. I believe that awareness by the patient of their destructiveness (and this is aided by our awareness of our own) is very important, but it is also crucial that there is recognition of the reality of our patients' experiences of profound trauma and, often, the transgenerational transmission of trauma. In all the patients I am talking about in this chapter, the idea that one can repair damage done to an internal object is sometimes rather far-fetched. The great disadvantage for our severely abused patients is that they have the right to hold a grievance with their objects for the rest of their lives.

This thought was disturbing for me, working at the Portman Clinic with perverse and violent patients, and at Chelsea and Westminster Hospital with borderline and psychotic patients. Was it just an omnipotence to engage with such disturbed patients and was I kidding myself that anything can be done? I still do not know the answer but "having a go" seems to be one possible way of counteracting some of the hopelessness that surrounds these cases. I have also been very surprised that the chance to think with someone, once weekly, has sometimes led to quite remarkable changes in some people.

I have been helped in this by my reading of Gianna Williams's excellent book *Internal Landscapes and Foreign Bodies* (1997). She provides a way of thinking about traumatized patients that is helpful. In a chapter entitled "Reversal of the container/contained relationship", she addresses the emphasis in psychoanalytic theory, particularly Kleinian theory, on the adult as a container for the child. When describing children exposed to being used by their parents as a receptacle of massive projections, she reminds us that it is the adult who should have provided the function of containment had she or he been fit to do so, but instead projects into the child or the baby, or indeed, I would say, the foetus.

One of the great difficulties of working with psychotic, borderline, perverse, or criminal patients, who enact their psychosis on the minds and bodies of others, is that for a great deal of the time, one has to bear the experience of sharing one's mental space with someone whose communications can at first, and for some time, feel quite mad. Suffering and bearing this experience seems to lead towards some understanding that has helped them.

My first experiences of thinking about apparently mad things were at the Maudsley hospital. I sat with two patients. The first was a writer who was admitted to hospital for standing on top of a government building and shouting down to the people in the street that the second ice age was coming. She also later told me that she regularly listened to the shipping forecast on Radio 4 because at some point there would be a specific message indicating to her that the second ice age was coming. Her response to this message was to cut her wrists as it would be her blood that would save the world. She told me this in a voice that seemed reasonably normal. There was some element of hysteria in her manner, but she led a seemingly average life with a career and a family.

Sitting listening to these kinds of communications, the first thing one feels is a pressure to make sense of their symbolic meaning, but the patient feels it is real and expects me to concur, not to start suggesting that it has symbolic meaning (for example, in the case just referred to, that the ice represents the patient's own destructiveness and that she is frightened it will destroy her world). To do this would seem to threaten her, suggesting that my reality is sane and hers insane. The transference, therefore, seems to be of one person with a very concrete sense of reality, while another person is in a state of confusion, trying to understand rather concrete thoughts which disorientate their own sense of reality. Thus, the first sensation one is forced to feel in these situations is anxiety and a sense that one should know how to communicate something meaningful. However, the latter is very difficult, for whatever reason, not least the patient's certainty that they are right.

Another patient, a manic depressive man, had been admitted because he was feeling driven to jump out of the ten-storey window of the research centre where he worked. He could not bear doing his job any more. It soon became clear that this man felt that he had been made to do everything that he had ever done in his life. It was as if he had never made a decision of his own. He had become a doctor to please his father. He had married because his (prospective) wife had told him she would leave him if he did not. He had been wearing the same pair of shoes, despite their having holes in them, because he could not go to a shoe shop and choose a pair for himself. His father would sometimes take him out shopping, select clothes for him, and buy them. His plea to me was, "Please tell me what I can do to stop feeling so awful." It felt very cruel not to tell him what to do. In these situations, some awful catastrophe is being communicated, but the only response to begin with may be to feel pressure and anxiety to say something—but what?

With both patients, it seems to me to be important to resist grasping at apparent answers or understanding and to bear being with very concrete experiences that, to begin with, seem to lack meaning. What is being communicated to the therapist is something very powerful: an experience of trying to find understanding in a world that lacks symbolism.

Another patient is a south London gangster, a hard man who has probably organized murders. He is admitted into hospital because he is being driven mad by a persistent auditory hallucination from radiators in his home and in the pub. The music has the sound of a dulcimer and it is driving him mad. Clearly, something is being broadcast by the radiator. If these were dreams, we could probably have some understanding, but the problem is they are not. We might understand that the gangster has placed his gentleness, his goodness, the music of his soul, into the radiator, a thing of warmth, and it is now persecuting him. But what good does this do the patient who seems to be locked in a world where there is no symbolic meaning? It is real.

A transsexual man tells me he wants to cut off his "old man", referring to his penis. When I suggest this might have something to do with his castrating father, he feels attacked and threatened, calling me a "mind fucker". I say it seems that I am not allowed to try to influence his mind but it is all right for him to mutilate his body. I am confronted by the spectacle of a man wanting to change into a woman, oblivious to what he is doing, and it is only I who has some feelings about his losing his "old man".

In these cases, there has been the introjection of an object performing the obverse of containment. In most of us, the introjection of an object that loves and protects the self, and is loved and protected by the self, is the basis of our security. Bion developed Klein's theory, stressing the function of this introjected object: to make things thinkable, understandable, and tolerable. He described the process of projective identification, whereby a child can have a parent into whom feelings can be projected, good and bad, for parental understanding. It is the parent who can name things and make sense of these sensations for the child, using their own experience of having been understood. Bion described these early proto-thoughts from the child as beta elements, and the mother's function of processing them as alpha function. The parent must have the capacity to bear the psychic pain the child cannot tolerate. Repeated experience of this process leads to an internalization by the infant of a thoughtful object, which gradually enables the child to deal with anxiety himself. I do not want to idealize this process—we can all be thoughtless at times.

As with the aforementioned Dr L, whose long history of hospital admissions began as a result of her being involved in abortions as part of her obstetrics and gynaecology training. In response to this, she developed a persistent hallucination of her mother telling her she should kill herself because she was evil. At some point in the psychotherapy, Dr. L became pregnant and was assailed by violent feelings towards herself and her baby. The feelings were strong, but another part of her resisted them. The experience of being with her in this conflict was almost unbearable for me. To feel responsible for an adult was one thing. To feel responsible for an unborn child was another. Dr L was communicating, in a profoundly confused way, something that was completely unconscious to her.

I gradually realized that it was possible, despite there not being any knowledge of her family history, even though there were volumes of psychiatric notes and files, to understand her apparently mad communications. They contained the profound impact of a traumatized mother on her infant. Dr L's mother had felt unable to face the awful experience of dead babies, feeling unconsciously that it represented something of her own murderousness. This was mirrored in my own countertransference feelings, in that my inability to feel able to help Dr L was a reflection of a mother's inability to give life to her children. Due to her own history, she was then ill-equipped to deal with her daughter's normal aggression, which then erupted in Dr L when she was required to participate in an abortion. She felt she was left alone in the world and accused of a crime, and probably persecuted by her mother's own unbearable guilt.

Dr L's feelings of culpability were an example of her attacks on a mother who, due to her own pain and guilt, was experienced as unable to detoxify her first child's aggressive impulses. Instead, she returned them to her child in a persecutory way. In enacting the abortion, Dr L was, in fantasy, becoming what her mother may have felt herself to be: a bad, murderous person who kills off other children and who deserves to die for these attacks on life. It was only very gradually, through a process of discovering whether I corresponded to this projection, that is, that I would hate her for what she had done, that the beginning of some other form of object relation began to develop.

Bion described this process, where the object is impervious to the child's projections. Not being acceptable to the object, they are returned unprocessed into the child and appear as a 'nameless dread'. Williams describes this process where the child is used as a receptacle for the parents' return of the projections into the child. As in the example of Dr L, these are still projections looking for containment but they are unlikely to be understood by the child, anymore than the mother's mother in this case could comprehend them.

As Williams (1997) says, this involves the introjection of an object which is not only impervious, overflowing with its own projections, but also is looking for a place to be understood, and comes to reside in the mind of the infant. I think this a profoundly important addition to our work with severely abused and traumatized children and adults. As she goes on to say, just as the introjection of the alpha function is helpful in establishing links in organizing a psychic structure, the introjection of the opposite disrupts and fragments the development of personality. Williams links this helpfully with current attachment theory and disorganized, disorientated, insecure, ambivalent, and avoidant attachment. The attachment theorists suggest that the attachment figures of children who have been traumatized have themselves experienced severe trauma.

I have in mind an adolescent patient, a victim of serious violence and sexual abuse as a child, suicidal, and having exhausted a number of other services.

Ms D was a concern to her parents because she was failing at school. Having initially been somewhat successful, she had become increasingly withdrawn. In our first meeting, she sat opposite me, and I asked her to tell me about herself. In the beginning, she was able to tell me that her parents had sent her to treatment, but then lapsed into silence, with a beseeching look that felt extremely uncomfortable. This continued until the end of the session. I felt rather trapped with this silently pleading patient, and I was confused and rather irritated when I brought the session to a close. I saw her for three months, trying to establish some contact, and each session was marked by this behaviour. She would sit opposite me and move as if she was going to speak, then fall back in her chair, apparently defeated, looking at me with this imploring expression. I found myself egging her on to say something, to let it out, or I would scramble around in my own countertransference, trying to find something coherent to say.

Of course, I now realize it was the incoherence I was being expected to bear. I was able to say something about her fear of the effect the words she wanted to say might have on me. But each session was the same, over and over, until I began to dread seeing her. I would hope that she would not come, but she did, relentlessly on time to every session, repeating the same behaviour. I would collect her from the waiting room, where she sat with a hopeful expression while I was feeling apprehensive about the next fifty minutes. Obviously, I knew that either something was being communicated or that I was being incompetent. As each session came and went, it added to the sense of cumulative dread and disappointment. I thought of bringing the treatment to a close or suggesting I bring in paper or pencils, which might relieve her need to put things into words, but she shook her head and seemed to indicate that she required me to bear this endless enactment.

For six months we continued with this perpetual, silent behaviour. My rather formulaic interpretation also continued, despite the fact that I was fed up with using it and had little belief that it would have any effect. Then, one day, she responded. I had said yet again that she was showing me what it felt like to be with someone who creates a feeling that something is about to happen, only to be disappointed; that this might actually have been her experience, or her fear of what might happen here, if she was able to speak. She whispered, "Yes." I felt anxious that the moment might be lost so I just responded with another yes, said in as unthreatening a way as possible. Then, in a very quiet voice, she told me about how her father had been visiting her room over the years, but not since she had started coming here, and that he would masturbate her and himself.

Suddenly, because she could put her experience into words, the behaviour I had been living through over six months seemed clearer. I said that this had felt very difficult to say to me, and up until now she had been showing me what had happened to her through her actions in the sessions. In some ways, she had to see if I could bear it before she could talk about this experience. She again whispered "Yes."

I had the usual anxieties that what was being communicated was a fantasy or, indeed, a communication more about what was happening between us: who was exciting whom? Who was abusing whom? But her profound need to begin to think about her real experience impressed itself upon me far more powerfully.

Of course, the enactment continued because I was now in the same position that she was in, with the knowledge of her abuse in my head. I had to know what to do about it. Should I remain silent as she had done? Should I assume that the abuse had stopped, which it may not have done? Or should I use the information she had given me, in confidence, to bring awareness of what had happened to the notice of the social services? Her dilemma, of when to speak or not, now became mine. I explored this with her, how it seemed I was at present really able to understand her dilemma, while she was watching me very carefully to see what care I had to give her at this moment. Her father had left her with the confusing problem of what to do with an adult who does not know the difference between hurting his daughter and taking care of her. She had now shared that difficulty with me, and I think she was wondering if I, as an adult, had any other way of dealing with it than keeping it quiet, as she had done.

She agreed. She said she did not want to hurt her father by getting him into trouble but she did not want what he was doing to continue. She was frightened because she felt it had only stopped because he was afraid that she would tell me. We were able to think about this together. Just as she wanted to share this problem with an adult, she was also aware that adults were not to be trusted and she was afraid I would do something with the information she had given me or, conversely, not do anything.

The question seemed to be about how we could help an adult who dealt with his own confusion about his sexuality by using her, and making her muddled about her own feelings. What seemed very important at this time was that I did not add to her distress and we could decide on a course of action together. It seemed that she was very frightened of my reaction to her revelation; I had first to relive the experience with her so as to gain her trust. When someone has been enacted on mindlessly, it seems it is necessary for the therapist to bear this experience long enough in the countertransference before any symbolic meaning of the experience can be communicated.

If a child has been the repository of cruel acts, however mitigated by the circumstances of the abuser's own formative experiences, is there any hope of reparation or any possibility of repair?

The sexual perversions I have witnessed in the patients I have seen seem to be a distorted development of the entire personality and mental structure. Sexualization and violence become a mental state that is used to withdraw from reality and the need to relate to the world. Unlike Freud's view of a development of infantile polymorphous perversity, a withdrawal into sexualized mental states means that any humanizing influences that may occur in that person's life have to be attacked. These sexualized states of mind obliterate the need for human relationships.

The clinical problem is how to help the patient benefit from treatment, as it appears in the beginning to be the analyst who must breach impenetrable barriers. Sometimes, the patients we see *have* to resist the powerful forces of humanization, love, concern, and the importance of ethical right and truth. These things, which we might consider to be life forces, are the very thing that is likely to make them aware of the paucity of their existence. Thus, what we think is life-giving to our patients is, in fact, perceived as a horrendous threat. A less disturbed analytic patient once told me that if she believed what I gave her in the sessions was what she needed, she feared she would become a ferociously greedy child, unable to control her needs, which would either destroy me or leave her to gorge herself on food until she killed herself with obesity. It is useful for her and me to imagine a part of her holding a ham roll to her head saying, "If you get any closer I'll kill myself with this." At one level, she is terrified of her need of me and the object. On the other hand, she is also aware that after a lengthy period of neglect at the hands of a very disturbed mother (she had been excommunicated from her mother at the age of twenty), she is justified in questioning if she did anything so awful to this parent.

Another patient I saw at the Portman was a young man who had come into treatment because he was unable to sustain a relationship. He was heavily into sado-masochistic practice. He did not want help with this aspect of his life: he just wanted help to meet someone who would participate in the sado-masochism with him. He told me that it was his sado-masochism that had saved his life. He and two friends had been arrested after political unrest in his country of origin, had been imprisoned and tortured. Both his friends had died in captivity, but he had survived and flourished in jail, and had even gained the admiration of his captors for his capacity to bear the pain inflicted upon him. It was his interest in sado-masochism preceding his capture, he said, that had sustained him. The other two had missed their families, but he had learnt to love his cruel persecutors. One could see why finding a partner might be difficult, but one had to sympathize with his view. Do these perversions, therefore, have a survival remit?

André Green, in many of his writings, considers the destructive drive to be aimed at destroying the meaning of everything and that good has to be rendered meaningless. Real destructiveness, or what he terms evil, is not the opposite of love, but coldness and absence of love are. Destructiveness is, therefore, an attack on the emotions and any relationship between human objects. No understanding is possible, as this is attacked because it involves taking account of another person and their needs and interests. These assaults are occasioned by a particular form of pleasure that makes annhilation preferable to any good. In its most primitive form, as seen, I believe, in sado-masochistic patients at the Portman, it is the fascination of absolute destruction and domination of the helpless victim which gives rise to pleasure.

This is at the more extreme end of what might be called identification with the aggressor, but it involves an attempt to rid oneself of all awareness of goodness. At times, I have felt sickened, rejecting, sometimes hatred, as a result of what such patients are putting me through, that is, hopelessness. I have often had to live with the guilt that if they did not attend again, I would be relieved. At other times, I have felt hope, but this is hard to sustain. I have had to overcome profound pessimism about my own capacities as a human being and as a therapist. The need for patients to have a bad object in these cases is paramount.

I hope that, in this chapter, I have demonstrated that with patients suffering the severity of difficulties that I have been referring to, psychotic, perverse, and forensic patients, what is required by the practitioner working with them, be that in a community, outpatient, or inpatient setting, is the capacity to try to bear emotional states of mind that can often feel unbearable, and sometimes are unbearable. It also requires the capacity to try to consider enactment as not only an evacuative process expelling these unbearable emotional states, but also as having a symbolic meaning. In as much as this is possible, and it is not possible without collegiate and institutional support, the beginning of understanding, rather than enactment, may eventually begin to emerge.

References

Freud, S. (1911b). Formulations on the two principles of mental functioning. *S.E., 12*: 213–226. London: Hogarth.

Hinshelwood, R. (1993). Locked in role: a psychotherapist within the social defence system of a prison. Journal of Forensic Psychiatry & Psychology, 4(3): 427–440.

Jackson, M. & Williams, P. (1994). *Unimaginable Storms:A Search for Meaning in Psychosis*. London: Karnac.

Williams, G. (1997). *Internal Landscapes and Foreign Bodies: Eating Disorders and Other Pathologies*. London: Karnac.

CHAPTER FIVE

Thinking about antisocial behaviour and mental health in Youth Offending Services

William Crouch

Introduction

Now a decade old, Youth Offending Services are the result of reforms of the youth justice system and, specifically, the 1998 Crime and Disorder Act (Home Office). At the centre of the new approach to youth crime was a duty placed on local authorities to provide interagency services to address offending by young people through the establishment of Youth Offending Teams (YOTs). More recently, many teams have expanded the services they provide and have become Youth Offending Services (YOS). Teams are multi-disciplinary, with social workers, probation officers, police officers, education workers, and health workers collaborating to meet the needs of the young people referred to them by courts, the police, and other agencies. The development of YOTs has resulted in mental health practitioners, mostly psychologists, being seconded to these teams from their health trusts.

The young people worked with by youth offending services are without doubt a group that need the help of specialist mental health workers. Research has highlighted that rates of mental health problems in adolescent populations are high: one in five children and adolescents experience mental health problems (Audit Commission,

1999) and one in ten in the 5–15 year-old age group experience a diagnosable mental disorder (Meltzer, Gatwood, Goodman, & Ford, 2000). Furthermore, there is considerable evidence that young offenders are at increased risk of mental health problems (e.g., NACRO, 1999). Kurtz, Thornes, and Bailey (1997) reviewed the mental health provision for children in the criminal justice and secure care systems for the Department of Health. They concluded that the mental health needs of young people who may be in trouble with the law are not well recognized, widely understood, or adequately met.

The work of YOTs is complex and arduous. The young people with whom they work are often very disturbed, with multiple needs. At the same time, they may be quite unwilling to engage with the services that might meet these needs. I argue that in carrying out this difficult task, it becomes a challenge for teams and individuals within it to think about their work. Thoughtfulness is too often replaced by action, or a turning away from reality (in a way that Steiner (1985) has referred to as "turning a blind eye"). I will argue that it is the potentially emotionally painful aspects of this work that drives the teams and individuals within them to resort to self-preservationist and primitive defences.

Psychoanalytic theory may be helpful in conceptualizing the organizational difficulties in YOT work: in particular, ideas about psychic defences that are both ubiquitous and necessary to the welfare of the conscious mind. Within the team, individual psychic defences contribute to a social defence system that protects the team from anxiety, guilt, doubt, and uncertainty. This sort of defence system was first described by Menzies Lyth (1970), following her work on hospital wards.

In this chapter, I use case illustrations to show the difficulties faced in thinking about the relationships of staff to young people, as well as the young people's mental health and emotional needs. I then make some suggestions as to how the organization can be supported in this task.

Striving for a psychological understanding of offending behaviour

Youth Offending Services rely heavily on structured assessments to appraise young people's risks and needs. Programmes of interven-

tion are designed to address the young person's antisocial or criminal behaviour. These draw mainly on behavioural and cognitive–
behavioural techniques to try to reduce impulsivity and heighten
empathy and social awareness. They are often quite successful;
however, the less bright, less motivated, and those who are more
entrenched in their offending behaviour may struggle to use them.
There is also a danger of the opportunity for forming a helpful relationship with a worker falling by the wayside.

Youth Offending Services in England and Wales universally use
the "Asset" tool to assess young people they work with (see Youth
Justice Board, 2003). This is a structured assessment tool used on all
young offenders who come into contact with the criminal justice
system. It aims to look at the young person's offence, or offences,
and identify a multitude of factors or circumstances (ranging from
lack of educational attainment to mental health problems) which
may have contributed to such behaviour. The information gathered
from Asset can be used to inform court reports, so that appropriate
intervention programmes can be drawn up. Particular needs or difficulties will be identified, so that these may also be addressed.
Asset will also help to measure changes in needs and risk of reoffending over time.

Tools such as Asset are psychometrically impressive in their
ability to predict risk of offending and recidivism, but add little to
an interpersonal understanding of the young person and their
behaviour (see Baker (2005) for further discussion of the positive
and negative effects of the use of this tool in the youth justice
system). Obviously, limited resources mean that the use of a reliable
and valid assessment tool can be valuable in directing team
resources and highlighting difficulties. However, they can also be a
part of an organizational defence that, while protecting against
anxiety, increases the struggle to reach an understanding of the
behaviour the team needs to work with.

The dynamics of youth offending

Psychological thinking about young people who commit criminal
offences owes much to Winnicott, paediatrician and psychoanalyst,

who had a particular interest in working with young people who engaged in antisocial and criminal behaviour. Winnicott, in his seminal paper, "The antisocial tendency" (1956), highlights the dynamic between the antisocial act and the environment. The anti-social act, according to Winnicott's thinking, is characterized by an element which compels the environment to be important and unconsciously compels someone to attend to management. The act committed by the young person then makes society, through agencies such as the police or Youth Offending Services, attend to the young person's needs. For Winnicott, the antisocial tendency, therefore, implies hope: "In the period of hope the child manifests the anti-social tendency" (Winnicott, 1956, p. 123). In contrast, a lack of hope is the basic feature of the deprived child who may not be antisocial, but may also be overlooked.

The work of helping antisocial young people, according to Winnicott, should be done in terms of management, tolerance, and understanding. He also attempted to provide some psychological understanding for antisocial acts. He suggested that, in stealing, the child is looking for something somewhere to meet a need, and when failing to find it, seeks it elsewhere. Hence, the stolen object is representative of something that the child feels that he or she was deprived of. He suggested that destructiveness is a seeking of environmental stability that will stand the strain resulting from impulsive behaviour. In both cases there is a search for environmental provision that has been lost: a human attitude that, because it can be relied on, gives freedom to the individual to move to act and to get excited.

Particularly because of his or her destructiveness, the child provokes total environmental reactions; Winnicott (1956) says that this is as if they are seeking an ever-widening frame, a circle which had as its first example the mother's arms or the mother's body. Despite this psychoanalytical formulation of antisocial behaviour, Winnicott famously maintained that the treatment of the antisocial tendency is not psychoanalysis, but the provision of child-care that can be rediscovered by the child. The environment must give new opportunity for relatedness, but must also be robust, so that, in it, the child can experiment again with basic drives and impulses (in adolescence these will be particularly sexual and aggressive drives and the impulse to act upon them).

The task of the Youth Offending Team

The primary task of the YOTs is to reduce youth offending in their locality: teams will work to this task in a number of ways. The team acts as a monitoring agency, ensuring that a sentence or order is carried out (there may be increased monitoring in the form of time spent with a mentor, or electronically monitored curfews). A sentence may include a condition that some reparatory work is carried out in the local community. Teams also work with young people to try to reduce their potential for reoffending: this will include trying to address any problem that the young person may have that increases their risk of becoming involved in offending (drug and alcohol misuse and exclusion from school are probably the most important).

It is important to note that the task of the mental health worker within the YOT is different. Although, as part of a team, they will engage with the wider YOT task, the mental health worker's focus is the mental health needs of the services users. This creates an interesting tension between the YOT task, which is driven by the needs of the community, and the mental health task, which is driven by the needs of the young person. This will be discussed further later in this paper.

Socially structured defence mechanisms in Youth Offending Teams

Why the social defence system is needed

Menzies Lyth (1970) suggested that social defences were needed to protect the staff of hospitals against the feelings that would otherwise be raised when confronted with the illness and death of their patients. The function of the defence system is then to allow a denial of feelings that might arise in the relationship with the patient. Menzies Lyth believed there was a core anxiety here that led to a detachment and denial of feeling. Furthermore, she found evidence of a history of collusive interaction between individuals to project and reify relevant elements of their psychic defence systems. There were then widespread organizational ideals of "a good nurse" that shunned ideas of relationships with patients. There was also found to be an elimination of decision making by ritual task performance and check and counter-check of work. The function of this was proposed to reduce the weight of responsibility on the nurses for the wellbeing of their patients. This meant that staff functioned in a rather robotic manner and the possibility of anyone forming a meaningful working relationship with a patient was minimal. Critically, she observed that the personal and institutional defences needed to be in tune, or there would be a breakdown, the individual not fitting in with the organizational culture.

Here, I propose some of the underlying anxieties involved in work with young offenders and link them to institutional defences that seem to be at play in the youth justice system. The defences employed to protect workers and the organization are primitive, and involve denial or a turning away from reality, splitting of people (both workers and young people) into good and bad, and manic enactments. These defences are in response to the underlying fear of the young people themselves, a fear of blame for what the young person does, guilt that the worker is not able to help, hatred of the young offender and the doubt and uncertainty they engender in the workers. The deployment of these defences means that building relationships with the young people who have offended is impeded, and addressing their mental health and emotional needs is then greatly affected.

Underlying anxieties in work with young offenders

There are a number of anxieties that, for the most part, remain unconscious, which affect teams working with young offenders.

Fear of the young offender

YOTs work with a variety of young people, most of whom have a history of only minor offences (often motor crime); however, some have committed violent and sexual offences. As there is also a drive towards keeping young people out of custody, YOTs increasingly take responsibility for high risk young people in the community. In my experience, there is little expression of fear among staff, even when working with the most potentially dangerous young people.

It would seem that to express fear runs counter to a culture of keeping such anxiety in the background. Since the service as a whole cannot refuse to work with a young person, this culture can be seen to be essential to the organization's survival. There is, then, often a denial of the danger, and workers expressing fear may be thought unsuitable to work with high risk cases.

> Steve was a large and intimidating young man of seventeen; he had been involved in a string of local street robberies. Young people had been threatened into handing over mobile phones and money. Following a review of his casework, it was noticed that he had not been attending all his appointments. His young, female case-worker was immediately replaced by an experienced male manager.

It seemed difficult to address the possibility of the worker being frightened of Steve, as well as the possibility that this might have led to his missed appointments going unchallenged. There was a sense that the organization must present a tough face that stood up to him. However, in doing this, the young and inexperienced case-worker had been undermined and Steve was left with the impression that he had got rid of her.

Fear of blame

Both nationally and locally, work in Youth Offending is highly politicized. The system has to publish quarterly statistics on a number of measures of how they are tackling local youth crime, as well as other targets. Everybody, understandably, wants the problem to be addressed efficiently, and there is a corresponding clamour for visible progress. There is little public tolerance for the complexity of the problems involved or for the struggles of those trying to address them. Hence, the whole system finds itself under continual scrutiny for what it is doing about much publicized youth crime issues. This pressure is then passed down through individual YOTs and services and on to individual workers, who need constantly to account for what they are doing. Local pressure comes, too, from town councillors, local press, and from other agencies. Fear of blame is inextricably linked to a drive to act: it seems the worst crime of a service is to have "done nothing".

Sarah was a fifteen-year-old girl who had been excluded from school for systematically bullying other girls. This behaviour included physical intimidation and threats, both inside and outside the school grounds. She was referred to the YOT following an apparently random assault and attempted robbery of a woman on the street. There was great anxiety in the YOT when the father of one of the victims of intimidation at school made a complaint to a local councillor that the local authority was not doing enough to protect his daughter from Sarah. There followed a number of meetings with the school to share plans for what would be done, despite the fact that Sarah had already been permanently excluded from the school.

There is a wish here for the system to show everything that it is doing to address the problem. The team seemed to so fear being blamed for not acting that it was driven to acting in what everyone agreed in hindsight was a rather thoughtless manner: putting a great deal of resources into a meeting to pacify the school. In doing so, the team disowned its authority to manage the young person who committed the offences and perhaps take the time needed to work with her complex problems.

Guilt

Broadly, people join teams like YOTs because they believe in what they do; indeed, they may also have deeply held wishes to help others, and not being able to help is then psychologically painful. The young people who attend Youth Offending Services are more likely than their peers to be disadvantaged economically, educationally, and in terms of the quality of their childhood upbringing. As making a change for such young people is so inherently difficult, workers are faced by the failure to bring about change. This brings great potential for feelings of guilt. Added to this, if they reoffend there will be also the guilt at what the young person has done to the victim of their offence, and the fear that the worker is also open to being blamed.

Tom was a fourteen-year-old when he first came to the attention of the YOT. Subsequently, he went on to commit an array of petty offences that brought him back to the YOT time and again until he was too old to receive a service from them. There was concern that, at his last court appearance, a judge had warned that he would go into custody if he offended again. His history was of disturbed behaviour dating back to an early age: it included conduct problems at home and at school, hyperactivity, difficulties in learning, and, in adolescence, violent outbursts and threats at home. Paediatricians, child psychiatrists, and psychologists had been involved with him and his family since his early childhood. Case-workers reported "heart-sink" when he was referred back to the team, and exasperation, thinking that his problems were surely a mental health issue. He was an infuriating young person to work with, but also evoked feelings of helplessness and failure in his workers at the YOT and in CAMHS services.

Sadly, it is likely that Tom is now in an adult prison. His behaviour was undoubtedly challenging and his very limited attention span made working with him exceptionally difficult. Part of the pain for his workers was a sense that the system was acting too late.

Doubt and uncertainty

The difficulties of this group of young people described above means that the workers are operating in an environment of continued uncertainty. These young people tend to lead quite chaotic lives, being more likely than peers to be out of school, and living in less predictable environments in terms of their homes and neighbourhoods. Their behaviour, too, is erratic: frequent missing of appointments, being out of contact, and late attendance is common. The chaos of the young person's world can lead to confusion in the worker, where they are left struggling to plan or work with the young person in a proactive way. Struggling with this projected chaos involves the worker feeling deskilled, confused, and useless. There is then an understandable wish to hold on to some certainty and take refuge in following preordained patterns of working that may be to the detriment of working with the young person as an individual.

Dylan was a sixteen-year-old when referred to the YOT for a number of motoring offences: essentially stealing and "joy riding" motor-scooters. A popular and good-looking young man, he seemed full of bluff and bravado. Workers moved quickly to offer him places on youth training programmes, including a motorcycle mechanics' course that they thought would engage him. He was initially enthusiastic about this change. There was fury and exasperation when he failed to turn up for several carefully organized appointments to discuss the training programme. At the same time, Dylan would turn up at the team offices without an appointment, asking to see social workers about various problems, his benefits, and having been thrown out of home by his mother.

The hatred of the young offender

It is a great challenge to ask professionals who dedicate their working lives to helping others to consider their hatred of their service users. The wider society, at a greater distance from these young people, perhaps finds it easier to hate the young offender, with more and more draconian measures called for to deal with youth crime (see, for example, BBC, 2005, 2008a,b).

Winnicott (1956) suggests, "Perhaps one of the reasons why we tend to leave the therapy of the delinquent to others is that we dislike being stolen from" (p. 123). These "others" Winnicott talks about are not only therapists like him, but staff working closer to the ground, such as those in youth offending services. There are then quite complex and often ambivalent feelings towards the young offenders. As with most helping professionals, youth justice workers have presumably found their way to this sort of work influenced by a number of conscious and unconscious factors that are important and deeply held parts of who they are. If there is an analysis of the self, these will usually involve wishes to be helpful, make better, or fix. However, it is unlikely that staff will be free from more hating feelings towards their service users.

> Jamal, aged fourteen, was referred to the YOT following a complaint that he had exposed himself to a woman on the street. He had been picked out at a police line-up by the woman, but maintained his innocence. His records showed previous complaints about indecent exposure. He was immediately almost universally disliked in the team: his lack of contrition was often cited, but the sexual nature of his offence almost certainly influenced this dislike. Jamal was several times taken back to court, having been judged to have breached the conditions of his order. This was done in a mechanistic fashion and without reference to anyone's feelings about the effect that his offence had on them.

It is perhaps easier to think about our hatred of sexual offenders. However, there is also a rapid and strong identification with the victims of any crime, or a more general sense of being part of a society that has been attacked or wronged. In helping the offender, there is then the potential to feel very conflicted, and there may be an array of defences employed to avoid this conflict.

Defences

As discussed above, defences are mobilized to protect against anxieties that might otherwise be overwhelming. The concept of the "manic defence" is useful in thinking about what happens when persecutory anxiety threatens to overwhelm. The manic defence is linked to a state of omnipotence, a state where reality is denied: by employing a manic defence, the persecutory anxiety is "blinded" (Klein, 1940). Klein puts this succinctly: "The sense of omnipotence is what first and foremost characterises mania and, further, mania is based on the mechanism of denial" (Klein, 1935, p. 277).

There is a danger that rapid action that serves to reduce team and individual anxiety may be a manic defence that will then impair the ability to see the problems clearly and work on them effectively, as can be seen in the illustrations of enactments to reduce anxiety below.

Another useful concept is that of "splitting". This is a phenomena first described by Freud (1927e, 1940e [1938]) as a process whereby a conflict between different points of view can be resolved in the mind. The concept was developed later by Klein (1946), who observed that children's views of the world often involve wholly good or wholly bad figures (in psychoanalytic parlance, the subject's "objects"). With development, the child needs to face the painful reality that this is not the case, and that people have both benign and malevolent parts. This is a difficult reality to face and continues to be a struggle into adult life: it will, then, be an ongoing struggle for the team. Hence, splits may become evident in views of young people, so that young people may be considered more or less bad or worthy of the efforts of staff: there may then be views of the young people that divide them into those who are unfortunate, needy, or "mad", and those who are just plain bad.

There can also be a wholesale denial within the workers of difficult feelings (such as hatred) about the young people.

The following case examples show how well-meaning attempts to manage alarming behaviour by young people can become manic enactments. These inhibit thinking about the young person's needs and effective management of their behaviour.

Manic enactment to reduce anxiety

Josey was a fourteen-year-old girl with a history of violent behaviour, alcohol use, and involvement in a street gang. She was on an intensive supervision and support programme following a community sentence for a serious assault on another girl. The programme of supervision involved a "mentor" (essentially a non-professionally qualified youth worker) spending a prescribed number of hours a week with her. In addition, she had to spend some hours in education (she was excluded from school) and had to observe an electronically monitored curfew. Her YOT social worker became concerned that Josey had complained that her mentor was using some of her hours with Josey to take her to church. This was reported to a manager, who promptly changed the mentor working with Josey.

It can be seen in this example that the decision to quickly change the young person's mentor immediately stopped any thinking about what was going on in the relationship between the young person and the mentor. The chance for understanding what that might mean for them, and possibly for the organization, was also lost.

It could be thought to speak volumes about under-trained and under-resourced staff working with troubled and disturbing young people whom they are struggling to start to relate to or understand. The, presumably religious, mentor probably thought that going to church would be a good socializing and spiritual activity for the young person. The young person may have thought that this was rather thrusting religion on her. Of course, we never found out what either thought about this incident. Instead, the young person found herself in the omnipotent position of having got rid of her worker, having split her off from the team management.

Splits in the team and young people

The criminal justice system lends itself easily to splitting in the minds of those observing it and working in it. Offenders are guilty or not guilty, behaviour considered good or bad. It is difficult in this context to consider the true nature of people and behaviour as more complex and harder to understand and, therefore, to work with.

> Ray was a fifteen-year-old boy who had been convicted of breaking into a flat and stealing a computer. He had committed the offence with a number of peers, but had been the only one caught. There was a suspicion that he had run up debts with a cannabis dealer. Parenting workers became involved when earlier minor offences had resulted in a Parenting Order. He was frequently non-compliant with the conditions of his orders, and there was a debate within the team over whether to breach his order and take him back to court. Some of the team thought that he needed to be taught a lesson and should be sent back to court, some thought that he could be worked with if he could be interested in some diversionary activity, such as a local motorbike project. Interestingly, the parenting worker reported that these splits paralleled the situation between his parents: his father believed that Ray needed to learn his lessons and that, if necessary, they should call the police in to deal with Ray's cannabis use; his mother took the opposite position, believing understanding to be the way to help Ray.

Of course, the splits that existed in how to manage Ray's behaviour at home were a big part of the maintenance of his difficulties, and helping the parents to work together to respond to his cannabis use and antisocial behaviour was effective in the long run in keeping him out of trouble. However, such splits in thinking about young offenders exist widely and at various levels.

What can be seen from the example of Ray is that the more caring role is split from the more limit setting role (sometimes, in psychoanalytic terms, referred to as traditional "maternal and paternal functions"). In order to work effectively with these young people both positions are needed.

Organizational issues

Negotiating relationships within the team can be difficult: for the mental health worker, there is often a sense of working in an alien culture, as most Youth Offending Services are dominated by workers from social services. Social workers can often find the mental health worker unreasonably demanding, perhaps a little precious in their requests for privacy and confidentiality around their work, as well as sometimes limited in what they can really offer to some of the very troubled young people the social workers want most help with.

Many workers from a mental health background will be used to patients being referred to them in a formal way, with appointments arranged for a particular time and place. Often, this is not the way that young people present to mental health workers in YOTs. Frequently, help is needed in some sort of crisis, and the mental health worker needs to be responsive to this. Young people have to be seen in a range of contexts very different from the consulting rooms that will be available in most Child and Adolescent Mental Health Service (CAMHS) bases.

There is a tension between the different tasks of the mental health service and the Youth Offending Service (mentioned above). Addressing a mental health need may occasionally conflict with addressing the need to reduce the young person's offending. This is often seen when there is a need to engage the young person in therapy at the same time as there is a need to enforce some sort of other order, such as a curfew or attendance at some offence-focused programme. The danger here is another form splitting: the mental health worker becoming the engaging, possibly "soft" or "good" figure and the social worker the enforcing, possibly "hard" or "bad" figure.

Working in a multi-agency environment requires staff from different agencies to get to know one another's expertise, ways of working, and needs. In a large team with high staff turnover, this may require rolling programmes of training on mental health, youth justice procedures, drugs and alcohol work, and so on.

Helping the organization to think

It can be all too easy to condemn teams and individuals as unthinking and stuck. There must be recognition of the difficulties that come with thinking. In asking workers to consider a young person's emotional needs and psychological state, as well as to understand their behaviour as something that has meaning, one is asking them to expose themselves to the doubt, uncertainly, fear, and guilt outlined above. It also requires a shift away from the organizational norms that are dominated by structured, prescribed assessment and intervention.

Conclusions

Against a background of a call for robust responses to the problem of offences committed by young people, it is difficult to maintain that there is also a need for greater consideration of young people's needs. But, over half a century ago, Winnicott (1956) advocated both robustness and understanding. This vision of treatment of antisocial young people presents a formidable task to Youth Offending Services and the people who work in them. Carrying out work of this nature involves a struggle with both the anxiety it potentially raises and the defences that are employed against this anxiety. This ultimately impairs the work, as well as relating, within the team and with the young people served by it. Supervision, network, and professionals' meetings are, therefore, essential. There also needs to be an awareness of how these can come to be about checking that tasks have been done, rather than a space to discuss the young person and work with them.

In Youth Offending Services, there is often a high turnover of staff, with new workers asked to "hit the ground running", taking on large case-loads. It is essential, therefore, that there is adequate induction of staff that includes some mental health training. In order for an organization to begin to think about the mental health needs of their young people, they need to address the needs of the workers.

When an organization can begin to think about the mental health needs of their young people, there is likely to be an uncovering of need and a demand for specialist help. Then, adequate CAMHS resources will need to be behind the mental health worker as the number of young people requiring this service increases.

References

Audit Commission (1999). *Children in Mind: Child and Adolescent Mental Health Services*. London: Audit Commission.

Baker, K. (2005). Assessment in Youth Justice: professional discretion and the use of Asset. *Youth Justice, 5*(2): 106–122.

BBC (2005) Curfews "demonise young people". Available at: http://news.bbc.co.uk/1/hi/england/london/4700581.stm: Wednesday, 20 July.

BBC (2008a). UK society "condemning" children. Available at: http://news.bbc.co.uk/1/hi/uk/7732290.stm: Monday, 17 November.

BBC (2008b). Are we negative about our children? Available at: http://news.bbc.co.uk/1/hi/uk/7732203.stm: Monday, 17 November.

Freud, S. (1927e). Fetishism. *S.E., 21*: 149–158. London: Hogarth.

Freud, S. (1940e [1938]). Splitting of the ego in the process of defence. *S.E., 23*: 271–278. London: Hogarth.

Klein, M. (1935). A contribution to the psychogenesis of manic–depressive states. *International Journal of Psychoanalysis, 16*: 145–174.

Klein, M. (1940). Mourning and its relation to manic–depressive states. *International Journal of Psychoanalysis, 21*: 125–153.

Klein, M. (1946). Notes on some schizoid mechanisms. *International Journal of Psychoanalysis, 27*: 99–110.

Kurtz, Z., Thornes, R., & Bailey, S. (1997). *A Study of the Demand and Need for Forensic Child and Adolescent Mental Health Services in England and Wales*. Report to the Department of Health. London: Department of Health.

Meltzer, H., Gatwood, R., Goodman, R., & Ford, T. (2000). *Mental Health of Children and Adolescents in Great Britain*. London: TSO.

Menzies Lyth, I. E. P. (1970). *The Functioning of Social Systems as a Defence Against Anxiety. A Report on a Study of the Nursing Service of a General Hospital*. London: Tavistock.

NACRO (1999). Facts about young offenders in 1997. *Youth Crime Section Briefing*. London: NACRO.

Steiner, J. (1985). Turning a blind eye: the cover-up for Oedipus. *International Review of Psycho-Analysis, 12*: 161–172.

Winnicott, D. W. (1956). The antisocial tendency. In: C. Winnicott, R. Shepherd, & M. Davis (Eds.), *Deprivation and Delinquency* (pp. 120–131). London: Tavistock, 1984.

Youth Justice Board (2003). *ASSET (summary)*. London: Youth Justice Board.

CHAPTER SIX

An alternative to "slapping": multi-agency working with excluded young people exhibiting antisocial behaviour

Mike Solomon

Contexts

There is significant overlap between young people's so-called "antisocial behaviour" in and out of school. Those school students excluded from school because of their behaviour are often also involved in antisocial behaviour in the community. This chapter discusses these phenomena, and different agency responses to working with such young people.

When students are permanently excluded from school, their local authority is obliged to offer them education. In the UK, this is currently most often provided by Pupil Referral Units. I work as a clinical psychologist in both a mental health institution and a Pupil Referral Unit (PRU). The PRU is in an inner-city authority, and offers education to students aged 11–14 who are in the first three years of secondary school (Key Stage 3 in the UK). Historically, such young people—challenging, vulnerable, and on the margins of mainstream society—would have been invisible to traditional, clinic-based child and adolescent mental health services (CAMHS). However, there is a growing recognition that these young people are among the most vulnerable and needy in our society, as well as being the most challenging. As a result, the growing presence of CAMHS professionals in specialist education settings is part of an attempt to make mental health services more accessible to a greater number of people who might have most need of them.

In addition to working directly with students and their families, clinicians can also make their contributions and perspectives available to other professionals. A great deal of my work in the PRU consists of working with colleagues, both the staff team within the PRU and the wider network of professionals from different agencies with whom we work. There is scope to make many, varied contributions as a clinician working within a multi-agency service based in education, as long as one enjoys being flexible.

In this chapter, I consider young people who are excluded from school, some characteristics of their families, the nature of their antisocial behaviour, as well as possible reasons behind it. I then discuss some of the societal responses to such behaviour. Given these contexts, I then introduce some practical approaches that try to foster alternative ways of responding to young people's antisocial behaviour. These include some of the contributions that a mental health professional can make within exclusion systems, together with the value of multi-agency working.

Excluded young people and their families

Children and young people are excluded from mainstream schools for a variety of reasons. Factors underlying school exclusion may be a temporary crisis in the young person's life, or may reflect more chronic situations (Rendall & Stuart, 2005).

Evidence shows that background family factors for excluded children include: early separation from a primary carer; bereavement; serious parental illness; mental illness in the family; as well as substance misuse and/or criminality in the family. It is very common for there to be multiple factors involved (Rendall & Stuart, 2005). In my experience, such factors are often combined with other background circumstances, including: domestic violence; abuse and neglect; children in public care; families who are refugees from conflict and war zones; dislocation, displacement, and trauma; as well as intergenerational patterns of behaviours and relationships.

While not all excluded students are involved in antisocial behaviour in the community, there is a great deal of overlap between such behaviour of children and young people inside and outside school. Some factors may underlie both exclusion from school and antisocial behaviour, including cognitive and learning difficulties, delayed language development, as well as impulsivity, hypervigilance, and sensitivity to violence that may follow children witnessing domestic violence.

Many excluded young people come to the attention of a range of other services around the same time as their exclusion from school, as their acting out begins to affect public spheres and be noticed by adult society. Around this time, such young people may start to become familiar to the police and youth offending services, together with specialist education, social care, and safeguarding services.

Young people and gangs

Young people excluded from school are commonly involved in anti-social behaviour in schools and in the community. They often belong to gangs, and become known to the police, youth offending, and criminal justice systems through theft, assault, and causing "nuisance" generally.

One way of thinking about gangs is that they provide a home for existential homelessness, a place in which some young people can feel they belong (Caviston, 2008). For some excluded young people who may have suffered neglect or abuse in their childhood, or witnessed domestic violence, an experience of "toxic shame" (Mollon, 2002) may need to be kept at bay. Gangs offer a way of warding off such shame, through hierarchy and persecution of others—either those outside the gang, or the weakest within it. Gilligan (1999) argues that shame can be a trigger for violence and other forms of antisocial behaviour.

On a more individual basis, those students excluded from school often have cognitive and language difficulties, as well as a lack of emotional literacy to communicate their experiences ver-bally and to ward off such shame. In these circumstances, a lack of verbal skills may well mean that shame must be kept at bay through behaviour instead, both in and out of school.

Societal responses

Before describing some practical ways of working with excluded young people, it is important to consider more widely the potential impact that the behaviour of such children, young people, their parents and families can have on professionals and agencies who act on behalf of wider society. Young people's antisocial behaviour often provokes a polarized reaction. Agencies do reject and exclude, most obviously from mainstream schools. However, there is a danger that other services working with excluded young people may themselves become embattled "advocates", friends, and defenders of their students/clients, committed to "include at all costs".

When faced with young people's antisocial behaviour, which may constitute attempts to ward off shame, an increasingly common response from statutory agencies is a determination not to be duped or shamed in turn by young people. It is a common adult experience to feel "shamed" by young people who laugh at, ignore, or abuse you. This can provoke a feeling of wanting to retaliate, to "make them cry instead", and maybe also to wish to act out of the unconscious pleasure derived from suppressing the enjoyment of others (Žižek, 1993). Recent UK government campaigns against antisocial behaviour, particularly concerning young people getting together, wearing "hoodies", even walking down a street or going into a shop, can be seen as examples of attempts at such retaliatory suppression. Increasingly repressive legislation prohibits such behaviour, expanding the range of what is "antisocial", while acting out the unconscious wish that "we must deny to others what we ourselves desire". Suppressing the enjoyment of young people may be a result of a collectively driven refusal of our own enjoyment. This may link with intergenerational envy: young people being increasingly persecuted and criminalized precisely because adult society envies their enjoyment and excessive pleasure.

There is a danger when this becomes acted upon through the use of legal and criminalizing frameworks. The United Nations has recently highlighted the extent of this situation in the present day UK. The UN Committee on the Rights of the Child (2008) states that the use of Anti-Social Behaviour Orders (ASBOs) and other measures, such as mosquito (noise deterrence) devices, "may violate the rights of children to freedom of movement and peaceful assembly".

The Committee goes on to say that "there is a general climate of intolerance and negative public attitudes towards children, especially adolescents, in the UK", offering a total of 120 recommendations, indicating the extent of the problem. Other evidence includes the fact that there are currently 3000 children under the age of eighteen in prison in the UK, a higher proportion than in almost any other country in Europe, and that the age of criminal responsibility (ten years old, eight in Scotland) is among the lowest in the world.

In my work with excluded children, I see this enactment most vividly in the increasing use of ASBOs. The symbolism of the language of a punitive societal response mirrors a common behaviour among young people. ASBOs are "slapped" on young people, just as they "slap" and "happy slap" each other and members of the public. In this way, our feelings of hatred, resentment, and violence can be projected on to and into young people. This is not interactive, relational, or "face to face". It is only a unilateral, unidirectional action—just like a slap.

However, punitive societal reactions may cause young people to feel less guilt about their actions, and are likely to make them feel more ashamed. The more harshly we punish children, the more violent they may become. It is a myth that you can "beat something out of a child". If societal reactions are punitive, then young people risk losing face, and feeling yet more "shamed". By attempting to do so, the risks of further, and more serious, antisocial behaviour are increased, as this is one way of warding off such shame.

ASBOs offer mainstream society an illusion that we can feel as if we are doing something, as if we can stop young people from being antisocial or engaging in criminal activity. Criminologists Loader and Walker (2007) have described this societal response as "get tough hyperactivity". When ASBOs are applied to our children, they constitute a delusional act of enforcement and control, which serves to criminalize increasing numbers of our young people.

Furthermore, there is a fundamental flaw in the culture of "slapping" ASBOs on young people, as if they were simply smaller adults. It ignores any sense of child and adolescent development, in which children and young people learn ways of behaving and relating from adults—and adult society—with whom they come into contact. Treating children as if they were adults ignores questions such as: how do children and young people learn? How do we help them change? How can adult society help children and young people to see things, themselves, and others, differently?

If the task is actually about reducing and managing the antisocial behaviour of young people, and supporting them by offering alternatives to criminal activity, it can be seen that ASBOs frequently work against this. They can stop young people from making use of facilities and services, by "banning" them from football pitches, from meeting their friends, from going to youth clubs, etc. This further increases their sense of exclusion. From a developmental perspective, the danger is that they will grow up experiencing society as persecuting and excessively repressive and punitive.

While a mature, adult response is necessary from agencies, efforts to try to change the antisocial behaviour of young people need to be informed by a developmental perspective, and to have at their heart an attempt to understand the reasons for such behaviour. As Loader and Walker (2007) argue, unless we understand, we cannot help young people to develop a language for responsibility and compassion. In my experience, there is little opportunity to contribute a developmental perspective to an ASBO consultation process, and it seems to be a case of a system designed for adults simply being applied to children and young people without thinking developmentally. The process really raises the question: what do children and young people learn from being on the receiving end of the ASBO process? Whether considered from a social learning (Bandura, 1977) or psychodynamic perspective, it appears that this process ends up promoting even more social exclusion among the already vulnerable, and results in more societal splitting between "us" and "them".

There is a need to "face" young people (rather than "react"), to try to work together to understand their experience, and to share our efforts with them. Without attempting to recognize and acknowledge their experiences, there is a danger of systems replicating the dehumanizing brutality of those who cannot manage their hate and rage.

Alternatives to "slapping"

As a CAMHS professional working within a setting for excluded students, I witness and play a small part in facilitating a number of different attempts at engaging children and young people and their families in conversations that seek to try to understand their experience. While responses that enforce clear boundaries are often necessary, they are part of proactive, thoughtful attempts to engage students and families consistently, rather than reacting to particular instances of challenging behaviour.

It can be difficult, within an education setting, with the inherent demands of the national curriculum and targets, to be explicit about offering children and families holistic, containing interventions. Nevertheless, if there is to be any hope of changing antisocial behaviour within or outside schools settings, it is essential to strive to offer students and their families an experience of feeling understood, or, at least, that professionals are trying to understand them and their experiences. This may open up the possibility of engaging them in beginning to think about their experiences of guilt, love, care, and concern. This process may ultimately bring hope and reparation.

It is possible to characterize a range of interventions at different levels in terms of facilitating "conversations that require courage". This involves a willingness to "face" young people, and to work alongside them and their families in order to try to help them "face" their experiences. It also involves working together with a complex array of various agencies, supporting whoever is most appropriate to try to have those conversations. By creating, supporting, and continuing be part of a network, the aim is to give young people and families a sense that professionals are trying to understand their experience and offer support consistently.

Direct "face to face" conversations can happen at different levels. I will describe four different types of conversations that I witness or in which I participate; daily phone calls home, restorative justice meetings, the internal consultancy offered by a mental health professional in a specialist education setting, and the work of a multi-agency network.

Daily conversations with parents/carers

The cornerstone of successful work with excluded students is a good relationship with parents and carers. Establishing this can be easier said than done, as parents often come with a history of difficult conversations and experiences with school, culminating in a permanent exclusion. Consistent contact over time can help to establish mutual trust and confidence, and an important way in which this happens is a daily phone call home at the end of the school day. This call highlights any difficulties there have been during the day, which can corroborate what students have said when they get home, or sometimes offer parents/carers a different version of events. What can be particularly powerful is the impact of a phone call home that lets a parent/carer know that their son or daughter has had a good day at school, and has done well. This can be the very first time that there has ever been "good news" from school. It can also introduce a more positive, hopeful narrative into conversations at home, and between home and school. Over time, as trust builds, parents may value these daily conversations as a way of sharing information and concerns about their children's behaviour out of school as well, so that all adults are better informed about what children may be doing.

Restorative justice

Inevitably, there are times when young people with a history of antisocial behaviour become involved in situations of conflict, either with each other or with staff. In particular, children exposed to domestic violence when young can become hypervigilant, may seek to defend themselves, and to avoid "losing face" in situations in which they feel threatened. This can be the case even in circumstances that might not seem threatening to others. Without a repertoire of alternative experiences or the necessary verbal skills to resolve or negotiate, some children may not be able to access ways of resolving conflict other than through verbal and physical violence.

After such incidents, staff in the unit will set up restorative justice meetings (Hopkins, 2004), in which both parties will describe their memory and experience of the incident, and will listen to the other party's point of view. This conversation is facilitated by a member of staff, who sets a clear agenda and offers a containing framework in which this conversation can happen. This approach offers children an opportunity to experience an alternative way of resolving conflict, and experience has shown that it can make a significant difference to how children subsequently respond. For example, when two twelve-year-old girls arrived at the unit, having heard that each of them was going to "batter" the other, they began to threaten each other. In a restorative justice meeting, they were able to tell each other about what they had heard about the other and reached an agreement that they would not act on what they had heard. While they did not become friends, they were subsequently able to tolerate each other and get along without any further conflict. (Note: All case material has been disguised and comprises composites of individuals with whom the author has worked.)

The CAMHS role as part of the exclusion education system: the "internal consultant"

As a mental health professional working as part of a staff team in a PRU, it is possible to contribute to building up an understanding of students and their families in different ways. One way of conceptualizing this is in terms of distinguishing between the role of "internal consultant" to the system within the unit, and the role of providing a mental health perspective to the multi-agency system surrounding the unit's students, developing more effective multi-agency working practice. These can be thought of as different levels at which attempts to offer understanding and to contain anxiety can contribute to a bigger picture of a holistic multi-agency response to excluded children and families.

As a clinical psychologist working half-time in a PRU, I work alongside the head teacher, and, although I am a health professional, I am part of the senior management and leadership team. I am embedded within the education system, and am "part of the team" rather than a visitor.

I am seen as a member of the staff team by students, their parents and carers, and by my education colleagues. My primary working relationships are within education, rather than CAMHS, making it quicker and easier to offer mental health contributions directly with teachers and other colleagues involved in the planning of students' education. Wherever possible, I am part of students' initial inductions in the unit, and contribute to initial assessments with students and families before and immediately following their arrival. By "being around", I am in a position to offer flexible and responsive clinical input to the unit, to individual students, their parents and carers, sometimes to whole classes, as well as to the staff team within, and the multi-agency network surrounding, the unit. I can offer my observations of the whole system, and continue to strive to keep this system open by developing and maintaining links with external agencies, including CAMHS.

A significant step has been to "embed" staff support systems in the unit. While different kinds of conversations about clinical work may be taken for granted in mental health service settings, case discussion and reflection can still feel new, unfamiliar, and uncomfortable in education contexts. However, over time, colleagues have come to value different fora in which thinking can develop. These include daily de-briefing meetings, weekly staff consultation meetings, and risk assessment meetings when needed. After a brief description of staff consultation and risk assessment structures, I will then outline the perspective that a CAMHS clinician can offer in specialist education provision.

Consultation with staff

Within the daily life of the unit, there are daily briefing and de-briefing meetings, planning and reviewing students' time, and for staff to share their daily experiences of being with the students. While these meetings are familiar to colleagues in education, we have also introduced an additional programme of weekly staff consultation meetings, in which staff can reflect at the end of the week, share experiences, thoughts, and feelings about students, as well as consider what they might bring up for the staff team as a whole. As a kind of "internal consultant" (Huffington & Brunning, 1994), I facilitate these meetings, and, while I may not be able to take up a more distant "objective" position, my own knowledge and experience of students seem to be valued by my colleagues. Often, discussions about challenging and stressful situations generate ideas for developing the work in the unit generally, or with particular students or classes.

For example, in one discussion of Anna, a thirteen-year-old girl whose behaviour had been very disruptive both in school and in the community, and who was due to return to mainstream school from the PRU, colleagues spent a lot of time talking about Anna's preoccupation with asking about whom she would be supported by on her return to school. Her mentor in the unit also worked in the mainstream school for part of the week. However, she said that she had told Anna that "there's another mentor in the school". I responded by saying how easy it might be to underestimate the importance of the attachments that students had formed to particular members of staff during their time in the unit. It seemed that there was a tendency to avoid, or at least minimize, the reality of the importance of those attachments, and the responsibilities that went with them, by depersonalization ("there's another mentor in the school"). This is one of the institutional defences against the anxiety of dependence found by Menzies Lyth (1959) in her seminal study of the nursing profession.

The discussion turned to thinking about the importance of students' attachments to staff during their time in the unit, and about what it might be like for students to be returning to mainstream school. The staff group became more able to think about reintegration as a "lived experience", rather than a depersonalized procedure. The group also became more able to think about what might be needed to manage that process successfully, in terms of the external and internal worlds of the students. In this way, the mentors became more able to think of themselves as transitional objects (Winnicott, 1965), secure and reliable attachment figures needed to support students to cross the organizational boundaries on returning to school.

Risk assessment

As an in-house clinician, I also facilitate the processes of risk assessment and risk management when required. Information is gathered from files and from all staff, individually and collectively, to create an initial risk assessment plan. This identifies risks and potential triggers, with clear strategies and responses to prevent, minimize, and then respond to any risky situations. This plan is shared with the young person and their parent/carer, so that everyone can refer to it if necessary. It is then reviewed regularly during the young person's placement in the unit, and may be shared with staff at their next educational placement. The process has a containing function for staff, and often for young people themselves, as they can be clear about the consequences of any behaviours that pose excessive risk.

Taking up a "third position"

By virtue of being a non-education professional within an education setting, a clinician can take up a "third position" that is different to students and families and different to schools, teachers, and other education staff. This can enable different kinds of conversations to happen in schools (Dowling & Osborne, 1994), creating a triad around a symbolic "triangular" reflective space in which new thinking and new patterns of relationships may be created.

Taking up a third position involves holding on to uncertainty, not knowing, curiosity, and ambivalence, while reflecting on the interactions and relationships between students and staff, home and school, as well as helping staff to reflect on their own roles in relation to their students. In such a way, a staff team can be helped to "think about itself while being itself" (Britton, 1989, p. 87), as in the example of the discussion of Anna, above.

For example, it becomes possible to think about patterns of relationships involving authority by having available someone who is neither student nor teacher to be curious about, and reflect on, the ways in which staff and students interact. Also, planning the reintegration of students into mainstream settings may be made easier if anxieties around mental health or behaviour issues are contained by the involvement of a mental health professional, particularly one who straddles boundaries themselves

It becomes possible to be curious about young people's relationships to authority in the community outside school, with the police and youth offending services, for example. This can be particularly valuable in opening up conversations about young people's own antisocial behaviour, without being seen by them as necessarily part of the statutory services that enforce various youth offending "orders".

Promoting "depressive position" functioning through containment and supporting management

As individuals, we can all move between more and less integrated emotional and mental states (Klein, 1959). When our anxieties are not contained sufficiently, we can be unable to tolerate our thoughts, feelings, and anxieties, and so may "split them off", and "project" them elsewhere. In Kleinian language, this state of mind is referred to as the "paranoid–schizoid position" (Klein, 1946). Emotional development can be thought of in terms of movement towards the so-called "depressive position" (not the same as "depressed"), in which anxieties, difficult thoughts, and feelings may be tolerated, and in which there is a capacity to think about them in a more integrated way. As individuals, we move between these two positions all the time.

Just like individuals, we can think of systems and organizations being more and less able to tolerate anxieties, and moving between paranoid–schizoid and depressive position functioning. Effective management and decision making needs, among other things, time, the capacity to tolerate uncertainty, and a wish to understand, as well as the ability to keep thinking under pressure. When organizations are not able to offer these conditions, decisions can be made reactively, with less thought or understanding, and the organization itself can be experienced as functioning in a paranoid–schizoid way. The pressures to act, and to re-act, may mean that the space for understanding that is essential for containment (Winnicott, 1971) is squeezed out, leaving less opportunity for depressive position thinking.

Mental health professionals can play an important part in facilitating shifts towards more depressive position thinking—with both education and multi-agency settings. They can offer a containing space in which thinking can develop that links with the painful reality of students' experiences, rather than simply reacting to their behaviour from a more paranoid–schizoid position (Klein, 1946).

Mental health professionals can make this contribution by providing arenas in which new ways of understanding students' behaviours, states of mind, and needs can be thought about and shared. The containment they potentially offer is, according to Bion (1962), the process by which experience is felt, processed and then fed back in a more digested form, that can then be integrated, thought about, and learnt from. This is most effective when combined with strong management, together providing "containing leadership that involves the creation of a relational and mental space that helps in the toleration of ambiguity, uncertainty and anxiety" (Simpson & French, 2005, p. 294). By providing contained and containing spaces for thinking, mental health professionals can help to address, manage, and ease anxieties of education colleagues, and, by so doing, can lead to increased understanding of, and empathy for, vulnerable and challenging young people.

In a hopeful context, an integrated mental health perspective can help to manage anxiety when students are reintegrating into mainstream schools after intervention in the unit. The presence of a CAMHS professional crossing the boundary between exclusion and mainstream setting, sharing an understanding of emotional and behavioural needs in general, and of the reintegrating student in particular, can go a long way to containing some of the fears and anxieties of the mainstream school. Previously excluded students can begin to be understood, their needs met and their voices valued, rather than simply being seen as "other". By crossing the boundary between exclusion and mainstream setting, the contribution of a CAMHS professional can both contribute to and represent this shift, accompanying reintegrating students in their journey from the margins back into mainstream, and helping to reduce the risk of any future or further antisocial behaviour.

It is possible to think about containment in different ways, as offered by different types of leadership. A more "maternal" form is offered by the process of listening to staff experience, putting difficult feelings and thoughts into words, and helping staff to feel valued, listened to, understood, and have their experience validated. Having the opportunity to think about and try to understand students' challenging behaviour is an essential part of working in a specialist setting, and yet can easily be overlooked. The job of being a teacher or member of support staff in a PRU can be extremely challenging, especially when staff may have "uncharitable" thoughts, feelings, or fantasies about their students. Feelings of resentment or even hatred may be thought to be "unprofessional", but must be voiced and acknowledged in a thinking space if they are not to be acted out (Winnicott, 1947). Other feelings, such as anxiety and stress, hopelessness, and helplessness, frustration, and anger, are more common, but it is just important to find ways of speaking and thinking about these, in order to support and sustain ourselves and each other in the work. This can be offered by a clinician "embedded" within the system, offering regular and frequent staff consultation meetings in order to contribute to the general health and wellbeing of the unit as a whole.

Another way in which to think about containment is the value of having systems, structures, and boundaries clearly and firmly in place. These are vitally important in an organization that must manage chaotic and out-of-control feelings and actions, as they must be maintained in order to keep staff and students feeling safe and secure. The importance of clear "paternal" management and leadership cannot be overestimated. While this comes from the Head Teacher as manager of the unit, managerial decisions are often informed by clinical discussions and thinking, including issues of working practices and risk. The close working relationship between Head Teacher and clinician, involving constant sharing and reviewing information, experience, practice, and hypotheses, means that the combination of both clinical and managerial containment contributes to the health of the unit, particular in times of stress and distress.

Multi-agency working

The networks of professionals working with excluded children and young people who come to the attention of various agencies are usually complex. In the Pupil Referral Unit, where this is almost always the case, we have established and developed a consistent, stable network of colleagues from our partner agencies. The aim of our multi-agency "reintegration forum" is to co-ordinate informa-tion, assessments, interventions, and referrals among representa-tives from a network of agencies.

Our multi-agency reintegration forum meets regularly, once every month, at the PRU. Membership has been reasonably stable, and includes colleagues from within and outside the PRU, from education, health, social services, youth, and youth offending services. From within the PRU, the teacher in charge, deputy teacher in charge, special educational needs co-ordinator (SENCO), senior behaviour support worker, safer schools police officer, and myself, the clinical psychologist, all attend. Other education colleagues are the SEN (special educational needs) placement and planning officer, the allocated educational psychologist, the educa-tional welfare and truancy officer, and school inclusion officer.

Colleagues from the local authority more widely include representatives from the Youth Offending Service, Safeguarding and Social Care, and Youth and Connexions Services.

There is always a danger with complex networks around children and young people with complex needs that services will, individually, pursue their own line of work in the belief that "we know best". The danger is that each service will consider each "bit" of the young person from their own perspective, and that the needs of the young person as a whole will not be considered. This can particularly be the case when young people exhibit challenging and anti-social behaviour, as the tendency to act to "stop the behaviour" may override attempts at understanding. While networks come together around particular children at given times, we aim to maintain an ongoing network of colleagues who share a mutual understanding of each other's roles and the complex issues in each other's agencies, while considering a group of young people as a whole.

As the in-house clinician, I chair these meetings, and I see my role as both offering a mental health perspective directly, as well as facilitating thinking and discussion among all parties generally. I see my role as being part of this multi-agency forum, rather than somehow separate from, or "consulting to", it. The role might be thought of in terms of an "internal consultant" (Huffington & Brunning, 1994), where the process of facilitating working together can be considered alongside addressing the specific mental health concerns of any particular young person. The aim is that the co-ordinated efforts of representatives from the relevant agencies involved in the lives of the children and young people will offer them and their families an experience of professionals working with them, getting alongside to try to see things from their point of view. The hope is that this will be felt as an acceptable, even welcome, way of supporting young people and their families to initiate changes, through reaching an understanding and "facing" the realities of their situations. When this is successful, excluded children and families experience this as supportive, rather than as an institutional "slap round the face".

The English Department for Children, Schools and Families has highlighted "success factors" for multi-agency working (DCSF, 2006). At a strategic level, these include having shared goals, building on existing partnership working, and having regular monitoring and reviews. On an operational level, success factors include establishing clarity of vision and purpose, having clear roles, and an exchange of information. Finally, in terms of evaluation, success factors include collaboration and co-ordination. Our experience is that, by meeting regularly "face to face", co-ordinating our work and, when necessary, challenging each other, our multi-agency forum strives to meet those criteria and helps to keep thinking alive.

So, what? The impact for students and their families

From the feedback from education colleagues, it seems clear that all staff working directly with excluded students have a better developed understanding of mental health difficulties in young people, and their impact on behaviour, as a result of having a mental health colleague as part of the staff team. Students and their families have appropriate access to support from CAMHS and other services, in ways that can be planned and negotiated from an informed position. At times of more acute concern, there is a flexible and immediate response available to requests from students and parents/carers, as well as to any crises that occur. There is also the capacity to offer a psychological and mental health perspective on antisocial behaviour to the police and youth offending services. There is a greater understanding of risk in the unit, and how to assess and manage it.

In addition, the multi-agency network of agencies works together in a more co-ordinated way, with each part of the whole system usually having a better idea of what other parts of the system might be doing, or contemplating. The experience of children and families is that agencies are better at talking to each other, not duplicating assessments, not contradicting each other, and not asking families to repeat their stories several times over.

One example of how this co-ordinated multi-agency working benefited a young person was John, a thirteen-year-old boy who was at the unit for over a year. His siblings were well known to the police, and when he arrived at the unit he was part of a gang involved in antisocial behaviour consistently in the community, and "was being considered" for an ASBO. He received consistent support from teachers and support staff over time in the unit, as well as mentoring support outside school through a local voluntary sector project. The youth service provided a continuum of support through a local youth club, and there was also consistent follow-up by education professionals with John and his mother to improve his attendance. Parenting support was also offered through the local Youth Offending Service. Our multi-agency forum played a key part in co-ordinating the work of so many different agencies, and continued to do so as John became less involved in antisocial and criminal behaviour locally, and began gradually to take up a place in a mainstream school. After successfully doing this, he also won an award for his contributions to local youth services.

Another example was the consistent support offered to Mushtaq, a thirteen-year-old boy whose attendance at the unit after his permanent exclusion was extremely poor. When not attending, he was frequently involved in violent and antisocial behaviour in the community. Through a combination of individual support to Mushtaq himself, when he attended, the work of family support workers with him and his family in his local community, and the work of our educational welfare officer, he began attending more often and more regularly, so that, by the end of his year in the unit, he was attending almost every day, a huge change from when he had first been placed in the unit. His behaviour in the community also changed significantly, as he became less involved in fights and other incidents.

Limitations

The reality of working across agencies with excluded young people who exhibit antisocial behaviour includes inevitable difficulties and limitations. First, joint working itself takes time: to build up under-standing, mutual respect, a common language, and new ways of working. This is consistently scarce, especially in a PRU where there are such insistent demands and challenges that need to be responded to quickly. There are also scarce resources in other agen-cies, where the vision and philosophy of joint working may not be shared quite as fully. Different agencies have different thresholds, either for responding to routine referrals or different meanings of what constitutes "urgent". In a multi-agency context in which there are different shades of commitment, resource, and capacity to respond, it can be very challenging to manage extremely stressful situations.

There are also occasions when in-house containment may not be sufficient. Part of the task of the unit is to assess students' needs and to clarify what kind of educational provision may best meet them. Very occasionally, it becomes clear that the unit itself cannot meet those needs sufficiently to carry out that task, and so alternative education provision must be found. Even then, however, structures such as the risk assessment process described earlier help to identify the limits of what risks are acceptable, and have been used occasionally to inform students, parents/carers, and colleagues from other agencies that other provision may need to be offered.

In terms of working across agencies, our own multi-agency network has no authority to direct other agencies to work collaboratively with us. Local services may come under particular pressure around young people's antisocial behaviour in the community, and may not have the capacity to share alternative approaches to understanding and intervening in young people's lives. One example of such limitations was our work with George, a thirteen-year-old boy who had been permanently excluded from his mainstream school. He was very bright, while adults in and out of school experienced him as loud and extremely active. There seemed to be a split between different parts of the system. While teachers and support staff in the unit were consistently supportive, he and his mother reported to me in my work with them that they felt that George was receiving unfair attention from local law enforcement agencies. George reacted by provoking and shouting at officials in the community, and was then given an ASBO. One condition of the ASBO was that he should not be seen with a good friend of his. Almost inevitably, for a thirteen-year-old, he was seen with this friend, and was judged to have broken his ASBO. He was subsequently labelled as a "criminal" and was sent to prison as a young offender.

Another example of some of the frustrations and limitations involved work around Leah, a bright fourteen-year-old girl who had been permanently excluded from her mainstream school for fighting. Leah's family were having a stressful time, and the housing service had become involved following complaints of noise from neighbours. The housing service was considering issuing Leah with an ASBO, adding to the pressures the family was under. We did not have enough time to work with Leah, her family, and the network before she had to leave the unit at the end of the school year due to her age, and so she was unable to have an opportunity to reintegrate into a new mainstream school.

Conclusions

I have tried to show how different ways of "facing" young people and their families with an institutional response that is seeking to understand, rather than punish, can make a difference to young people's lives, including their educational prospects, capacity to relate to others, and their behaviour in both school and in the community. If society is serious about trying to change some of the antisocial behaviour of young people, then more efforts need to be made to try to "get alongside" them and their families, to engage in "conversations that require courage", and to work together with them, their families, and others in their networks to start to reverse vicious circles of retaliatory behaviours on the part of both young people and adult society. If young people, already shamed and made vulnerable by their childhood experiences, are made to feel "slapped" and shamed further, they are likely to engage in yet more antisocial behaviour to ward off that shame. If, on the other hand, they are helped to feel more "held", held in mind and understood, then they become more likely to use other opportunities to engage in and with adult society more constructively.

This chapter has outlined a few ways in which young people and their families can be helped to feel more contained, held, and understood within a multi-agency context after exclusion from school. While this is not the sole prerogative of mental health professionals, they can still play a key role in supporting teachers and colleagues from education and other agencies who work with children and young people on a daily basis, as well as promoting the co-ordinated work of multi-agency systems.

In England, the Office for Standards in Education (OFSTED) inspects schools and education provision regularly, reporting on their findings. Their recent report has highlighted the importance and value of partnership working for supporting excluded students (OFSTED, 2007, p. 5). The integrated presence of a CAMHS professional can help to strengthen the exclusion setting as an "open system": not just an open education system, but open to contributions across service and agency boundaries. CAMHS professionals can make a key contribution in promoting the integration of Pupil Referral Units and other alternative education provision into a whole system of support for young people - an aim of the UK Government in its White Paper for provision in England, *Back on Track* (DCSF, 2008).

Multi-agency working has long been rhetoric of choice for policy-makers, while putting it into practice has traditionally been more difficult to do than say. This chapter has attempted to describe different ways in which the rhetoric can be made a functioning reality. Despite some limitations and frustrations, there are still many ways in which the lives of children and young people, their families, and those affected by their antisocial behaviour, can be made a little easier by effective multi-agency working.

References

Bandura, A. (1977). *Social Learning Theory.* Englewood Cliffs, NJ: Prentice Hall.

Bion, W. R. (1962). A theory of thinking. In: E. Bott-Spillius (Ed.), *Melanie Klein Today,* Vol.1 (pp. 178–186). London: Routledge.

Britton, R. (1989). The missing link: parental sexuality in the Oedipus complex. In: R. Britton, M. Feldman, & E. O'Shaughnessy (Eds.), *The Oedipus Complex Today: Clinical Implications* (pp. 83–101). London: Karnac.

Caviston, P. (2008). Youth violence: it's all the rage these days! Presentation to OPUS (Organisation for the Public Understanding of Society) Scientific Meeting, London, 25 June 2008.

Department of Children, Schools and Families (DCSF) (2006). *Every Child Matters: Cross-government Working with Local Partners to Achieve Better Outcomes for Children and Young People.* London: HMSO.

Department for Children, Schools and Families (DCSF) (2008). *Back on Track: A Strategy for Modernising Alternative Provision for Young People.* London: HMSO.

Dowling, E. & Osborne, E. (1994). *The Family and The School: A Joint Systems Approach to Problems with Children*. London: Routledge.

Gilligan, J. (1999). *Violence: Reflections on our Deadliest Epidemic*. London: Jessica Kingsley.

Hopkins, B. (2004). *Just Schools: A Whole School Approach to Restorative Justice*. London: Jessica Kingsley.

Huffington, C., & Brunning, H. (Eds.) (1994). *Internal Consultancy in the Public Sector*. London: Karnac.

Klein, M. (1946). Notes on some schizoid mechanisms. *International Journal of Psychoanalysis, 27*: 99–110.

Klein, M. (1959). Our adult world and its roots in infancy. *Human Relations, 12*: 291–303.

Loader, I., & Walker, N. (2007). *Civilizing Security*. Cambridge: Cambridge University Press.

Menzies Lyth, I. (1959). The functioning of social systems as a defence against anxiety: a report on a study of the nursing service of a general hospital. In: *Containing Anxiety in Institutions: Selected Essays* (pp. 43–85). London: Free Association Books, 1988.

Mollon, P. (2002). *Shame and Jealousy: The Hidden Turmoils*. London: Karnac.

Office for Standards in Education, Children's Services and Skills (OFSTED) (2007). *Pupil Referral Units: Establishing Successful Practice in Pupil Referral Units and Local Authorities*. London: HMSO.

Rendall, S., & Stuart, M. (2005). *Excluded from School: Systemic Practice for Mental Health and Education Professionals*. London: Routledge.

Simpson, P., & French, R. (2005). Thoughtful leadership. *Organisational and Social Dynamics, 5*(2): 280–297.

United Nations Committee on the Rights of the Child (2008). *Consideration of Reports Submitted by States Parties Under Article 44 of the Convention: Concluding observations—United Kingdom of Great Britain and Northern Ireland*. Geneva: United Nations.

Winnicott, D. W. (1947). Hate in the counter-transference. *International Journal of Psychoanalysis, 30*(2): 69–74.

Winnicott, D. W. (1965). *The Maturational Process and the Facilitating Environment*. London: Hogarth Press.

Winnicott, D. W. (1971). *Playing and Reality*. Harmondsworth: Penguin.

Žižek, S. (1993). *Tarrying with the Negative: Kant, Hegel, and the Critique of Ideology*. Durham, NC: Duke University Press.

CHAPTER SEVEN

Managing difficulty: a journey with a murderous adolescent by a CAMHS psychiatrist and team

Rosemary K. Richards

Introduction

The encampment sites from where Bronze Age families kept watch over the sea-plains now lie empty and windswept above the market town. Those families were well practised in survival and social skills that families in the early twenty-first century may not possess. As a child and adolescent mental health service (CAMHS) team, we work in a semi-rural locality with families experiencing problems with a child or children from birth to eighteen. We are a tier three service, so practise at a district general hospital level of specialization. The team comprises a consultant psychiatrist (me), two nurses, two psychologists and some additional psychotherapy and occupational therapy time. We receive 1880 referrals annually from a population catchment of 128,200 children and young people. Although the county appears affluent to outsiders, there are pockets of real poverty in both town and country.

This piece is about a patient, Migel, an adolescent in whose care we were heavily involved over four years. It gives some account of how we tried to manage a difficult case with grossly sub-optimal staffing (25% of the nationally recommended minimum), how we offered a lead in containing anxiety through multi-agency work, and the learning I have gained in the process. For confidentiality reasons, I have disguised the patient and family details, although the dynamics of the actual case have been preserved.

First presentation

Migel was nine years old when he was first referred. He was described as stealing other children's jackets, subsequently hiding them at home, behaving aggressively to other children, and sometimes slapping them. He would also hide his own uniform blazer around the school and subsequently accuse other children of taking it. Migel's mother did not let her husband know about these difficulties, as she felt that he would be too angry with him. At asssessment, there were complaints about Migel's behaviour at home as well as his general lack of co-operation. It was noted that both mother's parents were killed in her country of origin during the early years of the marriage before the pregnancy with Migel was confirmed. These losses seemed to have affected the early relationship between mother and son.

My predecessor advised a low-key response including a restructuring of the family day in the evenings so that Migel had some personal time with parents after his adopted younger sister had gone to bed. At follow-up three months later, he seemed to be doing well and was therefore discharged.

Second presentation as an emergency

At fourteen, Migel had a diabetic crisis which required hospital treatment. The diagnosis of diabetes was confirmed, and he was started on long-term treatment to prevent further attacks, which included "funny turns" when he would become aggressive. These were attributed to hypoglycaemic episodes, with organic confusion and agitation. At this time, he was noted by the paediatrician to have multiple self-inflected lacerations on his legs. A referral was made back to child and adolescent mental health services. Seven days later, he presented in casualty with further burns which were cleaned and dressed.

Migel was seen by our music therapist for a generic assessment, then began individual work to help him think about processing his feelings. By agreement, the music therapist liaised with the family social worker and the school. Migel's ability to manage both school and home without becoming involved in swearing and aggressive acts was diminishing. His head teacher noted that he had a history of inflicting burns with matches on his arms and forehead between lessons. The family attributed this to worry over his diabetes.

Now in Year 11 (fifth form, 15–16-year-olds), he was reported as showing erratic behaviour: fine and pleasant on some days, but on others rude, defiant, and sometimes violent. He had pushed school staff whom he disagreed with on several occasions, giving them a hard shove. He had poured ink on another pupil's face and at times was very intimidating to pupils in other ways, such as by shouting abuse. In one episode, he sat on the roof for twenty-five minutes, refusing to move, without any apparent reason.

Initial management

I met Migel for the first time when he was fifteen. He was obviously bright, although lacking in social skills, very obese and clumsy. He was not depressed, not experiencing psychotic episodes, and did not meet the diagnostic criteria for Asperger's Syndrome, though he tended towards this end of the spectrum. He was interested in planes, lacked empathy, and was somewhat solitary.

The family attributed Migel's psychological problems to the stress of diabetes and possibly to some other unknown diagnosis. Throughout my contact with them all, they returned to this belief. It was a belief that prevented them from engaging in conversations that would help them to think about other explanations. The paediatrician and I wondered if we had missed something, but we thought not. We referred Migel for more specialist neurological assessment as a response to the family's view that more could be done.

The police picked him up behaving dangerously when he got through the side fencing of a railway station and walked too close to the tracks, apparently caring nothing for his own safety or the trains. A visitor to the home reported that Migel showed off his collections of tarantula spiders and scorpions in a manner that was intimidating and that (we realized later) was sadistic.

The team's music therapist was working with Migel in a weekly session. The clinic was held in an out-of-the-way location in the hospital and there were no panic buttons. I was aware of increasing concerns about Migel; then the therapist came to see me urgently to tell me about a threat Migel had made to her. She said that she was not willing to work with him any longer.

Her account was that the session was coming to an end, and Migel's mother was due to collect him to return him to school. He stopped packing up the materials from the session, picked up a drumstick, stood between the door and the therapist, menacing her with threats to poke out her eye.

The therapist and I had differing views about how to respond to this incident. It was clear that we needed to make the environment around Migel safer in terms of potential weapons and availability of other staff. I disagreed with her view that Migel was too dangerous for us to see. I considered that the team still had a duty to care for him and needed to find an approach that would still enable him to engage therapeutically. I felt angry with my therapy colleague and experienced her abrupt withdrawal from the case as something of an abandonment. I had to mobilize myself to manage the increased level of danger that I felt surrounded direct clinical contact.

As it happened, there was an outpatient appointment scheduled in the same clinic suite for me to review the patient a few days later. I decided to use this opportunity to explain to him and his mother that we would need to move the appointment venue to my team base so that we could keep Migel and staff safe during sessions. I explained that the music therapist was no longer able to work with him due to the drumstick incident.

Although they accepted this situation, which involved a location for appointments that was not easy to get to, both mother and son denied the threatening behaviour.

Thinking one: being afraid

At the weekly team meeting, I raised the case. There were polarized views. The music therapist maintained her opinion that we should no longer see the patient due to the risk he presented. At that time, Migel was still attending a local comprehensive school, helping out in a corner shop, and attending a local boy scouts club. There were significant concerns about his behaviour, including aggressive acts to other children, stealing, and bullying.

As a psychiatrist, I needed to be confident about diagnosis. Migel had been treated for diabetes for eighteen months by a paediatric colleague, having been admitted with a "funny turn". He was on insulin medication and appeared to be stable with no further episodes. However, was diabetes contributing to or causing some of his behaviours? Was he mentally ill, perhaps in early psychosis? Was the family making a valid clinical point when they spoke of "funny turns" which they could not describe and which no one else had seen? I told my team that I considered I had to see the patient and that I had a duty of care to him. There was also a multi-agency context to which we might need to contribute: local social workers were working with the family on parenting issues. Unfortunately, the music therapist cut off from the conversation, which made thinking about alternatives for Migel difficult. Migel's self-harm to forehead and arms had ceased with mental health input, so I knew that something helpful had been provided for him which needed to continue, but I also realized that the intimacy of individual music therapy in a small room with a consistent presence might have been too much for him. I knew, too, that I had a key responsibility to keep myself safe.

When I was training in a London hospital, a social work colleague was mortally knifed from behind by a mentally ill patient in one of the long hospital corridors. Ever since, I have been very aware of safety. Doctors are explicitly trained to take charge of risky situations with direct interventions and generally to wield authority. I have learnt that although this attitude in itself can bring danger to the doctor, the multi-disciplinary team setting has helped me to keep some kind of dynamic balance between being able to work in clinically difficult situations (potency) and setting myself up to do nothing or the impossible (impotence and omnipotence). I used to work in a team that could not have these conversations, where I felt very unsupported.

My present team is warm, frank, and robust. They appreciated that a male therapist would be particularly helpful for the work with Migel and also to me, since I was now afraid of him. It was decided that a male psychologist would join me; we would manage the case together. It was important for me to experience the support of the team, to know that my decision had been scrutinized by them, and that they had acknowledged the reality base of my fear.

It is very unusual for me to be afraid of patients, although I have observed that in district general CAMHS teams, the setting is often one that is intrinsically unsafe. In fact, this is the only patient I have been afraid of in the last nine years. I am still not sure if this represents my realization of his risk or my professional inadequacy. I know that I do not feel guilty about the care I provided for him, but I do wonder if I could have done it differently and perhaps more effectively.

First hospital admission

About seven months after I first met him, Migel's behaviour escalated. At school, he was oppositional and aggressive, threatening people with scissors that he had stolen. He took his church youth worker into his home and frightened her badly with his dominating manner. He took tarantulas out of their cages to "show" her; consequently, she felt very threatened.

I became increasingly concerned that he might have some other problem I could not elucidate. I negotiated an inpatient admission to a national specialist unit where young people can be remotely monitored for seizure activity twenty-four hours a day. I remember wondering whether I was a "good enough doctor". I urged my colleagues to push him up the priority list as he became excluded from school and presented an unknown risk to the community.

Migel was admitted voluntarily under parental authority to a mental health unit for observation. The parental script was still that all his difficulties were caused by diabetes. They and he were hugely resistant to any formulation that disagreed with this. Neither the parents nor Migel wished to consider any responsibility they might have for the present difficulties .

The national specialist hospital began a full assessment, which was brought to a halt four weeks later. Migel's violence to other younger children in the unit was considered to put them in unacceptable danger. He had also blocked toilets and caused bathrooms to flood repeatedly.

He came home just before Easter to await specialist clinical psychology assessment.

Thinking two: multi-agency work

At home, we wondered how to manage him. I faced a familiar dilemma in my job. How do I create/find time to consider his needs? My work life is busy; there are competing demands. I train junior staff, I am on call out of hours, and I am responsible for emergencies. The kind of thinking we are talking about requires reflective space and room for uncertainty. In CAMHS, we often turn to multi-agency work to obtain a multi-dimensional picture, a shared risk assessment, and holistic plan for care. Yet, in this work, we find that colleagues look to us for a lead, for clarity, and for answers.

We had a multi-agency meeting about Migel and his return to education. The consultant from the national unit attended. She explained that he had behavioural problems of the type that psychiatrists label "unsocialized conduct disorder", but no other psychiatric diagnosis such as Asperger's syndrome, early psychosis, or depression. His diabetes was well managed, in their specialist opinion. She spoke strongly of the need to support, help, but not to demonize him.

In the meeting there was awkward manoeuvring between some professionals, who keenly felt their responsibility to protect the community's children, and who advocated supportive action as well as attempting to understand Migel. In the end, the need to protect other children took priority: Migel was permanently excluded from school.

In a multi-agency meeting, we learnt that over the previous months he had exhibited explosive anger in Boy Scouts in the presence of the troop leader over previous months. There had been an episode where, in the presence of an archdeacon, he had attempted to stab a fellow scout with a penknife. I think this was the first recorded of a number of occasions when it required more than one adult to prevent Migel from completing a dangerous assault.

Migel and his parents were most indignant that educational provision had not been found sooner. They saw it as his right and could not accept the lists of concerning incidents. They dismissed and minimized professional concerns.

From my point of view, it was both a worry that he was receiving less supervision than he would had he been in school, and that his church youth worker was not at work. I had referred Migel to our regional forensic CAMHS service. As he had no diagnosis of mental illness and was not deemed detainable under the Mental Health Act, he could not be assessed as an inpatient in secure conditions. The team were somewhat dismissive of my referral, but agreed to put him on their community assessment waiting list.

The Education Authority offered Migel reintegration tuition, which depended on appointing a male tutor for the purpose and Social Services providing a social care assistant for additional supervision. I remember feeling rather overwhelmed by my own responsibility, as well as other agencies' anxieties, but not being able to think clearly about how to move forward.

Another hospital admission: forensic assessment

At this stage, I was still trying to establish a consensus medical diagnosis that the patient and his family would buy into. I did not think that he was psychotic or depressed. I knew very little about his early medical history. I had difficulty in obtaining other specialist opinions because he was either not "bad enough" or "too bad". The family still believed that diabetes was the problem. While he was waiting for inpatient assessment, the forensic CAMHS team undertook their outpatient assessment. This made clear that a community team should be able to manage Migel and his risks. They suggested that he be placed in a residential establishment with tripartite input from health, education, and social services. No such placement existed for an adolescent in the county. The emotionally and behaviourally disturbed boarding schools were not suitable. We were advised that an out-of-county placement would not be funded, and, in any event, we could not identify a possible placement.

I felt let down by the lack of advice and support. I also felt let down by my colleagues, and I remember believing that I had overestimated the risk. I felt incompetent and troubled—Migel was not engaging with either me or the psychologist.

Migel went into the specialist adolescent psychiatric unit (Tier 4). He failed to engage there, too: he was oppositional and declined to participate. There had been heavy pressure from local agencies for me to detain him under the Mental Health Act, but I did not think he met the criteria, and nor did my colleagues at the unit or peers in the county. When the unit staff stepped up the pressure for Migel to involve himself in unit life, he absconded and refused to return.

He was back in the community. I continued to see him, very slowly reducing his benzodiazepine (hypnotic/anxiolytic) that had been part of his earlier paediatric management. This type of medicine has been associated with aggressive behaviour and, although I did not think that it played a causal role, there was a possibility. He had not experienced a seizure for over two years, but continued to assert that his "funny turns" had caused his aggressive behaviour. There were no observations to back this up. Migel and his parents still said that I was failing to recognize the central role of his diabetes. With advice from the specialist adolescent unit, I referred him to an ultra specialist in liaison adolescent psychiatry at a national outpatient clinic for a final opinion.

Multi-agency work

At this time, the continued low-level physical aggression towards his mother and sister was escalating. Migel made phone calls to the National Society for the Prevention of Cruelty to Children (NSPCC) and social services alleging severe physical punishment from his father. A child protection investigation was initiated; as this got under way, Migel viciously attacked his sister. He was removed into voluntary care.

Multi-agency meetings at that time included the Youth Offending Service, education, CAMHS, and social care. There was a lot of anxiety, which we explicitly recognized and tried to work with. A joint care plan would have been a good idea, but was too difficult to achieve at the time. I find it difficult in complex cases like this to carve out enough time to deal with them and to appropriately prioritize various other equally needy cases that have waited a long time.

Gratefully, I stepped back a bit, and my psychology colleague led on multi-agency work and co-ordination. There was some antagonism between agencies about the quality of their work, and there was significant avoidance of difficult issues (myself included). My psychology colleague undertook some careful chairing of meetings, but we still had to work with managers weighing in on the "side" of their junior staff members with the risk of losing focus on the patient.

Thinking three: risk and violence in outpatients

Migel was still attending outpatient sessions, arranged around when his mother could bring him at the end of her night shift. His father was not available due to work, so CAMHS family work could not take place. Our waiting room is narrow and small, and I fielded concerns from colleagues that he might harm a child in this confined space with him. We made sure to pick him up promptly.

Our reception area is in a corridor with a glass screen, the other side of which is an office in which three young staff members can be seen working. Following the assaults on his mother and sister, I thought Migel could pose a risk to these people, who he came to recognize, so we securely locked the door for the duration of his visits. I felt that I received pitying looks from the music therapist for my stupidity in continuing to work with Migel. It was difficult to hold my course, especially as the lead psychotherapist in my service had said that he could not work with a particular six-year-old because he was too violent.

I think that I stopped contemplating carefully enough the risk and violence at this time. I was having to overcome reluctance to meet the patient. My team was still very supportive and the psychologist ensured that he was available to join all my appointments.

At about this time, we determined major issues with boundaries within the family. Professionals had long been uncomfortable with the nature of the mother–son relationship. Now that Migel was in care, staff noticed sexualized behaviour between Migel and his mother, as well as Migel and his sister. Staff intervened when they saw Migel lying on top of his sister and moving up and down on her lower body. Migel and his mother were seen to kiss, both with open mouths, on a number of occasions. Female staff reported that he touched them inappropriately, especially bottoms and groins. There was an episode when a male member of staff challenged him over throwing a hot drink and he responded with physical threat and sexualized, racist verbal abuse.

One morning, we saw Migel in a clinic room quite a distance from the reception area. At the end of the appointment we agreed to bring mother in for feedback and an update. The psychologist apologized for having to leave before we had finished. After agreement with Migel, I left him in the room and went to get his mother. When we returned to the room, Migel was crouching, invisible, behind the door, and he jumped out towards my back making "Grrh" noises. I moved quickly away and, although he did not touch me, I was terrified. I felt as if I had been attacked. He is physically tall and large. Migel's mother was laughing, and neither she nor her son could understand my view that his behaviour was inappropriate. (He has a normal–superior intellect.) They saw it as a "joke". Although jumping out is an act we often see in younger children, this act by a fifteen-year-old seemed very threatening. I now think it was his sadistic response to my inadvertent threat to his core complex.

Later on, in clinic visits, he took to calling me by a pet name that my family happen to use and by which I am never called at work. I took charge in my doctorly way, and told him that it was not in order. I did not recognize that he felt threatened by the powerful engulfing mother. I just experienced my boundary as being breached. I was thinking on my feet in the waiting room. Now, I think that I understand the therapeutic tight-rope which I needed to walk the first time he did this: acknowledging the strength of the other's anxious state without challenging it so far as to give an experience of humiliation to the person and trigger a fight response.

Throughout my contact with this patient, I had been aware of struggling to discharge my responsibility. I was glad that, when I took up my appointment, I had insisted on preserving a space for specialist supervision, which was infrequent, but a good time for thought both in the session and travelling to it. I had made an agreement with my Trust to pay for it. Truthfully, I cannot say that

I used the supervision to arrive at profound analytical understandings. It was more about helping me hold together and not feel overwhelmed, so that I could, in turn, help the system to hold and contain my team's patients.

Social care: a dangerous task

Looking in from the outside, I could see how structually split the system was. Migel was housed in a children's home in the county capital where the Youth Offending team worked and saw him nearly daily. He travelled to my town for a CAMHS appointment. He used public transport extensively to travel to his college. He also had weekly counselling, yet in a different town, a decision that was not at first shared with us and arose out of a sense that CAMHS was not doing enough. I remember discussing the risks of this unsupervised movement through the community.

By this time, Migel was accumulating a list of charges for threatening or actual assault and a variety of thefts. Then a frightening episode occurred. One evening, he was picked up for inappropriate behaviour in the care home by a senior worker. He withdrew to his room where he set his bed alight, covered it with the duvet and left the room. He saw the male staff worker sitting on the top of the stairs. Migel went towards him, putting his hands round the worker's neck tightly, so that the worker felt he would be throttled. Several staff were needed to disentangle them. He absconded and stole a boat, floating away from the search for him. The fire smouldered in the bed, but was discovered and put out by the fire brigade without harming anyone.

Some ten days earlier, Migel had been taken to a coastal resort by care staff on a day out. He disappeared. The coastguard was called and a search mounted, including a helicopter, over some hours. He was found bobbing up and down in the sea watching the activity.

I could perceive that Migel's behaviour was escalating as the care staff attempted to manage him on tight behavioural contracts. The firesetting and involvement of the emergency services led to the system round Migel disintegrating. There was a strong view that he should be locked up, but this could only happen through the criminal justice route. The charges and the hearings took time.

I continued to explain that he could not be placed in a secure forensic adolescent unit because he did not have a mental illness to account for his deterioration, even though he was dangerous. There was intense pressure on me to "do something". I listened to staff, supported them, and tried to explain why doctors considered that "funny turns" were not the cause of his behaviour. I resisted pressure to change the medication regime. I experienced first hand the power of social pressure to define a person as mentally ill so that social control could be achieved.

Risk realized

Migel began attending college in the town where his family lived and he had been to school. One Saturday, still living in the same care home, he went out for the day with permission. He travelled there to see a friend, a girl of thirteen he had been to school with. They walked from the town centre across some fields to a secluded area with an isolated beach in a shallow mere by the sea. The two lay down on the sand and kissed for a while. Then they walked to a place under a rock and sat there on an upside down boat. The girl gave evidence that he pushed her off the boat, that she fell into the water, that Migel held her head under the water, punching her body but mostly her head. When she managed to get to her feet, he continued to attack her head, pushing her back in the water with his hands round her throat so that she lost consciousness.

Later, she was dragged out of the water. Migel telephoned his mother to say he had had a "funny turn", she told him to call an ambulance, which he did. The ambulance crew had to cross the fields to find the two and was directed by Migel from his mobile. The victim told paramedics that she thought she would die.

The victim's injuries required intensive care for five days. She had stream water and sand in her lungs, extensive facial injuries, including a cheekbone fracture, a nose fracture, multiple bruises and lacerations, several fractured ribs, as well as contused kidneys. There was no sexual assault.

Migel described the victim as his girlfriend, although it seems that this was the first time they had spent any time together on their own. We presume that he made an advance to her that she rejected, but he has steadfastly refused to discuss the episode.

Conclusion

Migel was charged with attempted murder and convicted; he was sentenced to nearly four years in custody with a period of eight months having been spent on remand. He is currently in a Young Offenders Institution, but will probably serve the last part of his sentence in an adult prison. Once Migel was sentenced, all four local agencies co-operated to write a joint report for the Youth Justice Board. We believe this was unprecedented.

What risks can we anticipate when he comes out of prison? I remain fearful of Migel, having written a court report for the youth justice proceedings. I am left wondering how I could have dealt with my responsibilities differently. Could we have managed this situation in the community more safely?

CHAPTER EIGHT

The interface between forensic psychiatry and general adult psychiatry

Richard Taylor

Introduction

T he relationship between forensic and general adult psychiatry has, in recent years, generated a lively and, at times,
heated debate. In the past three decades, forensic psychiatry
as a sub-speciality has expanded rapidly in England and Wales, and
to a variable extent in other jurisdictions. In the UK, forensic psychiatry arose from the branch of psychiatry dealing with prisoners and
high security hospital patients (such as at Broadmoor Hospital). As
the deinstitutionalization of asylum psychiatry proceeded, forensic
and general adult psychiatrists have needed to liaise and collaborate in a number of ways. Forensic psychiatrists have perceived a
difficulty in discharging patients with the stigma of criminal
convictions and offending histories to community care (see case
two, below). (All case material in this chapter is disguised and
fictionalized, in order to preserve confidentiality and anonymity.)
Conversely, general adult psychiatrists may complain that their
most disturbed and high-risk patients do not benefit from the relatively well-resourced forensic services (for example, by an admission to medium security) until an offence is committed (see case

one, below). Both groups of psychiatrists need to communicate about risk, which has led to professional conflict and debate about how to conduct robust risk assessment and what resources to use in risk management.

In the UK, the interface between the two specialities promoted, in the late 1990s, a debate about the aftercare and community management of mentally disordered offenders. However, as mental health services have evolved, for example, by the commissioning of prison inreach mental health teams, the building of more low secure beds (reinstititionalization, as described by Priebe and Turner (2003)), the interface is evolving at different levels: in prisons, intensive care units (PICU), the community, and in the provision of speciality placements in the private sector. In psychodynamic terms, many forensic patients will have experienced conflicted parental relationships and disruptions in their early attachment relationships in childhood. Disputes between psychiatric teams about, for example, who should supervise a patient after discharge, may risk recapitulating early parental disputes. Discontinuities in attachments to professional figures at the point of transfer may, by the same mechanism, increase risk of reoffending. This has been recognized in an attempt to provide continuity of forensic psychotherapy for patients moving down from high security, through medium security, to the community (Minne, personal communication).

Case one

Mr Z was admitted to a local psychiatric intensive care unit (low security) after being found behaving bizarrely in a public place from where he had been removed by police under their powers to transfer a mentally disordered person to a place of safety (section 136 of the Mental Health Act 1983 in England and Wales). He had a diagnosis of treatment-resistant schizophrenia with a history of five previous admissions to local open and locked ward facilities. After a four-week admission, he had failed to respond to being re-established on an adequate dose of clozapine (an antipsychotic used in treatment-resistant schizophrenia) and continued to describe symptoms of thought broadcast and derogatory hallucinations in the third person. There were several assaults on staff, requiring periods of seclusion. He was referred to the local medium secure unit for advice on management with a request that he be transferred to the higher level of security, because of his violence. He was assessed by a consultant forensic psychiatrist, who agreed with the diagnosis of treatment-resistant schizophrenia, and suggested persevering with adequate doses of clozapine for a further period of time. However, transfer to medium security was not offered.

Approximately eight weeks later, he had continued to fail to respond to maximal doses of clozapine and there had been two further episodes of seclusion. A second referral to the forensic service resulted in suggestions about management, but did not recommend admission to medium security. Several weeks later, there was an unprovoked attack on a fellow patient motivated by a derogatory auditory hallucination. Mr Z attacked the patient with a ballpoint pen, which he had concealed in his pocket, inflicting serious injuries to the other patient's eye. He was again secluded, and a third referral was made to the forensic service. On this occasion, it was decided that in view of the new index offence, the matter should be reported to the police and he should be referred urgently for a high secure opinion. After being treated in seclusion for a period of five days, he was seen urgently by a high secure hospital and transferred. Representations were made to the police for evidence to be gathered to support a prosecution so that he might later be detained on a hospital order by order of the criminal court with special restrictions. (Under this order, sanctioned by sections 37 and 41 of the Mental Health Act, there are greater safeguards on leave and discharge of mentally disordered patients, as the process is overseen by the ministry of Justice in England and Wales.) The general adult psychiatrist in charge of the PICU expressed disappointment that the previous referrals had not resulted in a transfer to a higher level of security, that is, medium security, given the identified risk factors. The patient was only thought suitable for treatment in a forensic setting once an offence had been committed. A psychotherapist who gave evidence to the serious untoward incident panel suggested that the patient's violence had been a communication of internal distress that had not been heard by the team.

International perspectives

As described by Arboleda-Flórez (2006), and Velinov and Marinov (2006), forensic psychiatry has undergone many changes world-wide during the past decades. Forensic psychiatrists are today widely expected to provide a competent opinion in difficult judicial situations. Arboleda-Florez (2006) argues that modern forensic psychiatry has benefited from four key developments: an evolution in the understanding and appreciation of the relationship between mental illness and offending; the evolution of legal tests to define insanity; new methodologies for the treatment of mental conditions providing alternatives to custodial care; and changes in attitudes and perceptions of mental illness among the public. He goes on to state that from an obscure and small group of psychiatrists who dedicated their efforts to the study of mental conditions among prisoners and their treatment, forensic psychiatrists have now developed into an established and recognized group of "super-specialists", an influential group that is transforming the practice of psychiatry and that has made deep incursions into the workings of the law.

Forensic psychiatrists are also facing ethical and professional difficulties in their everyday practice, especially when they have to address the conflicts between the patients' rights and the imperative for public protection. Despite some similarities, there are important differences in forensic psychiatric practice worldwide. In many countries, forensic psychiatry is not a separate sub-speciality of psychiatry with a parallel training programme, but an area of special interest for some general adult or child psychiatrists. The different legal framework for criminal responsibility and court-mandated disposal of mentally disordered offenders make comparison and international standards problematic. For example, in the USA, a prerequisite for entry into hospital treatment for seriously violent mentally disordered offenders is that the court must make a finding of not guilty by reason of insanity (or of permanent adjudicative incompetence). This is such a high legal threshold that many psychotic offenders, although clearly mentally ill at the time of their offence, receive prison sentences and thus require "correctional" psychiatric treatment in a prison setting. In England and Wales, a hospital order can be made if psychiatric treatment is thought appropriate, irrespective of criminal responsibility. Even in the event of a mandatory life sentence for a murder conviction, a hospital transfer can occur and can result in lengthy hospital treatment (under sections 47 and 49 of the Mental Health Act, 1983). In other jurisdictions, for example the Netherlands, there is provision for a "sliding scale" of criminal responsibility for personality disorder, which can result in a sentence split between prison and a treatment facility (the TBS system). In Bulgaria, as described by Velinov and Marinov (2006), education in forensic psychiatry has been introduced in the curriculum of medical students as well as general practitioners and all psychiatric trainees. Among the problems in Bulgaria is the scarcity of outpatient services for the reintegration/ aftercare of patients, a common theme in all jurisdictions that have developed a forensic psychiatric service. It has been argued that the World Psychiatric Association has a significant role to play in promoting an international consensus on the basic terminology in forensic psychiatry, the core forensic psychiatry sub-speciality curriculum, and the services which should be available for forensic psychiatry practice in high, medium, and low income countries. As forensic psychiatric services develop, there is potential for the tensions with adult psychiatry observed in the UK in recent years to be replicated elsewhere.

UK perspectives on the community interface

Gunn (1977) provides the earliest UK description of different models of aftercare for the management of the mentally abnormal offender. He suggests that in a choice between integrated or parallel services, there are advantages in having specialist forensic teams for mentally disordered offenders, as these may be more attuned to risk factors for reoffending and able to liaise more effectively with criminal justice agencies such as probation. Many parts of the UK have set up (often with minimal initial resources) specialist forensic assertive aftercare teams (forensic outreach) in parallel with existing community mental health teams, with the aim of de-silting expensive medium secure beds and improving post discharge risk management, albeit in the absence of a robust evidence base for their efficacy. These often have lower patient numbers and more experienced staff, but may lack access to other resources, such as day hospitals and community occupational therapy. Buchanan (2002) describes the various legislative changes during the 1990s, including the advent of the more structured Care Programme Approach, and the short-lived supervision register in the wake of the Clunis enquiry (a man with schizophrenia and poor quality community care who committed a homicide (Ritchie, Dick, &

Ingham, 1994)). The development of forensic outreach services continued in the 1990s with much variation nationally.

More recently, there has been a lively debate between general adult and forensic psychiatry about the relationship between the two sub-specialities (Gunn, 2008; O'Grady, 2008; Turner & Salter, 2005, 2008). Forensic psychiatry is criticized for failing to bring about a decline in offending behaviour by individuals with mental illness, despite substantial investment in inpatient facilities. It is suggested that forensic service development has been driven principally by a concern about risk assessment (Turner & Salter, 2008) and forensic psychiatrists are criticized for both failing to appreciate the dynamics of risk and for inappropriately fulfilling political demands for a robust and coercive response to dangerous patients risk. Turner and Salter (*ibid.*) argue that forensic services keep patients who have offended seriously as long-stay inpatients long after the dynamic risk factors have been reduced. Conversely, the forensic psychiatrists suggest that the criticism arises from a misunderstanding about the origins of the recent expansion of forensic services: O'Grady (2008) makes the point that forensic psychiatric services have developed in the context of the liberal public policy tradition of diverting mentally disordered offenders from prison to health and social care. One of the fundamental points of disagreement in this debate appears to be about the very history of the development of forensic psychiatry and the way that it has attracted resources. The rapid expansion of forensic psychiatry in terms of increased consultant posts, expanded training schemes, inpatient facilities, and funding is resented by general adult psychiatrists, who find themselves, particularly in inner-city settings, with high caseloads, high staff turnover and a requirement to manage increasing numbers of referrals on a fixed budget, whereas in forensic psychiatry the funding typically follows the patient. In order to examine this debate, it is necessary to consider both this historical development and the different ways in which the driving forces behind it are perceived by the two camps.

Case two

Mr B, a twenty-one-year-old man, transferred to a medium secure admissions ward from a remand prison, was charged with the attempted murder of a family member. He had developed first onset psychosis with six months of gradually increasing symptoms, including the delusion that a microchip had been implanted in his brain by his mother, that his father was controlling his body, and that his mother intended to kill him. The index offence against his mother was accompanied by a suicide attempt with self-inflicted serious injuries. He remained psychotic in prison, and gradually responded to oral antipsychotic medication when transferred to the medium secure unit. He undertook individual psychology sessions addressing his substance misuse and his insight into his illness. After a period of thirty months rehabilitation in medium security, during which his mental state remained stable, he was referred for discharge to a twenty-four-hour staffed hostel and follow-up by a community mental health service. There were considerable delays identifying a suitable catchment area team. The community mental health centre suggested that he be referred to the early intervention psychosis service. However, the latter service was unwilling to provide supervision and a community social work needs assessment was unforthcoming. After a delay of many months a formal opinion was eventually obtained from a community consultant, who stated they were not willing to supervise the case as it was considered too high risk, given the possibility of a reoffence. The forensic service was in the process of setting up a parallel forensic outreach service, and it was only after this team was operational, following a further ten-month delay, that Mr B was conditionally discharged to a hostel.

The historical relationship between forensic and general psychiatry in England

In the nineteenth century, general and forensic psychiatry were briefly located alongside each other. Following the case of Daniel McNaughten, a psychotic man who committed a homicide in the context of delusional beliefs about the prime minister of the day, Sir Robert Peel, and the consequent emergence of the concept of not guilty by reason of insanity, a criminal lunatics' wing of the Bethlem Hospital was built as an addition to the main asylum. The establishment of Broadmoor Hospital and subsequent transfer of Daniel McNaughten there in 1868 led to a lengthy period when forensic psychiatry was essentially a small branch of the profession, principally involving high secure care, initially at Broadmoor, and later at

Rampton and Ashworth as "special" hospitals. Prison psychiatry emerged later, notably with the appointment of joint Home Office/ NHS consultant psychiatrists in the 1970s.

The modern expansion of forensic psychiatry has occurred at the same time as the pattern of asylum closure and subsequent rein-stitutionalization of the seriously mentally ill, although it has not necessarily been driven by this process, as Turner and Salter argue (2008). A key turning point in this development was the publication of the Butler Report (1975), the recommendations of which were given added impetus by the care in the community "scandal of the day", the case of Graham Young (Bowden, 1996). Young, otherwise known as "the St Albans' Poisoner" was released from Broadmoor Hospital (high security) into the community only to reoffend, killing a number of people with poison, having originally been committed to Broadmoor for poisoning his mother. Subsequent analysis of the case suggests that he may have had unrecognized Asperger's disorder. The lack of aftercare for such a high-risk offender leaving a high secure hospital caused concern and added impetus to the expansion in forensic psychiatry already under con-sideration. The Butler Report also expressed concerns that there was hostility in the National Health Service to treating offender patients in hospital. It was suggested that offender patients could harm the image of the local care facilities, as mental illness could be further stigmatized by the notion that mentally ill people would have to "rub shoulders" with an antisocial minority. There was additional concern about the risk to NHS staff when admitting such offenders. One could argue that the Butler Report was ahead of its time in pointing out that risk assessment was fraught with prob-lems. The report recommended a review of all sentences, especially indeterminate ones (a recommendation which has only recently been implemented). It also recommended training and treatment for "dangerous antisocial psychopaths". Other recommendations were that restricted patients be reported annually to the Home Office to ensure they were not detained longer than necessary, and that there be continuity in the treatment of offenders between insti-tutions and their return to the community, including the provision of hostel accommodation. Interestingly, the report rejected the suggestion of an emergency reception centre for Section 136 cases, that is, patients brought to a place of safety by the police as a result of disturbed behaviour in public, anticipating the development of adequate psychiatric facilities in district general hospitals and teaching hospitals to deal with such patients.

The Butler Report had interesting comments to make about co-operation among the professions. The effect of treatment of mentally disordered offenders was said to include resettlement in the community, and forensic psychiatric services were proposed to be essential for this rehabilitation. Butler suggested that forensic secure units should be urgently established in each NHS region, the long-term objective being to develop close links between all services engaged in providing care. It was proposed that the main emphasis should be on community care and outpatient work, and the principle should be that treatment should always be provided as close to a patient's home as possible. Although forensic services would be under the NHS, prison doctors would be seconded to forensic psychiatric services for training. Closer links with community social services should be fostered, and the report thought that effective forensic psychiatric services would be an impetus towards the realization of the long desired aim of strengthening the links between the prison medical service and the National Health Service. The units were required for those mentally disordered persons, offenders and non-offenders alike, who did not require the degree of security offered at the special hospitals (which were found to be overcrowded) but, who, none the less, were not suitable for treatment in the open conditions pertaining in local psychiatric hospitals.

O'Grady (2008) argues that forensic psychiatry essentially evolved, in the wake of Butler, to deal specifically with mentally disordered offenders, that is, patients at the interface of law and psychiatry. This work involves liaising with criminal justice agencies, such as prisons and courts, to meet their needs. Preoccupation with risk appears to have come somewhat later. In 1990, the Home Office/Department of Health produced *Circular 66/90*, which essentially proposed that mentally disordered offenders should be treated within the National Health Service rather than the penal system. It is a feature of English mental health law, unlike, for example, in the USA, that Section 37 of the Mental Health Act 1983 allows for a hospital order to be made so that a mentally disordered offender can be treated in hospital even if they have been found guilty of a very serious offence. Any visitor to forensic hospitals in the USA will be surprised at the level of attention given to the different legal interpretations in each state of aspects of the McNaughten insanity rules. This is because there it is the only means by which somebody with serious mental illness can escape a prison sentence. O'Grady argues that the UK has, by contrast, an enlightened and liberal attitude towards offender patients.

The development of medium secure services during the 1980s and early 1990s was a result of central government funding of the development of regional secure units as recommended by Butler. This middle period of the development of the forensic psychiatric speciality is interesting in how different approaches to regional secure units later fell foul of the way that health services were reorganized and then redeveloped along internal market lines. One of the principles of the Butler Report was that treatment should be as near as possible to the patient's home. An early pioneering unit was the Denis Hill Unit in south London. The model for this facility was a central secure assessment unit (SASS) at the Bethlem Royal Hospital site, with the development of satellite units at Hellingly in Sussex, Cane Hill in Surrey, and The Bracton Centre in Bexley. The idea was that the initial remand assessment could take place in the centralized specialized unit, with rehabilitation and integration into the community being performed more locally. With the wholesale reorganization of the funding of health services in the early 1990s and the development of the internal market, care consortia, the purchaser/provider split, and the rigid sectorization of mental health care provision, this model proved to be less effective. Other units, for example, the Reaside Clinic in Birmingham, which had opted for a more centralized service, prospered under the new regime. Regional secure units developed on the centralized model, for example, in other parts of the London area, expanded rapidly.

While most forensic psychiatrists would not accept that a preoccupation with risk has been the only driving force behind the early development of the service, the case of Christopher Clunis in 1994 (Ritchie, Dick, & Ingham, 1994), and the subsequent decade-long preoccupation with the homicide inquiry, has clearly had an influence on the development of the speciality. Turner and Salter's (2008) argument that forensic psychiatry is essentially risk averse and reluctant to discharge patients may have some validity when one considers the length of stay of forensic inpatients, particularly over the past fifteen years. Forensic medium secure inpatients are expected to jump through an increasing number of hoops prior to discharge. These may include a willingness to accept depot antipsychotic medication, and participation in group and individual psychotherapies addressed at offending behaviour, substance misuse, relapse prevention, etc. On the one hand, it is argued that this is appropriate treatment, providing necessary rehabilitation and allowing transition to the least restrictive care environment. On the other hand, general psychiatrists might argue that the process has become unnecessarily protracted and that patients remain in medium security beyond the point at which their risk is acceptably reduced, whereas more acutely disturbed patients in need of interventions available in forensic units are denied admission.

The continual expansion in secure bed numbers would suggest that there is a process of reinstitutionalization. Regional secure units in the early 1990s, which were effectively gatekeepers for their own service, began to identify mentally disordered offenders who needed their treatment but for whom there was not a bed. These patients were typically placed in the private sector and funded via extra contractual arrangements, latterly known as OATs (out-of-area treatment services) or SPS (speciality placement service). The rising cost of these financial arrangements, principally because of the increased use of the private sector and the increased patient numbers, were then used as arguments by forensic services to expand their inpatient units to repatriate these patients from the private sector to new, expanded NHS facilities. This must be contrasted with the situation in general adult mental health, where small, open, acute units with community mental health services have increasingly had to decide how to spend their resources, regardless of patient numbers. This is one of the sources of resentment between the two camps. Added to this problem has been the fragmentation of community health services, in the face of central government targets and ring-fenced resources. The requirement for crisis resolution, home treatment teams, early intervention services, and assertive outreach teams has led to a reduction in resources in generic community mental health teams and an overall fragmentation of community services. Thus, the choice for community aftercare is no longer a simple one between a parallel or an integrated service, but a confusing plethora of often understaffed, specialist teams. Priebe and Turner (2003) argue that signs of reinstitutionalization are clear. The number and cost of forensic beds is rising in both the National Health Service and in the private sector. It is, however, noteworthy that a similar process appears to have occurred in other countries, for example, in Germany and Austria.

Turner and Salter (2008) also suggest that attitudes to compulsory treatment have changed. Although the increase in supported housing and assertive outreach can be thought of as representing a form of reinsitutionalization, albeit in a community based resource, it may also be argued that twenty-four-hour staffed specialist forensic hostels may represent the least restrictive form of care available for some of the more disturbed patients forensic psychiatrists have to deal with. In the wake of the 2007 revision of the Mental Health Act (1983), there has been a surge in applications for supervised community treatment, which may represent a further form of increased coercion, albeit in a community setting.

The current situation is that there has been a substantial expansion of regional (medium) secure inpatient beds, but there also appears to be an element of silting up of the system, so that regional secure units (RSUs) are having difficulties admitting acutely disturbed mentally disordered offenders from prison (because of the difficulty discharging patients). Recent attempts to improve the response from regional secure units have suggested a much shorter fourteen day time limit for the transfer of a psychotic prisoner (in Sweden, the target is twenty-four hours). However, it is not unusual to find individuals with a diagnosis of schizophrenia, charged with homicide, waiting on remand for more than twelve months for an RSU bed. There may be disagreement about the reasons for this, the lack of available step-down facilities being one problem, as patients who have recovered cannot be discharged. Continued reluctance by general adult services to accept mentally disordered offenders with the stigma of a serious or high profile index offence may be an issue, although the organization of community mental health services varies around the country.

General adult and forensic psychiatrists at court

A complete analysis of medico-legal work is beyond the scope of this chapter; however, in this area there may be a further source of tension between forensic and general adult psychiatrists, which arises in discussions over the provision of psychiatric opinions in legal proceedings. Many aspects of psychiatry overlap with the criminal and civil justice systems, for example: child psychiatrists advising the family courts in child-care proceedings, liaison psychiatrists commenting on medically unexplained symptoms in personal injury litigation, and forensic or general adult psychiatrists advising on issues of criminal responsibility or mental health disposals in the criminal courts. The role of expert witnesses is increasingly under scrutiny after Professor Meadows' difficulties, with formal guidance now available for civil and criminal procedures (Rix, 2008; Taylor & Buchanan, 1998). Turner and Salter (2008) have suggested that forensic psychiatrists in the UK should consider restricting themselves to medico-legal practice; however, in my opinion, this may risk throwing the baby out with the bathwater. Forensic psychiatrists certainly find that their opinions are more respected in court jurisdictions where they are also able to provide appropriate inpatient treatment for mentally disturbed offenders. Moreover, many general adult and liaison psychiatrists provide reports in personal injury cases, the usefulness of which may be undermined if they were not engaged in treating the illnesses they are assessing. The Butler Report rejected the notion of panels of psychiatrists with responsibility for only preparing reports. In the USA, there is a clearer demarcation between psychiatrists who treat patients and forensic psychiatrists who are assessing patients and providing an opinion. Establishing a boundary between the activities of therapeutics and evaluation may be said to prevent a conflict of interest between therapeutic and judicial responsibilities. In the UK, personal injury and family litigation is such that there may be a good argument for separating the two roles, especially where a psychiatric assessment may have a negative impact that could undermine the therapeutic relationship. However, in the arena of criminal law, it is common for treating psychiatrists to comment on the index offence, mental responsibility, risk assessment, and disposal. It is likely that expert witnesses, whether general adult or forensic, will be subject to greater scrutiny and regulation in the future.

Risk assessment at the interface

There is clearly a correlation between having major mental illness in the form of schizophrenia and increased rates of offending behaviour in general and violence in particular (Wallace, Mullen, & Burgess, 2004, Walsh, Buchanan, & Fahy, 2001). Maden (2005) argues cogently that the evidence on risk assessment in relation to both forensic and general psychiatry patients is unequivocal. He suggests the best assessment of violence risk in an individual patient is provided by structured clinical judgement. The question remains as to whether this should be conducted by a specialist forensic psychiatrist or by general adult services. One of the most widely used of such risk assessment tools, the Historical Clinical Risk 20 (HCR-20) (Webster, Douglas, Eaves, & Hart, 1997) begins with historical variables that provide a summary of actuarial risk. This tool also measures five clinical variables which are concerned with present mental state (and represent changeable or dynamic factors) and, five risk management variables that are concerned with future management, treatment and destabilising factors. Training requires a three-day course, including training on the Psychopathy Checklist Screening Version (PCL: SV) Hart, Cox, & Hare, 1995), which is one item on the HCR-20. It may be seen as impractical for all community mental health practitioners to be trained in this risk assessment tool, and, if that is the case, forensic services may continue to be requested to conduct these assessments.

Understandably, forensic psychiatrists have developed an interest in risk, partly because they have seen many cases of mental illness that have resulted in serious violence. As Mullen (2006) points out, the annual homicide rate in the UK is about one per 100,000, so even a tenfold increase in risk amongst those with schizophrenia will not necessarily affect an individual psychiatrist. By contrast, forensic psychiatrists will have seen many more cases where mentally ill patients have become seriously violent and, therefore, may be more finely attuned to the potential for bad outcomes. It could be argued that this makes them biased and, therefore, likely to overestimate risk, although, of course, assessments such as the HCR-20 are designed to minimize this. Turner and Salter (2008) argue that mental illness is only a modest risk factor for the occurrence of violence, whereas Mullen (2006) highlights that there are a variety of factors among mentally ill populations, including active psychotic illness, personality disorder, and co-morbid substance misuse, which can mediate violence. It is important not to minimize the correlation between violence, offending, substance misuse, and personality in major mental illness (O'Grady, 2008). Given that there is much overlap between forensic and general adult populations, should psychiatry develop services designed to meet the particular needs of this group? O'Grady proposes that we need not only a radical expansion of low secure provision, but also the development of pathways of care that emphasize the need for long-term rehabilitation, including adequate community provision of specialist housing in areas not blighted by drugs and high crime rates. Ultimately, in an increasingly risk averse and blame driven society, all psychiatrists will be expected to assess risk. If resources become more constrained in over-stretched community mental health teams, then they are likely to look to their better-resourced forensic colleagues to provide the necessary in-depth assessments. Multi-agency public protection arrangements (MAPPA) are dealt with elsewhere in this volume and will not be covered in depth here. However, there is anecdotal evidence to suggest that general adult psychiatrists may welcome the opportunity to share risk across agencies, whereas forensic services may be more reluctant to share information, partly because of concerns about confidentiality, but also in the context of higher confidence (justified or otherwise) in the ability of mental health services to manage their own high risk cases (known as level one, single-agency management, in MAPPA terminology).

Personality disorder across the interface

Forensic psychiatrists have been criticized for following a political agenda in agreeing to staff and run the so-called "dangerous severe personality disorder" units (Mullen, 2007). However, both general and forensic psychiatrists have hitherto neglected individuals with primary personality disorder. Of course, many patients with serious mental illness, in both general adult and forensic services, have a co-morbid personality disorder, and both general and forensic psychiatrists are familiar with dealing with patients who remain antisocial and troublesome despite having active symptoms brought under control by antipsychotic medication. However, the neglect by psychiatrists of individuals with a primary diagnosis of personality disorder was firmly identified in the Department of Health (2003) document, *Personality Disorder—No Longer a Diagnosis of Exclusion*. While the expansion of non-forensic community personality disorder services is advocated, their availability remains very patchy and subject to individual local champions (Bateman & Fonagy, 2004). Since that report, there is increasing evidence that the speciality of forensic psychiatry has begun to grasp the nettle of personality disorder, although it could be argued that there remains a long way to go. The welcome development of pilot medium secure personality disorder units has filled another gap in services. Individuals who previously would have languished in prison, or caused mayhem in the community, now have an opportunity for more intensive long-term treatment. The units are currently undergoing evaluation, and early anecdotal evidence suggests that those run on therapeutic community lines may be having fewer institutional problems. Suffice it to say there will be further debate about the interface between general and adult services when attempts are made to discharge these individuals in a step-down manner to community settings.

Prison inreach services

It has been argued that the failure of stretched mental health services to respond to the needs of seriously mentally ill have increased the workload of the criminal justice system. Taylor and Gunn (1984) argue that those who have committed violent acts are more likely to be remanded in custody, by being perceived as more dangerous if they have mental illness and, therefore, more likely to be refused bail on grounds of risk to the public. Court diversion services have attempted to divert patients into treatment, often without success. Forensic psychiatrists argue that prisons were never intended to accommodate a large mental health burden and are ill equipped to do so. The prison regime can be a toxic environment for individuals with major mental illness or psychotic symptoms, and the principal aim of forensic psychiatric services over the past twenty-five years, whether in regional secure units or based in prison clinics, has been to divert seriously mentally disordered offenders into appropriate hospital treatment. With the further reorganization of prison inreach services in recent years, with the result that many are now run by general adult services rather than specialist forensic services, there seems to be an emerging perception among general adult psychiatrists that patients can be returned to ordinary prison accommodation once they have had a brief period of inpatient treatment in a psychiatric unit. To a forensic psychiatrist, this may seem counterproductive, as the prison regime invariably leads to relapse and a further need for return to hospital. Turner and Salter (2008) argue that low secure or psychiatric intensive care units should be reserved for the short-term stabilization of disturbed patients from open acute wards, and not used as a convenient place to park a low-level mentally disordered offender while court proceedings are dealt with. The following case illustrates this dilemma.

Case three

Ms C was remanded in custody charged with an offence of wounding. She had attacked a member of the public in response to delusional beliefs that she was about to be abducted. When assessed in prison she was found to be floridly psychotic, with grandiose and persecutory delusions as well as auditory hallucinations. A diagnosis of schizoaffective disorder was made. She was referred to the low secure unit for treatment, transferred to hospital under a Section 48 and commenced on antipsychotic medication. After three weeks of treatment, her mental state had begun to improve, although not all symptoms had resolved: she remained guarded and mildy suspicious, but without hallucinations. A decision was taken by the psychiatric intensive care unit to refer her back to prison for ongoing treatment, pending her court case, as she was not aggressive in behaviour and other, more acutely disturbed, patients had been referred from open wards. In the prison, her mental state gradually deteriorated. After a further two-month period in prison, she was transferred again to a different low secure unit run by a forensic psychiatrist. During the second admission, her psychotic symptoms took much longer to resolve. She was eventually dealt with by way of a hospital order with a restriction under Section 41 of the Mental Health Act. When the case was reviewed at a placement meeting, the general psychiatrist in charge of the PICU stated that it was not appropriate for patients to remain in a low secure environment beyond the point at which their acute disturbance had been treated, and that prison was an appropriate place for her to wait, pending outcome of the court case. The forensic psychiatrist protested, stating that prison is a toxic environment and that she should have remained in hospital for a longer period as the early relapse might have been avoided.

General adult psychiatry has been required to manage a large catchment area population with finite resources in terms of hospital beds, hence the need to prioritize bed occupancy on open or PICU wards by admitting the most disturbed patients and discharging the least disturbed. Case three, above, could easily have been thought to justify a medium secure bed, in which case the funding could have followed the patient via a specialist placement in the private sector. Forensic psychiatry has the relative luxury of being able to consider what is in each patient's interest, regardless of resources.

Conclusion

Thus, the nub of the problem in this debate can be viewed as a conflict between the needs of the non-offender community mentally ill patient and the mentally disordered prisoner. As general adult psychiatrists gain more experience of working in prison inreach teams, perhaps it will be recognized that there is considerable overlap between these groups, an overlap that may become more evident in an increasingly resource-strapped mental health service. There clearly needs to be a care pathway at every level of security for all mentally disordered individuals who find themselves involved in the criminal justice system. A patient with chronic schizophrenia who shoplifts will benefit from diversion to hospital as much as a more serious offender with the same clinical presentation. The role of prison inreach mental health teams must be to identify mentally disordered individuals in custody, provide short-term treatment to ameliorate the deleterious effects of custody, and liaise with the courts in order to effect the appropriate therapeutic outcome.

In terms of resource allocation, general adult services could consider employing some of the politically savvy strategies of forensic services, such as admitting all deserving acutely disturbed patients to an open bed, which may, by necessity, be in the private sector. This will not be easy, with bed managers and crisis teams gate keeping finite acute beds in an increasingly lean public sector financial climate (post the 2008–2009 banking credit crisis).

It is my view that well-resourced forensic services should accept that advising on risk assessment and management, however fraught, is the business of forensic services, and should be offered as part of the core service of the regional secure unit. Where the clinical assessment and HCR-20 suggest that the risk is high, then, in appropriate cases, transfer from low to medium security could be offered more frequently than it is (before an index offence is committed). This would be to honour one of the key recommendations of the Butler Report (described as the forensic psychiatrists' *vade-mecum* (Bowden & Bluglass, 1990)) and to foster a better relationship with general adult services.

References

Arboleda-Florez, J. (2006). Forensic psychiatry: contemporary scope, challenges and controversies. *World Psychiatry*, 5(2): 87–91.

Bateman, A., & Fonagy, P. (2004). Treatment of borderline personality disorder with psychoanalytically oriented partial hospitalization: an 18-month follow-up. *American Journal of Psychiatry*, 158: 36–42.

Bowden, P. (1996). Graham Young (1947–90); the St Albans poisoner: his life and times. *Criminal Behaviour and Mental Health*, 6: 17–24.

Bowden, P., & Bluglass, R. (1990). *Principles and Practice of Forensic Psychiatry*. London: Churchill Livingstone.

Buchanan, A. (2002). *Who Does What: The Relationship Between Generic and Forensic Psychiatric Services in Mentally Disordered Offenders in the Community.* Oxford: Oxford University Press 245–263.

Butler, R. (1975). *Report of the Committee on Mentally Abnormal Offenders.* London: Home Office, Department of Health and Social Security, CMND. 6244.

Circular 66/90 (1990). London: Home Office, HMSO.

Department of Health (2003). *Personality Disorder—No Longer a Diagnosis of Exclusion.* London: HMSO.

Gunn, J. (1977). Management of the mentally abnormal offender. *Proceedings of the Royal Society of Medicine, 70:* 877–880.

Gunn, J. (2008). Correspondence re "Forensic psychiatry and general psychiatry: re-examining the relationship" by Turner & Salter (2008). *The Psychiatrist, 32:* 197.

Hart, S., Cox, D. N., & Hare, R. D. (1995). *The Hare Psychopathy Checklist: Revised Screening Version.* Toronto: Multi Health Systems.

Maden, A. (2005). Violence risk assessment: the question is not whether but how. *Psychiatric Bulletin, 29:* 121–122.

Mullen, P. E. (2006). Schizophrenia and violence: from correlations to preventive strategies. *Advances in Psychiatric Treatment, 12:* 239–248.

Mullen, P. E. (2007). Dangerous and severe personality disorder and in need of treatment. *British Journal of Psychiatry, 190:* 3–7.

O'Grady, J. (2008). Time to talk. Commentary on . . . forensic psychiatry and general psychiatry. *Psychiatric Bulletin, 32:* 6–7.

Priebe, S., & Turner, T., (2003). Re-institutionalisation in mental health care. *British Medical Journal,* 326: 175–176.

Ritchie, J., Dick, D., & Ingham, R. (1994). *The Report of the Enquiry into the Care and Treatment of Christopher Clunis.* London: HMSO.

Rix, K. J. B. (2008). The psychiatrist as expert witness. *Advances in Psychiatric Treatment, 14:* 37–41.

Taylor, P., & Gunn, J. (1984). Violence and psychosis. *British Medical Journal, 288*:1945–1949.

Taylor, R., & Buchanan, A. (1998). Ethical problems in forensic psychiatry. *Current Opinion in Psychiatry, 11*(6): 695–702.

Turner, T., & Salter, M. (2005). What is the role of the community forensic mental health team? *Psychiatric Bulletin, 29:* 352–353.

Turner, T., & Salter, M. (2008). Forensic psychiatry and general psychiatry: re-examining the relationship. *Psychiatric Bulletin, 32:* 2–6.

Velinov, V., & Marinov, M. (2006). Forensic psychiatric practice: worldwide similarities and differences. *World Psychiatry, 5*(2): 98–99.

Wallace, C., Mullen, P. E., & Burgess, P. (2004). Criminal offending in schizophrenia over a 25 year period. *American Journal of Psychiatry, 161*:716–727.

Walsh, E., Buchanan, A., & Fahy, T. (2001). Violence and schizophrenia: examining the evidence. *British Journal of Psychiatry, 172*: 4777–4784.

Webster, C., Douglas, K., Eaves, D., & Hart, S. (1997). *HCR 20: Assessing Risk for Violence*. Toronto: Psychological Assessment Resources.

CHAPTER NINE

Multi-agency public protection arrangements (MAPPA): can we work with them?

Jessica Yakeley and Richard Taylor

Introduction

Multi-agency public protection arrangements (MAPPA) were introduced in England and Wales in 2000 with the aim of minimizing the risk of sexual and violent offences to the general public posed by identified high risk individuals living in the community. These arrangements developed in the 1990s, against a background of increasing social and political concern about violent and sexual offenders, which led to legislation requiring the police, probation, and prison services to work together as the "Responsible Authority" to oversee statutory arrangements for public protection by the identification of high-risk offenders, the assessment and management of their risk, and the sharing of relevant information among the agencies involved.

In this chapter, we will review the legislative changes that led to the formation and subsequent development of MAPPA, summarize the structure and functioning of the MAPPA framework, and, most importantly, examine MAPPA's relationship with mental health services, illustrating this with clinical vignettes. The relationship of MAPPA with mental health is an area of intense controversy, raising questions about whether to prioritize the protection of the public, or the rights of the individual's privacy and confidentiality. Many see MAPPA as part of a trend of retributive legislation, in response to exaggerated public fears about the risks posed by offenders, particularly paedophiles, and the failure of prison and probation services to detain and punish them. This parallels increasing public concern during the past decade about the risk of violence in people with mental illness, which has contributed to the current culture of blame and homicide enquiries that castigate the mental health professionals involved who are perceived to be guilty of failure. The media has been accused of fuelling this panic by unbalanced reporting, raising public fears instead of promoting thoughtful debate. Politicians may also be guilty of responding too quickly to public outrage and pressure, which has led to rapid changes in legislation and restructuring of services that have been destabilizing and demoralizing for both professionals and service users.

The social and political concern about violent and sexual offenders fostered closer working relationships between the police, probation, and prison services in the 1990s. The co-operation between these services was incorporated in legislation in the Criminal Justice and Court Services Act 2000, and was developed further by the provisions of the Criminal Justice Act 2003. This legislation establishes these three services (police, probation, and prison) as the "Responsible Authority" to oversee these statutory arrangements for public protection by the identification of high risk offenders, the assessment and management of their risk, and the sharing of relevant information among the agencies involved. These arrangements are required to be regularly reviewed and monitored by area Strategic Management Boards (SMBs) in each of the forty-two administrative areas of England and Wales, with the publication of annual reports on the operation of MAPPA. The SMBs also identify and plan the training and developmental needs of those working in MAPPA.

Public concern

The recent legislative changes in the UK can be understood against a background of increased international concern, particularly about sex offenders (Kemshall & Maguire, 2001, 2002). For the past fifty years in California, in the USA, sex offenders have been required to register, and, in 1995, a child molester identity telephone line was set up. In 1996, "Megan's Law" was introduced in Washington State, after the parents of Megan Kanka, a child who was raped and killed by a known paedophile who had recently moved into a residential area, launched a campaign as they had received no information about the risk their daughter was exposed to. This law requires law enforcement authorities to make information regarding registered sex offenders available to the public. Many American states now list sex offenders on the Internet. In Louisiana, personal e-mail alerts can be set up by any member of the public, who will be sent a message if a paedophile moves into their area. In Oregon, convicted paedophiles are required to place a sign in their window. In Washington State, police conduct house calls. In California, there is specific provision that any harassment of sex offenders identified under Megan's Law constitutes an offence in itself.

Not surprisingly, there have been problems with the American experience. There have been several documented cases of vigilantism and violence directed against known offenders. In the USA, only 80% of known sex offenders actually register, raising concern that offenders are "going underground". Where limited information is disclosed, this information can quickly spread, for example, via handbills on telephone poles or adverse press coverage. There are human rights issues around the stigmatization of offenders and the right to privacy. Furthermore, there is concern that focus on stranger paedophile risk diverts attention away from child sexual abuse within families.

In the UK, the much publicized killing of Sarah Payne in Sussex led to a News of the World campaign to protect children from sex offenders. This newspaper campaigned for a "Sarah's Law", along the lines of the American Megan's Law. Subsequent publicity, including the publication of details of known sex offenders, led to widespread public disorder, including an attack on the home of a paediatrician, presumably mistaken for a paedophile, in Portsmouth. Alongside issues about sex offenders, concern arose after the Michael Stone case about the risk posed by those suffering from personality disorder. Michael Stone was a man with a diagnosis of personality disorder who killed a mother and her daughter in Southern England in

1996 after having been discharged from detention under the Mental Health Act 1983 as he was deemed untreatable. This contributed to the policy to establish a new categorization of people with "dangerous severe personality disorder" (DSPD), with initial proposals for legislation requiring psychiatrists forcibly to detain people who may commit some dangerous act in the future. Pilot DSPD units offering treatment for such patients were set up around the country, but have been beset with difficulties and are likely to be discontinued.

Legal history in England and Wales

The issue of monitoring potentially dangerous offenders in the community has a long history. In the early 1970s, Graham Young was released from Broadmoor High Security Hospital, where he had been detained following homicide by poisoning. Upon release from Broadmoor, within a few months, he committed further serious poisoning offences. While the Butler report (Home Office and Department of Health and Social Security, 1975) led to the development of regional secure units, and the Aarvold Committee (Home Office and Department of Health and Social Security, 1973) established guidelines for those leaving high secure hospitals, indeterminate sentences for dangerous offenders were at that time opposed on humanitarian grounds.

Since the political impetus for increased attention to law and order in the 1980s, there has been a gradually increasing legislative framework for the management of perceived dangerous criminals in England and Wales. This has included introducing limited parole for sex offenders and a requirement that they register with the police upon release from prison (HMSO, 1997), longer sentences for certain types of offence (HMSO, 1994), the introduction of MAPPA (HMSO, 2000), and new sentences to protect the public: an indeterminate sentence for public protection (IPP) and an extended sentence for public protection (EPP) (HMSO, 2003). Release from the IPP is at the discretion of the Parole Board on grounds of public safety, and the EPP allows for supervision of offenders in the community for an extended period. In 2003, the Sexual Offences Act extended the orders that can be used in the management of sexual offenders and introduced new civil orders that can be used to protect the public, especially children and vulnerable adults, which restrict the sex offender's activities. These orders include Sexual Offences Prevention Orders (SOPO), which aim to prevent preparatory behaviour by convicted sexual offenders. These can include specific conditions such as: banning the offender from entering a park or taking a recreational walk unless accompanied by another adult, prohibiting him from seeking the company of children, and banning him from accessing the Internet or possessing equipment capable of creating photographs of children.

Recent legislation in England and Wales has also affected the rights of mentally ill offenders. In 2004, the Domestic Violence, Crime and Victims Act (HMSO, 2004) extended the rights of victims of domestic abuse, including the right of a victim of a mentally disordered offender detained in hospital to receive information about that patient's discharge. In 2007, the revised Mental Health Act (HMSO, 2007), among other changes, introduced supervised community treatment (SCT) for patients following detention in hospital, to allow them to live in the community while subject to certain conditions to ensure they continue with medical treatment.

The MAPPA framework

The MAPPA framework is made up of four overlapping and complementary core functions, which the Responsible Authority (police, prison, and probation services) must ensure are established across the agencies involved. These core functions are:

- the identification of MAPPA offenders;
- the assessment of the risk that these offenders pose;
- the management of that risk;
- the safe and secure sharing of relevant information amongst the agencies involved in assessing and managing the risk of MAPPA offenders;
- the identification of MAPPA offenders.

Offenders who fall within the MAPPA remit are divided into three broad categories specified in section 327 of the Criminal Justice Act 2003:

Category 1: Registered sex offenders—offenders required to comply with the notification (registration) requirements set out in the Sexual Offences Act 2003.

Category 2: Violent offenders sentenced to imprisonment of twelve months or more, other sex offenders not required to register, and offenders detained under hospital orders or guardianship, either under the Mental Health Act or after being found unfit to plead or not guilty by reason of insanity.

Category 3: Other offenders who do not fall into categories 1 or 2, but, because of the severity of the offences committed by them, are considered to pose a risk of serious harm to the public. "Serious harm" is defined as "Harm which is life threatening or traumatic and from which recovery, whether physical or psychological, can be expected to be difficult or impossible".

Category 3 is intentionally broad, and most of the offenders in this category are those who have committed serious violent or sexual crimes prior to the introduction of MAPPA legislation. The majority of all MAPPA offenders come from within the prison system, but some have received hospital disposals. Less than 5% are assessed as posing the highest risks or most complicated management. A list of all MAPPA offenders is kept by the Violent and Sex Offender Register (ViSOR), a database developed by the Police and Probation in England and Wales, and is currently accessible to the three Responsible Authority agencies.

Risk assessment

Since their introduction, multi-agency public protection panels (MAPPPs) have increasingly made use of structured risk assessment tools and, currently, three main instruments are approved for use by MAPPPs in England and Wales: the Offender Assessment System (OASys) (Home Office, 2002), the Risk Matrix 2000 (RM2000) (Thornton et al., 2003), and Asset (Youth Justice Board, 2004). OASys is an assessment tool incorporating both dynamic and actuarial measures that can be applied to all offenders and is the agreed tool used by the prison and probation services. The RM2000 is a simple risk assessment tool for adult male sexual offenders that uses solely actuarial measures of risk and then looks at aggravating factors to assign a category of risk. Asset is a risk assessment instrument used in respect of young offenders. These tools are used to identify factors that have contributed to offending, assess risk, and help decide options in managing those assessed by MAPPPs.

The OASys provides a standardized categorization of risk, the categories determining the function of the different levels of MAPPA. The categories are *low* (no significant current indicators of risk of harm), *medium* (identifiable indicators present with the potential for harm, but the offender is unlikely to cause harm unless there is a change in circumstances, e.g., loss of accommodation, break-up of relationship), *high* (identifiable indicators of risk with the potential for serious harm at any time), and *very high* (an imminent risk of serious harm). The OASys also determines the likely object of that harm, whether it be any member of the public, a specified sub-group, such as children or prisoners, or an identified individual, including the offender himself.

However, the use of these assessment tools is not without confusion or complication. The OASys and RM2000 may sometimes identify different levels of risk for the same individual offender, because the OASys incorporates both dynamic and actuarial factors whereas the RM2000 is based only on static factors. Moreover, these tools do not provide a comprehensive assessment of all aspects of dangerousness, but are designed to trigger further assessment, including mental health assessments. In the past twenty years, a risk assessment industry has burgeoned, with the creation and proliferation of risk assessment schedules for every conceivable risk, many of which are no better than their predecessors. Negotiating this landscape requires considerable expertise and understanding of the complexities involved in risk prediction. In the mental health arena, the actuarial model of risk assessment has been prioritized over clinical judgement, and it is argued that forensic psychiatrists should be expected to use structured risk assessment tools. However, more recently, researchers in the field of psychiatric assessment of dangerousness have begun to recognize some of the limitations of the actuarial method and have incorporated more dynamic clinical variables into risk prediction instruments (Maden, 2007). Clearly, the choice and interpretation of the tools used by MAPPA in the assessment of risk requires a degree of professional skill, which is founded upon the availability of adequate training of those involved. In practice, the different agencies involved in the MAPPA process have tended to use different forms of risk assessment, which may give conflicting results, and then require expert professional judgement and discussion to agree on the most accurate level of risk to be recorded.

Risk management

Recent MAPPA guidance (Ministry of Justice, 2009) defines risk management as the "process of ensuring that there is an effective risk management plan which addresses the identified risk of serious harm factors by putting appropriate plans into place". It is acknowledged that this is a complex and difficult task, as risk is a dynamic variable influenced by a variety of factors and circumstances, which need regular monitoring, and cannot be eliminated altogether. Risk management is carried out on a case by case basis in which the different agencies collaborate in identifying and managing the risks posed by relevant offenders, focusing on those offenders whose identified risks are highest, or whose management is recognized as complex.

There are three tiers, or levels, to the MAPPA management system at which risk is assessed and managed:

Level 1: ordinary risk management

This level is used in cases where the risk posed by the offender can be managed by one lead agency, such as police or probation, or where there is another active risk process in place, such as within the health service. Offenders managed at this level tend to have been classified as low or medium risk (see above). In 2007, just over half of all MAPPA offenders in London were managed at Level 1 (Ministry of Justice, 2009).

Level 2: Local inter-agency risk management

This level is for offenders whose management requires the active involvement of more than one agency. The work is co-ordinated at monthly multi-agency meetings held in each borough and chaired by either a senior police or probation representative. Permanent representation of the core agencies of the police, probation, and prison services is mandatory, supplemented by representatives of other involved agencies where needed. In practice, housing and social services are usually routinely present at such meetings, whereas the representation of health authorities and mental health trusts is more variable, depending on local resources and attitudes towards working with MAPPA, as well as the perceived conflicts of interests regarding confidentiality and disclosure (see below).

Level 3: Multi-Agency Public Protection Panels (MAPPP)

Level 3 is reserved for those offenders who are considered as posing the most serious risk and/or requiring complex risk management (assessed at high or very high risk). This small group of most serious cases have become known as the "critical few". Level 3 is also used for those offenders whose risk is not high or very high, but where the likelihood of media scrutiny is high. These cases will be discussed at the regular monthly Level 2 meetings, above, but also at emergency meetings (Level 3), which may be held at short notice and which senior members of the relevant agencies are expected to attend. In London, less than 1% of MAPPA offenders are managed at this level. At Level 2 and 3 meetings, the prime goal is to co-ordinate an effective multi-agency response and ensure that adequate arrangements exist for risk management, and are implemented and reviewed, while allowing the case-work to remain the responsibility of individual agencies.

An effective risk management plan for an offender at any of the above three levels must contain strategies shown to reduce the risk of reoffending behaviour, or minimize the risk of serious harm. Such strategies may include monitoring the offender (such as surveillance and electronic monitoring), addressing accommodation requirements, external controls and sanctions prohibiting behaviour (as contained within licence conditions), or by use of one of the civil orders, for example, a Sexual Offences Prevention Order, in the Sexual Offences Act 2003), intelligence and information sharing, including limited disclosure to third parties where necessary, treatment programmes such as those for alcohol abuse, and contingency plans and rapid response arrangements in case of risk management failure or changing circumstances.

Critics of the MAPPA process may point out that the work is focused primarily on changing external circumstances or limiting the behaviour of offenders rather than attempting fundamental change. To its credit, the latest MAPPA guidance (Ministry of Justice, 2009) on effective strategies does include cognitive–behavioural programmes to address the causes of offending, together with "interventions that emphasise self-risk management and which promote the use of internal controls over the longer term". Nevertheless, particularly for convicted sex offenders, or even suspected offenders (as in a Risk of Sexual Harm Order), the recent legislation encourages the use of orders with conditions that can severely restrict the offender's behaviour and freedom, which may impinge on their human rights. In contrast with the common practice in mental health, where the patient is routinely invited to attend his or her regular Care Programme Approach meetings, the MAPPA offender is not invited to attend, he is often unaware he is being discussed, and he does not have legal representation. He also has no right of appeal against the decisions of a MAPPA meeting, although there are formal complaint procedures within the police and probation services. The situation of the MAPPA offender is, therefore, much more restricted than the patient detained under the Mental Health Act, with its inherent system of tribunals and appeals.

Information sharing

The MAPPA process promotes the sharing of information across the MAPPA agencies with the aim of improving the quality of risk assessments and risk managements plans. It is argued that public protection may be compromised unless all relevant information on MAPPA offenders is made available to those carrying out the assessments and drawing up the risk management plans. The MAPPA guidance (Ministry of Justice, 2009) specifies that such information sharing must be lawful, necessary, proportionate, secure, and accountable. It cites the legal basis for data sharing as the Criminal Justice Act (2003), the Crime and Disorder Act (1998a), and the Data Protection Act (1998b), which put controls on data sharing so that responsible information may be shared for legitimate purposes. The guidance also aims to improve trust between MAPPA agencies without undermining professional integrity. However, serious reservations about the legality and ethics of the MAPPA information sharing process have been voiced, in particular from members of the mental health professions, which will be discussed in more detail below.

The duty to co-operate

The Criminal Justice Act 2003 introduced a "Duty to Co-operate" for a range of agencies involved in MAPPA. The purpose of this clause is intended to enhance multi-agency work by the co-ordination of the involvement of different agencies in assessing and managing risk, and to "enable every agency, which has a legitimate interest, to contribute as fully as its existing statutory role and functions require, in a way that complements the work of other agencies". These Duty to Co-operate agencies, as defined in the Act, are social services, youth offending teams, Job Centre Plus, local housing authorities and registered local landlords, electronic monitoring providers, Strategic Health Authorities, Primary Care Trusts and other NHS trusts. Although GPs and Accident and Emergency departments may be the first to witness the sorts of behaviour that MAPPA are established to prevent, it is primarily the Mental Health Trusts, and in particular forensic mental health services, with whom the Responsible Authority will deal with most frequently, as many MAPPA offenders have a history of mental illness and / or personality disorder.

However, from MAPPA's inception, many have vigorously argued that psychiatrists should have nothing to do with MAPPA, that this involvement could be seen as a further erosion of the boundaries between mental health and the criminal justice system, and that psychiatrists are at risk of becoming agents of social control. There are concerns about information sharing and protection of patient confidentiality, and that further preoccupation with risk damages the therapeutic relationship with patients. An important question is whether the public protection function is appropriate, or compatible with that of a medical duty of care.

Not surprisingly, therefore, there has been much debate about the exact meaning of the Duty to Co-operate. Section 325(3) of the

Criminal Justice Act 2003 specifies that "health agencies have a duty to co-operate in the establishment by the Responsible Authority" of MAPPA. Although some have interpreted this as meaning that the Duty to Co-operate does not extend beyond the setting up of MAPPA (Hewitt, 2004), most understand that the legislation requires more long-term participation in the MAPPA process. The Responsible Authority is required to negotiate "memoranda of understanding" with each Duty to Co-operate agency, including Health Trusts and Authorities. The most vigorous debate has been over whether the Duty to Co-operate implies a duty to disclose information.

Confidentiality and disclosure

All doctors and other health professionals owe a duty of confidentiality to their patients (Department of Health, 2003). This is both a statutory duty as defined in law, and an ethical duty as enshrined in the relevant professional regulatory bodies' codes of conduct and ethical guidelines. For doctors, this is set out by the General Medical Council (2009), amplified by guidance from the British Medical Association (BMA, 1999, 2002) and the Royal College of Psychiatrists (RCPsych, 2010). In law, a duty is owed to patients under the European Convention on Human Rights under article 8, the right to respect for privacy and family life, and there is also a duty under the Data Protection Act 1998 only to disclose patient-identifying information with the prior consent of the patient, unless certain conditions are satisfied. The recently amended Mental Health Act 2007 also includes references to confidentiality and information sharing regarding patients detained under the Act. Medical confidentiality may, therefore, be considered to be different and more restrictive than the codes of the other Duty to Co-operate agencies, being a common law duty which is closely defined in the above guidelines, and breaking these guidelines may leave the doctor open to both court action and GMC sanctions.

Confidentiality may only be breached under certain restricted conditions. The Royal College of Psychiatrists states that, in certain situations, it may sometimes be justifiable for a doctor to pass on patient information without consent or statutory authority. Such situations include: where serious harm may occur to a third party, whether or not a criminal offence; when, without disclosure, the task of preventing or detecting, or prosecuting a serious crime would be prejudiced or delayed; where a doctor believes a patient to be the victim of abuse and the patient is unable to give or withhold consent to disclose; and where, without disclosure, the doctor would not be acting in the overall best interests of a child or young person who is their patient and incapable of consenting to disclosure. Any decision to break confidentiality must be the result of careful consideration and judgement that public protection outweighs that of the confidentiality of the individual concerned. The risks of such disclosure must also be anticipated, such as damage to the therapeutic relationship, decreased likelihood that the patient may engage in treatment in the future, or decreased public confidence in health professionals in general. In other words, the risk of disclosure may outweigh that of non-disclosure in some cases. The extent of information to disclose must also be considered, with only the minimum necessary for the purposes of protecting the potential victim(s) being revealed. Each case for disclosure must be considered individually on its own merits, and while it is recommended that doctors anonymously consult colleagues, their defence organization, or seek other professional advice, the decision whether or not to breach a patient's confidentiality is ultimately a matter for the clinical judgement of the doctor concerned, and that doctor must be prepared to defend his or her decision.

The decision by a clinician to disclose information about an individual may be further complicated and present more difficulties and pitfalls if that person is, or could be considered to be, a MAPPA offender, than if the person was solely a patient under the clinician's care. The National Service Framework (Department of Health, 1999), a government plan which sets standards for mental health in England and Wales, emphasizes the need for good risk management and for clinicians to "work in partnership in the delivery of health services", and there are precedents for health professionals to be involved in multi-agency working with the Care Programme Approach and in child protection. However, clinicians who participate in the MAPPA process may be unprepared for the, sometimes subtle, pressures placed upon them to disclose information in the context of an organization committed to public protection rather than patient care. For example, just because a request for information about a patient comes from a MAPPP, this does not in itself justify the release of this information. It is the doctor, not the MAPPP meeting, who should decide whether, in a given situation, confidential information about a patient should be released. The doctor cannot simply accept the views of the panel, but is required to weigh the evidence, some of which may be factual and some speculative, to reach his or her own decision as to whether criteria for breaking confidentiality are satisfied. Doctors have to weigh up whether a perceived harm can be better averted by making a disclosure or by maintaining the trust of an individual while attempting to persuade him or her to disclose voluntarily. The subject of the potential disclosure must be consulted before disclosure, and his or her consent sought, "unless to do so would enhance the risk of harm or inhibit its effective investigation" (BMA, 1999). This judgement has to be made by the doctor, not by the MAPPP.

If a former patient is no longer under psychiatric care, or has served a term of imprisonment, this does not absolve the doctor of his duty of confidentiality. Furthermore, there may be conflicting views between health professionals and the Responsible Authority as to at what stage in the process of risk assessment such information should be disclosed. The original MAPPA process envisaged information sharing by relevant agencies as part of the risk assessment of an offender. This would mean that a clinician might be obliged to release confidential information before he or she would have been able to assess the risks of such disclosure. The current MAPPA guidelines are somewhat ambiguous, stating, "Unless all relevant information is available, in good time, to those making the assessments and drawing up the risk management plans, public protection may be compromised" (Ministry of Justice, 2009).

The prospect of having to engage with MAPPA may pressure some doctors to become overly cautious or defensive in their clinical practice. Medical reports, letters about patients to other professionals, and even hand-written entries in medical notes, might be restricted on the basis that otherwise the information risks being divulged to other non-medical parties in the future. This raises questions as to whether all interactions with patients should involve a preliminary warning that confidentiality may be breached under certain circumstances, and how this would interfere with engaging the patient in a therapeutic relationship.

These are just some of the questions raised and examples of situations highlighting differences of opinion between professionals involved in the MAPPA process as to when and how confidential information should be released. These conflicts and confusion among clinicians led the Royal College of Psychiatrists to issue recommendations for psychiatrists on how to engage with MAPPA (RCPsych, 2003), which includes guidelines on how to assess whether information release is justified. Since then, there has been extensive consultation between those involved in the evolution of MAPPA and shaping MAPPA policy, and its "Duty to co-operate" agencies, including the health profession, to reach agreement on issues such as the sharing of information, without compromising professional integrity. The latest national MAPPA Guidance (Ministry of Justice, 2009) goes some way towards achieving this aim, although there remain inconsistencies between agencies regarding the threshold for disclosure which are subject to ongoing debate. It is the our personal experience that, at all Level 2 and 3 MAPPA meetings that we have attended, each offender's case is discussed sensitively and at length, with much consideration and compassion given to the rights of the offender, as well as those of potential victims.

Initially, there were discrepancies between the views of the Royal College of Psychiatrists and that of the MAPPA. The most important was the interpretation of "the risk of serious harm" and the threshold at which confidential information could be released without a patient's consent. The Royal College of Psychiatrists' guidelines (RCPsych, 2003) specified that "not only must the threatened harmful behaviour be serious, but the probability of its occurring must be high, and *the risk immediate*". In our view, adding the criterion of "immediacy", which was absent from other guidelines, raised the threshold for disclosure so high that psychiatrists may be prevented from disclosing at all except on the rare occasions when the risk posed was thought to be "immediate", a judgement that could be very difficult to make with any accuracy. This created confusion among psychiatrists working with MAPPA, but the issue has, one hopes, been resolved by more recent guidelines by the Royal College of Psychiatrists (RCPsych, 2010) which have removed the criterion of immediacy.

Involvement of mental health trusts with MAPPA

Clearly, the extent of mental health services's involvement in MAPPPs remains a controversial area, with many concerns about information sharing and protection of patient confidentiality, as detailed above. Moreover, no additional funds have been provided for Health Authorities or PCTs for their work with MAPPA, and they are expected to develop and implement the necessary arrangements within existing budgets. Nevertheless, it is clear that MAPPA continues to evolve and cannot be ignored. Our view is that it is possible to work with them fruitfully, without damaging professional integrity.

The MAPPA originally envisaged potential roles for psychiatrists and other relevant mental health professionals in the MAPPA process as the identification of relevant cases, participation in Level 2 and 3 meetings and in their area SMBs, and the provision of information. In our view, mental health professionals could also offer an important educative and advisory role, not just in specific cases offering their expertise on assessment and management, but also in shaping MAPPA policy.

The relationship between MAPPA and mental health services can usefully be divided into five categories:

1. As a source of information about patients, particularly restricted patients in the community, which would not otherwise have come to the attention of their psychiatric supervisors (e.g., a consultant forensic psychiatrist attended a MAPPP and found out that one of his patients under supervision was being investigated for a series of aggravated burglaries, of which he was not aware).
2. As a source or conduit for referrals. Referrals could come direct from a MAPPP, or from partner agencies, such as social services or probation. Direct referrals are often accepted by forensic services from probation, usually for people involved in criminal proceedings. The sorts of cases seen by MAPPPs may be at a slightly different stage of the process; for example, having been released from a determinant prison sentence or under investigation for a possible criminal charge. Another example would be when a patient is discharged unexpectedly

by a Mental Health Review Tribunal from a high secure hospital. The local MAPPP may now become the agency tasked with co-ordinating a response from local services. One advantage of having some involvement of mental health services with MAPPPs is the ability to regulate the caseload and to avoid inappropriate referrals. Although cases with some form of mental disorder under the scrutiny of MAPPPs are likely to be the remit of forensic psychiatrists, there is sometimes an indication for involvement of both forensic and community mental health services.

3. Requests by MAPPPs for information from mental health services, either about patients currently under the care of mental health services, or patients who have been in the past. This area is the most fraught with difficulty, as discussed above, and it is here that there is a need to establish clear information sharing protocols.

4. Requests from MAPPPs for a mental health professional to become involved in the assessment of a MAPPA offender. Here, it is important that the informed consent of the offender is gained first and that the resulting report is limited to information of relevance to the MAPPA process. Offering opinions on offenders without interviewing them in person, or those with no history of mental disorder, should be avoided.

5. A purely advisory role where, for example, a psychiatrist or social worker sits on a panel to give expert advice. The MAPPA Guidance recommends that each Mental Health Trust should appoint a senior clinician (usually a consultant forensic psychiatrist) and senior manager to engage with MAPPA in their area by being a member of their local SMB as well as attending Level 2 and Level 3 meetings.

As the number of cases being referred to mental health services via MAPPPs is increasing, the possibility of service level agreements and funding needs to be considered. However, it is important to recognize that of the large number of individuals considered by a MAPPP (several hundred in inner-city boroughs), only a very small proportion will require mental health intervention. It is also not clear as yet how patients who may also be MAPPA offenders and who are being cared for by private health care organizations or individuals (for example, a sex offender being treated privately by a forensic psychotherapist) should engage in the MAPPA process.

Clinical examples

One of the author's (RT) experience of cases that have been subject to MAPPA consideration referred to community forensic outreach services in a London borough since 2001 may be instructive. Some referrals come via the usual routes of referral, including court diversion schemes, referral by community mental health teams, referral by the probation service for a pre-sentence report, or referral by a prison mental health in-reach team. During the course of ongoing assessment, it becomes clear that these cases are subject to MAPPA consideration. Other referrals may come directly from the MAPPP, or are cases that are discussed at MAPPP meetings, but then channelled via other individual agencies such as the probation service or child and family social services. In general, as one would expect, the offending histories of the individuals concerned are serious: for example, homicide, attempted murder, harassment, rape, and arson. Referral is usually made because mental disorder is suspected, and concern often centres around confusion as to whether the offender suffers from psychosis or personality disorder. One notable feature of these cases is the frequent difficulty in getting individuals to attend outpatients for interview voluntarily, which often results in formal assessment under the Mental Health Act. It is not possible to present the flavour of all these cases, but three are described in more detail for the sake of discussion. The following vignettes are fictional but based on real cases.

Case one

Mr A was raised at a MAPPP in 2002. He had been detained in prison on remand for a charge of arson with intent, having set fire to his house containing his wife and children, but had been released on a legal technicality. Mr A had a long history of treatment for schizophrenia prior to this offence, and had been violent to his wife many times while psychotic, accusing her of being unfaithful to him. He had a diagnosis of delusional (morbid) jealousy, in the context of schizophrenia, and had several previous admissions under the Mental Health Act, during which he was treated with antipsychotic medication and his symptoms would improve. However, on discharge, he would repeatedly return to his country of origin, stop taking his medication, and relapse. Despite many incidents of domestic violence, he had never been convicted of an offence as his wife was too terrified to testify. Following his release from prison, he was under the care of the assertive outreach team, who made an urgent referral to forensic services as he was actively delusional and making threats to kill his wife and children. Forensic psychiatric assessment confirmed this, and, as he was unwilling to accept treatment voluntarily, a decision was made to formally assess him for admission under the Mental Health Act. The local police were contacted for their assistance, but told the assessing psychiatrist that they did not have the necessary manpower on that day, as their forces were currently being deployed on other pre-booked Mental Health Act assessments. By chance, the consultant forensic psychiatrist supervising the case was attending the monthly local MAPPP the following day. In view of the seriousness of Mr A's risk to his wife and children, which he assessed as imminent, he decided to disclose information about Mr A and asked the MAPPP for advice. The Chief Inspector chairing the MAPPP mobilized the necessary police assistance and Mr A was found at his home and admitted under the Mental Health Act to a medium secure unit within twenty-four hours.

Mr A's case illustrates the benefits of co-ordinated multi-agency working with the sharing of relevant information that can enhance risk assessment and lead to appropriate intervention. The seriousness of Mr A's mental disorder, and, most importantly, the associated risk to his wife and children when psychotic, had not been apparent until the MAPPP meeting, where discussion could take place between the different agencies involved. Significantly, social services had been unaware of the family until then, and it was only their presence at the MAPPP that alerted them to the serious risk to the children and led to the initiation of child protection proceedings. This case occurred before the implementation of the Domestic Violence, Crime and Victims Act in 2004, which would have made a prosecution of Mr A more likely.

Case two

Mr B was mentioned at a recent MAPPP meeting by representatives of the prison service. He was due for release from prison after serving a three-year sentence for manslaughter. Prior to this offence, he had a history of treatment for schizophrenia. The index offence involved him stabbing his wife many times while floridly psychotic. Following this offence, he absconded to another European Union country, where he was eventually arrested, detained for psychiatric treatment, and subsequently deported back to the UK. Pre-sentence reports did not consult his catchment area psychiatric services, and a prison sentence was given in the absence of a possible mental health disposal. Psychiatric services were not involved in his treatment in prison, or in plans for his care following his release. At the MAPPP, it became evident that Mr B would imminently need psychiatric supervision, which should be organized before his release.

In this sort of case, it can be seen how the MAPPP may be a conduit for referring worrying cases for assessment, whereas previously prison medical services in dispersal prisons may not have been able to identify all high-risk inmates about to leave custody. A local body such as the MAPPP, receiving information from multiple sources, would appear to be in a better position to do this. This may also apply when an individual is discharged from a high secure hospital by a Mental Health Review Tribunal (an independent body which reviews patients' detentions and allows right of appeal) against medical advice. In these circumstances, co-ordination of a response via a MAPPP may be particularly useful, even if local mental health services are not able to offer any appropriate treatment.

Case three

Mr D was coming to the end of his six-year sentence for rape, and was due for release into the community. He had a history of previous rape convictions, and his probation officer working in the prison was concerned about his risk, as he had refused to engage in the sex offender treatment programme offered. A Level 3 MAPPP meeting was convened within the prison, and this led to a referral to his local forensic mental health services to consider treatment under the Mental Health Act. Psychiatric assessment concluded that he fulfilled criteria for antisocial and borderline personality disorder, as well as the criteria for Dangerous Severe Personality Disorder (DSPD), including high scores on the Hare Psychopathy Check List—Revised (PCL—R) (Hare, 1991). He was not considered suitable for his local forensic mental health services, but was referred to the DSPD Unit at a high security hospital.

This case highlights the controversy regarding the management of offenders diagnosed with personality disorder, or psychopathy, who are considered to be very high risk. Historically, the probation service has felt overburdened with such individuals, to whom they can offer limited treatment opportunities with which they are unlikely to engage. The current blame culture feeds into the fear that if all interventions, including mental health treatments, are not exhaustively pursued, then the professionals involved will be blamed for any future adverse outcome. This may lead to a wish to detain offenders for as long as possible, either in prison, or under the Mental Health Act. The question is whether the category of DSPD was helpfully applied to a group of mentally disordered patients who had been historically neglected and were now offered the treatment they needed (Mullen, 2007), or whether this was a stigmatizing label given to individuals who were forced into a treatment facility against their will, where they were unlikely to engage, but in which they could be detained indefinitely.

Conclusion and psychodynamic overview

Public protection from danger and the wish to eliminate risk appear to be major preoccupations of contemporary society, so that MAPPA could be seen as an inevitable outcome. The intense emotions, both conscious and unconscious, that are provoked by the violence and aggressive sexual behaviour that MAPPA is meant to defend us from can themselves, if not fully understood, give rise to defensive retaliatory behaviour in those who are given the task of limiting such violence. "An eye for an eye, a tooth for a tooth", the law of talion (the principle developed in early Babylonian law and Roman law that criminals should receive as punishment precisely those injuries and damages they had inflicted upon their victims), reigns in the violent internal world of the offender, but also, to some extent, in the unconscious of us all.

Although in this chapter we have not considered the personal histories of the MAPPA offenders, many will have experienced abusive and neglectful childhoods which will have had a serious impact on their adult personality, pathology, and functioning, and significantly contributed to their offending behaviour. Although only a minority may be suitable for formal psychotherapeutic intervention, an understanding of the dynamics of the offender's relationship with others, which will be based on his early parental relationships, may be helpful in formulating his overall management. For example, many offenders have had absent or abusive fathers, which has contributed to their distrust of authority figures such as the police. Here, the MAPPA agencies may again be experienced as persecutory and punitive parental objects, repeating the cycle of abuse that the offender unconsciously perpetuates by his rebellious attitude and offending behaviour. Real disagreements and impasses in inter-agency working may be experienced by the offender as an all too familiar pattern of parental conflict. Such management is unlikely to create an atmosphere of safety in which the offender can feel contained, but, instead, may create conditions that increase the risk of offending.

From a psychodynamic viewpoint, such splitting between agencies may, in part, be due to the projections of the offender, but also due to our own projections as professionals anxious to defend our individual identities, being suspicious of different attitudes and ways of working that can seem alien and threatening. Such anxieties exist in all institutions, which may be useful in fostering rivalry and competition necessary for survival and growth. However, when such anxieties become tinged with paranoia, relationships may break down and effective functioning is stifled or prevented. If the wish to denigrate or even deny the existence of the other predominates, independent agencies may end up working in isolated and precarious ways. By contrast, if different agencies and the professionals working within them can relate to each other in a more healthy and less paranoid manner, the capacity for genuine growth and understanding can be enhanced. Our own experience is that meeting in person the different professionals involved in MAPPA work can go a long way to allay anxieties on both sides about incompatible attitudes and conflicts of interest. Thoughtful involvement and discussion with each other can lead to helpful compromises, solutions, or, sometimes, the acceptance of difference. Such collaboration can be seen as representing a healthy parental couple, capable of resolving conflicts, a novel experience for the offender who has never had adequate parental guidance or supervision.

MAPPA continues to be an evolving process, and it is important that we, as mental health professionals, remain involved, to contribute to the public protection debate and to promote the interests of our patients while being mindful of the rights of others, in the knowledge that the complete elimination of risk is a utopian fantasy.

References

British Medical Association (BMA) (1999). *Confidentiality and Disclosure of Health Information*. London: British Medical Association.
British Medical Association (BMA) (2002). *Patient Confidentiality – Guidelines*. www.bma.org.uk/ap.nsf/Content/PatientConfidentiality guidelines.
Department of Health (1999). *National Service Framework for Mental Health—Modern Standards and Service Models*. London: Department of Health.
Department of Health (2003). *Confidentiality: NHS Code of Practice*. London: Department of Health. Available at: www.doh.gov.uk/ipu/confiden/protect.
European Convention on Human Rights. Available at: www.hri.org/docs/ECHR50.html.
General Medical Council (GMC) (2009). *Confidentiality*. London: GMC Publications.
Hare, R. (1991). *Manual of the Revised Psychopathy Checklist*. Toronto: Multi Health Systems.
Hewitt, A. (2004). An added duty of risk assessment. *New Law Journal*, 23 January, p. 87.
HMSO (1994). *Criminal Justice and Public Order Act 1994*. Available at: www.opsi.gov.uk/acts/acts1994/ukpga_19940033_en_1
HMSO (1997). *Sex Offenders Act 1997*. Available at: www.opsi.gov.uk/acts/acts1997/ukpga_19970051_en_1
HMSO (1998a). *Crime and Disorder Act 1998*. Available at: www.opsi.gov.uk/acts/acts1998/ukpga_19980037_en_1

HMSO (1998b). *Data Protection Act 1998.* Available at: www.uk-legislation. hmso.gov.uk/acts/acts1998/ukpga_19980029_en_1

HMSO (2000). *Criminal Justice & Court Services Act 2000.* www.opsi. gov.uk/acts/acts2000/ukpga_20000043_en_1

HMSO (2003). *Criminal Justice Act 2003.* Available at: www.opsi.gov. uk/acts/acts2003/ukpga_20030044_en_1

HMSO (2004). *Domestic Violence, Crime and Victims Act 2004.* Available at: www.opsi.gov.uk/acts/acts2004/ukpga_20040028_en_1

HMSO (2007). *Mental Health Act 2007.* Available at: www.opsi.gov.uk/ acts/acts2007/ukpga_20070012_en_1

Home Office (2002). *Offender Assessment System (OASys): User Manual Version Two.* London: National Probation Directorate, Home Office.

Home Office and Department of Health and Social Security (1973). *Report of the Review of Procedures for the Discharge and Supervision of Psychiatric Patients Subject to Special Restrictions (Aarvold Report) Cmnd 5191.* London: HMSO.

Home Office and Department of Health and Social Security (1975). *Report of the Committee on Mentally Abnormal Offenders (The Butler Report) Cmnd 6244.* London: HMSO.

Kemshall, H., & Maguire, M. (2001). Public protection, partnership and risk penalty: the multi-agency risk management of sexual and violent offenders. *Punishment and Society,* 3(2): 237–264.

Kemshall, H., & Maguire, M. (2002). Community justice, risk management and the role of multi-agency public protection panels. *British Journal of Community Justice,* 1(1): 11–28.

Maden, A. (2007). *Treating Violence: A Guide to Risk Management in Mental Health.* Oxford: Oxford University Press.

Ministry of Justice (2009). *MAPPA Guidance 2009,* Version 3.0. London: National Offender Management Service, Public Protection Unit.

Mullen, P. (2007). Dangerous and severe personality disorder and in need of treatment. *British Journal of Psychiatry,* 190: 3–7.

Royal College of Psychiatrists (RCPsych) (2003). *Psychiatrists and Multi-agency Public Protection Arrangements—Guidelines on Representation, Participation, Confidentiality and Information Exchange.* Available at: www.rcpsych.ac.uk/members/currentissues/publicprotection.aspx

Royal College of Psychiatrists (RCPsych) (2010). *Good Psychiatric Practice: Confidentiality and Information Sharing Council Report CR133.* London: Royal College of Psychiatrists.

Thornton, D., Mann, R., Webster, S., Blud, L., Travers, R., Friendship, C., & Erikson, M. (2003). Distinguishing and combining risks for sexual and violent recidivism. *Annals of the New York Academy of Science,* *989*: 225–235.

Youth Justice Board (2004). *Asset—Young Offender Assessment Profile.* Available at: www.yjb.gov.uk/en-gb/practitioners/assessment/ asset.htm

CHAPTER TEN

Gut feelings

Rob Hale

T here can be few judgements more crucial or finely balanced than the decision to release someone from a medium or high secure hospital back into the community from whence they came. In fact, it is rarely straight back into the community, but instead to an organization with lesser control over their actions, with increasing independence and autonomy accorded to the patient. Who makes these decisions, and how they are made, is the subject of this chapter. In writing it, I am effectively the scribe, the amanuensis, for the professionals to whom I have consulted over many years: the senior nurses, the psychologists, and the doctors at Ardenleigh Women's Unit, the Bracton Clinic, Reaside Clinic, and the Trevor Gibbens Unit. I have also consulted, with my colleague Stanley Ruszczynski, to Ashworth (high secure) Hospital. The responsibility for the content below is mine. The consultations, which usually take place on a weekly basis, are work discussion groups of five or six professionals, who may be from a single profession or from a mixture of trainings and identities. The focus is usually a clinical case or an institutional problem, examined from a psychodynamic perspective. In those units where continuing care in the community is possible, the relationship with other organizations comes into focus.

My own training was as a general psychiatrist and a psychoanalyst; my clinical responsibility has been at the Portman Clinic, where patients come voluntarily, usually following release from prison or a secure psychiatric setting. In that sense, the decision about release from detention has already been made, but it is a platitude to say that when a person regains their liberty, the possibility of a further offence increases dramatically, and, with it, anxiety in the professionals.

Having consulted to these groups over many years on topics which were of their own choosing, I decided to ask them, as a sort of roving focus group, what factors they considered to be important when a patient is to be transferred to lesser security. "Security" itself is perhaps an inappropriate word, a euphemism, because the security these institutions provide is not primarily for the patients but for the larger community; to the patients, it is restriction or detention. That being said, there is a sane part of a patient's mind that wants to be protected from the actions of the insane part. They are, in part, locked up for their own good.

Let me start by asking the question, "how does a complex organization reach this decision? And how is it ratified or discounted by outside opinion: in England, the First-tier Tribunal (Mental Health) and the Ministry of Justice?". I want to concentrate primarily on the first question, not that the second is unimportant.

Within a hospital, each profession has an appointed role and each professional is exposed to and responds to a different part of the patient's mind. The nursing staff are in permanent, twenty-four-hour contact with both the psychotic part of the patient and, probably more painfully, the psychopathic part of their mind. Theirs is the daily containment, care, and empathetic understanding of the patient; they communicate their experience of him or her to the larger ward group: the patient's capacity to control and look after themselves. It is a daunting role, and ironic that nursing staff are often, though not always, the least trained and the poorest paid.

The psychologists' role is to categorize, calibrate, and offer a psychological model of the patient's mind and their behaviour; where possible, they engage the patient in psychotherapy of whatever theoretical persuasion. They communicate their experiences to the larger team: the patient's capacity to think and to feel.

Occupational therapists (OTs) explore and develop the practical capacities of the patient to engage in everyday living. Through art, drama, music, dance, and other therapies they develop the patient's creative and restorative capacities. Again this, the patient's capacity to "do", is told to the larger team.

To the medical staff falls the responsibility of formal diagnosis and medical treatment. The consultant is both the titular head of the team and the decision maker in matters medical. Their role is as the Responsible Clinician and, ultimately, the decision to recommend release is theirs. In their medical role, they engage with the patient's propensity for psychotic functioning and his or her expression of affective distress.

The social worker is concerned with the external world, both present and past, from whence the patient came into security and to which they may return: the patient's external sources of support or tribulation.

All these people make the team. Collectively, they make the decision, but pivotal to this process is the ward manager, usually, but not always, a nurse. Apart from the overall organization of the ward (a not inconsiderable role in itself), it is the manager's role to collate and co-ordinate all of the information from other nursing staff, from psychologists, from OTs, from the social worker, and to present it at the weekly "ward round" to the consultant, where the decision as to when to recommend transfer is made. It is my observation that the opinion of the ward manager is crucial, and is rarely overridden by the consultant. The actual decision is made by an iterative process between the two. Assuming that a patient is detained on a court order, rather than a civil section, the consultant's final recommendation will obviously be subject to the deliberations of the Ministry of Justice and the Tribunal.

This enormously simplified schema of the process does not in any way do justice to the many complex interactions between professionals, their conflicts and their rivalries, as well as their synergies and congruencies. The central point to be made, however, is that each profession becomes the spokesman for, the representative of, the various functions of the patient's mind—the feeling, the thinking, the remembering, the hoping, and the doing. The final decision represents an integration of these various functions. It is this very capacity to recognize and integrate that the patient has lost in his "psychotic" breakdown, which culminated in the index offence that led to his or her detention. How far the patient has recovered these capacities for himself is a complex judgement the team must make when lesser security is contemplated.

The criteria (as opposed to the method) by which this judgement is made is a remarkably little discussed and written about topic. It is almost a folklore—there is remarkable consistency, but not much overtly articulated.

The purpose of the rest of this chapter is to expand on the above and to suggest four separate psychological functions we are assessing.

Two negative:
    Psychotic functioning
    Psychopathic functioning
Two positive:
    Ego maturity
    Superego maturity

While there are many (apparently) objective psychometric tests that can be and are employed, it is, I would suggest, the nature and content of our conscious and, more particularly, unconscious communications with our patients which also ultimately informs and directs our decisions.

Let us start with the two negative functions. It is generally assumed that a psychotic illness is a medical condition analogous to pneumonia or diabetes, which runs a natural course and manifests itself in specific psychological symptoms or behaviours. There are various non-specific factors that will make the appearance of the illness more likely. Biochemical, neuroanatomical, and neurophysiological abnormalities have been and continue to be identified, but no overall explanatory theory has been established. To the extent that pharmacological treatments are effective, there is progress in identifying the mechanism of action and the sites and systems within the central nervous system on which the drugs have their effects.

Psychopathy, on the other hand, is seen as enduring character pathology, with its origins in genetic endowment and early life experiences. It manifests in disturbed, often antisocial behaviour in childhood, adolescence, and adulthood. Genetic predispositions have been identified as having neuroanatomical and neurophysiological differences. It is seen as treatment refractory, and often not the province of psychiatry, an opinion confirmed by Cope's 1993 study. Most secure units are reluctant to admit a person solely on the basis of psychopathic personality disorder; prison is seen as the appropriate container.

In effect, however the distinction between psychotic illness and personality disorder is, to put it mildly, blurred. It is further complicated by drug abuse / addiction, which is seen as a separate diagnosis. The compromise struck is "dual diagnosis" (two separate entities existing in the same person), psychosis and drug abuse, with the latter obscuring underlying psychopathic personality disorder.

When one looks at patients in secure hospitals, only a minority have a normal or neurotic history and personality structure which has broken down into overt psychosis, with the (usually violent) index offence ensuing and being the reason for their admission. A far larger proportion would be classified as dual diagnosis.

My own view (Hale & Dhar, 2008) is that we are frequently observing a single entity: a stable psychopathic state which, under the influence of drugs, breaks down into frank psychosis, leading to the index offence. The psychopathic state is a partially successful, but ultimately flawed, defensive structure in which all anxiety and other disturbing affect is, by the patient's actions, projected into those around them. The individual continues to create mayhem, while apparently unrestrained by responsibility, shame, or remorse. There is an intimate relationship between anxiety and paranoia. The psychopathic defensive state wards off psychotic breakdown, but, under increasing external pressure coupled with the effects of large amounts of drugs (usually cannabis), it fails and the underlying psychotic state is exposed.

The effectiveness of neuroleptic medication is due to a reduction in arousal and perceived anxiety to a level where the psychopathic defence can reassert its control. Reduced access to cannabis, etc., is also an important factor.

This model proposes a very different model of mental functioning, taking a more dynamic view of personality as a form of defensive structure which we all employ to deal with unwanted or unacceptable affect, and specifically intolerable anxiety. When there is one specific defence which has developed (as a result of early experience) to the level that it dominates all mental functioning and personal interaction, we label this a personality disorder—obsessional, hysterical, antisocial, and so on. When, for whatever reason, this defensive structure fails, illness takes over. But illness itself is a way of coping: external reality is distorted so that it represents a form of internal reality (based on unconscious memory), thereby reducing the tension between the two. It is a compromise, but it wards off total psychic disintegration, the bedrock of fear. This model sits uneasily with, indeed in opposition to, current psychiatric classification, but, to me, makes more sense of the observable clinical phenomena in a significant proportion, perhaps even a majority, of the patients who are in secure hospitals. Such people would otherwise be placed in the "dual diagnosis" category: I will arbitrarily call them "type D". This is not to say that there are not those in secure hospitals who, in the course of a long-term psychotic illness, carry out a violent act and with little evidence of a psychopathic personality. These I will call "type P". Equally, there are those who do have an antisocial, psychopathic personality, but with little evidence of frank psychosis. They are usually there, rather than in prison, because the nature of their index offence was particularly bizarre, defying any understanding. These I will call "type A". Rarely, there are those in secure hospitals who have a purely affective disorder, but they tend to be cared for in general psychiatric units.

Let us return to the three areas of psychological functioning proposed above, starting with psychoticism and psychopathy. The starting point must be Hinshelwood's 1999 paper "The difficult patient", in which he explores our countertransference reaction to psychotic as opposed to psychopathic patients. The psychotic patient challenges our logical understanding of the world. His perception of the world and the meaning and intention ascribed to the actions of others is outside our normal experience or understanding (except in our dreams). We are, however, at a distance from him. We can sympathize but not empathize. It is our cognitive self, rather than our affective self, which is challenged. We feel emotionally uninvolved by him. By comparison, the depressed patient makes us feel depressed, the manic carries us along in their mania. We empathize and want to alleviate their distress.

Compare this with the psychopath, a term I am using in a qualitative sense. Easily recognized but hard to define, their capacity to alienate sources of help is a notable hallmark. My own definition of a psychopath is "someone who brings out the worst in me or an institution". At the centre of the psychopath's psychic structure is a very limited capacity to recognize or to tolerate negative affect: anxiety, loss, despair, nausea, anger. It is, instead, projected into all those around him by his actions, forcing them to react in a way which is often restrictive, dismissive, or overtly punitive. An alternative is to collude in what we know to be the psychopath's system of moral corruption. We ourselves then become either corrupt or sadistic and feel ashamed of ourselves. Of all of these interactions and his own destructiveness, the psychopath is only vaguely aware. It is by examining our own reactions, either singly or collectively, that we recognize the quality of psychopathy, it is a "diagnosis" made in the countertransference. Ours is a feeling response, but, unlike our empathetic response to the neurotic person's suffering, we end up hating the psychopath. To quote Glover (1960, p. 149) "the psychopath assaults the physician's most treasured possession, namely, his capacity to heal". The complex interweaving factors that generate this defensive structure I have tried to enumerate in a paper (Hale & Dhar, 2008). Suffice it to say that if ever there was someone who is trapped by the misfortunes of their own childhood, it is the psychopath.

Psychosis

I want now to consider how this conceptualization of the patient's pathology and our response can help us in understanding how we reach decisions involved in transfer to lesser security. Let us start with psychosis. The easiest part is to recognize the presence or absence of overt psychotic symptoms, hallucinations or delusions, although patients are often secretive and hang on to vestiges of their symptoms. Why not hang on to something that has served you well? After all, the psychosis has served a function: to distort reality to the extent that the index offence seemed necessary and permissible, or to provide a refuge from the guilt associated with it. Our assessment is to judge the extent to which the patient can cope without the psychosis. Can they join with us in the recognition (re-cognition) of the distortions of the psychotic state? Can they acknowledge their own propensity for descent into psychotic func-tioning, the part that drugs may play in provoking such states, and the probable continuing need for the protection of medication? Some would call this insight; others would use the term "illness awareness". In all events, it is an agreement with the patient to share the same understanding (in truth, our understanding) of the events and the psychotic phenomena. It is an agreement made largely at a cortical level in the two parties, and, while it challenges our understanding and arouses our anxieties about relapse, it does not really disturb us at a subcortical level. The greater the danger-ousness of the index offence, the more certain we must be that psychotic processes are not in active operation, and the greater the need for a compact between patient and clinician.

Psychopathy

Turning now to the quality of psychopathy there are two sets of papers that I think are seminal, apart, of course, from Cleckley's *Mask of Sanity* (1964). The first is Symington (1980), who explores the nature of the psychopathology and our countertransference reaction. He sees the "fault" in the psychopath as emerging from disturbance at the most primitive level.

> The psychopath's loss has occurred at the earliest stage, when the infant is still stretching for his object and holding it to him in a tactile way, and before he can internalise it within the unconscious. The psychopath has suffered a loss when the mother and child were still a unit. In Kleinian language, the infant has sustained a loss while in the paranoid–schizoid position. The projective and introjective processes by which the infant separates himself from his mother have not yet completed their work. The infant, thus, has not just lost a mother but part of himself. [pp. 293–294]

More specific to the subject of this chapter are the papers by Murphy (2004), and Slovic, Finucane, Peters, and MacGregor (2002), both of which look at the way decisions about dangerousness are made and conclude that such judgements are fundamentally influenced by "gut feelings". A problem that arises from this approach is that it may be harder to defend legally when things go wrong. It has been commented that gut feelings become more important in "grey" cases where the judgement is far from easy. It is also pertinent to ask the question, "what is the difference between those cases where your guts say 'yes' and those where they say 'no'?"

My own development of this idea, which I believe to be fundamentally true, is to explore what I consider is the essentially psychosomatic nature of the countertransference in psychopathy. The commonly used tool for assessing psychopathy is the Hare Psychopathy Checklist (PCL-R) (Hare, 1991), which is based on Cleckley's work. It depends on an extensive audit of the individual's life history, including their antisocial and criminal past. For my purposes, however, it does not explore sufficiently the nature of the disturbances and disruptions of early object relations, either in what is known historically or what can be gleaned from adult attachment patterns or projective testing. The other part of the PCL-R is an assessment of the way in which the individual currently relates to his or her objects. This is, apparently, an objective process but it is, I would propose, an interpersonal subjective process, an account of the countertransferential experience. It includes such qualities as "conning, manipulative, glib, superficial", all terms that, if they were applied to ourselves, we would regard as insulting. They also have strong moral judgements in them, reflecting the psychopath's troubled relationship with his own superego, his disowning of his own responsibility, and his leaving it to others to provide the containment normally afforded by one's own superego. It may seem that I am being critical of the PCL-R, but I am not: I am merely concerned that it can be presented as an entirely objective tool when, in fact, it, appropriately, depends on much that is interpersonal and subjective.

What are the emotions projected by the psychopath into those he/she encounters? I would suggest that there are two: fear and nausea, both basic emotions of the five proposed in Johnson-Laird and Oatley's schema (1992), the others being anger, sadness, and happiness. Psychopaths are usually divided into an aggressive–violent category and a sexually perverse category, both falling under the heading of antisocial (i.e., we do not like them). The feelings they stimulate in us are experienced primarily at a subcortical level. In fact, we initially experience these feelings in our autonomic nervous system, that part of the brain concerned with the control of visceral activity: heart rate, blood pressure, respiration, intestinal activity, and sexual function, to name but a few. Alteration in these functions is relayed to our cortex, where the disturbance is acknowledged, made conscious, and the appropriate action taken. We all have found ourselves blushing before we knew we were embarrassed. We all have experienced that lurching feeling in our stomachs at a near miss in a car before we recognized the nature of the danger.

I would suggest that the actions of the two types of psychopath stimulate different parts of the autonomic system. The violent psychopath stimulates our sympathetic system, the part responsible for fear and the fight or flight response. The sexual psychopath, on the other hand, stimulates the parasympathetic system: more specifically, the area concerned with nausea, a system designed to expel noxious substances that have invaded our bodies. I have tried to document the origins and mechanisms of these processes within the psychopath in another paper (Hale & Dhar, 2008). What I want to emphasize now is the extent to which he involves us at a visceral level in maintaining his psychic equilibrium. As professionals, we develop a carapace which allows us to believe we are not affected by our patients. Not only is this not true (Hale & Hudson, 1999), it also deprives us of a crucial means of assessing the depth of the psychopathic defence. It is instructive to listen to non-professionals' responses to the actions of the psychopath. They express a realistic, if perhaps somewhat exaggerated, fear of bodily damage to themselves or those close to them at the hands of the violent: "The streets aren't safe with these people free to roam". The sexually perverse psychopath, on the other hand, evokes a very different response: "It's revolting, disgusting, filthy pervs, they deserve to be castrated".

If we can recognize our true response to the actions of the psychopath (for it is his actions, not his thoughts, which disturb us so profoundly), we have made a start. The problem is that the patient has not, protected as he is by the excitement of transgressing society's accepted moral code. It is his revenge, his means in adult life of reversing the traumata of childhood in a way that he feels he can now control omnipotently. We, and society at large, are now the victims.

The advantage of the relatively long time that patients spend in medium or high security is that it often represents the most stable period of concerned care and containment they have ever experienced. It is the responsibility of the institution to be benign, responsive, thoughtful, and just. The danger is that the institution will slip (or be drawn) into retaliation or thoughtless cynicism; it will then be caught in its own psychopathic reprisal and there will be no possibility of therapeutic progress. If, however, the institution can remain healthy, it will provide a template for a new way of relating between the patient and those around him, both patients and staff, providing an opportunity for another go at childhood.

In the course of the therapeutic encounter within the institution, it is important to try to establish the circumstances that were so overwhelming that they propelled the individual into the index offence. As a generalization, it is my experience that violence is triggered by perceived psychological intrusion or by humiliation. On the other hand, sexually perverse acts are more likely to be provoked by being deserted, abandoned, or let down by someone on whom the offender has come to depend, although humiliation may also be a trigger. I would suggest that the efficacy of the treatment can be judged by the patient's ability to recognize the negative affect—a paranoid anxiety in the case of violence, sadness, humiliation, and loss in those with perversion—and contain it within their own psychological system. The extent to which they have failed to make this necessary transition (the reciprocal of success) can be gauged from their continuing capacity, in the case of the violent, to stimulate our sympathetic nervous system and instil fear in us, often by threat or intimidation. In the case of the perverse, it will be their capacity to seduce us to into their corrupt view of the world, to contemplate their index offence with equanimity, while the disgust and moral outrage is located in us and experienced as parasympathetic disturbance. The question with either group would be, "have they made the transition from a system in which anxiety/affective disturbance can only be contained by recruiting and infecting another, an interpersonal system, to an intrapsychic system in which the anxiety can be contained within their own psychosomatic apparatus?" In other words, can *they* now experience the sympathetic or parasympathetic (autonomic) disturbance within themselves?

With regard to morality and superego functioning, we need to be aware of the extent to which they have been able to develop their own reliable and non-corrupt system, where the opposite previously existed.

Ego maturity

The third quality we are examining is the positive capacity for sublimation, the capacity to delay gratification and to tolerate frustration. Can they plan ahead, take responsibility for their actions, perceive the needs of others, and act appropriately? Do all impulses result in physical action, or can they be recognized as emotions and expressed thoughtfully? Can they share? Can they create and sustain friendships? The infant, of course, can do none of these. He is entirely self serving and immediate. So, too, the regressed patient we encounter on admission. As the "normal" child matures, he gradually develops positive capacities. The question we must ask when contemplating transfer to lesser security are: "What is the predominant emotional age at which they are functioning? What age of child are we observing? How much independence and responsibility would we give a child of that age, and how much external containment and support would the child need from adults?". The answer to these helps us to determine for the patient the degree of external support and containment they now need. If we judge that they are functioning at the level of, say, an eight-year-old, the external provision must be appropriate for a child of that age. For many of our patients, independent healthy adult living is something they will never achieve. Their capacity for working and loving, as Freud describes in *Civilization and its Discontents* (1930a), will always be constrained.

Superego maturity

The superego in the psychopath has long been recognized as being distorted and deficient. It is variously seen as sadistic and retributive, inconsistent, needing to be challenged, or essentially corrupt and unpredictable. It is this last quality of corrupt agency which, for me at least, characterizes the psychopath's superego. During their stay in the secure unit, the patient will come constantly into contact with a system that is predictable, consistent, and above all benign (i.e., wishing them well). When contemplating transfer, what we have to consider is the extent to which they have developed their own sense of morality and fairness. This comes from the gradual, largely unconscious, assimilation of our set of values, the crucial question here being, "have they merely learnt it, or do they really feel it?" This change may be most apparent in the way they relate to their fellow patients, where there is likely to be no power differential, and, of course, reciprocally, how other patients regard them. Which part of the brain in the patient or ourselves is involved in these processes is, I understand, as yet unclear.

Conclusion

In this chapter, I have tried to explore some aspects of decision-making processes. The professional network making the decision must be collaborative and integrative, capacities so often absent in the parents and families (or lack of them) of the psychopath. The criteria used by the team will be the extent to which traumata of childhood and the pathological defensive structures derived from these experiences have been altered by the therapeutic processes within the secure setting. In gross oversimplification, "have they been able to benefit from the opportunity of the second go at childhood afforded them by their stay in a secure institutional environment?"

Case history

Dr Rajeev Dhar has provided this account with the patient's knowledge and permission.

> This man presented with a long history of violent offending behaviour. He had been previously admitted to a secure facility, with a provisional diagnosis made in prison of schizophrenia. He was subsequently treated with medication, and his psychotic symptoms abated very

quickly. He then proved to be difficult in terms of drug abuse, but his behaviour settled. He was eventually discharged from hospital into the community, where he was placed in a hostel. It was also recognized that he had a severe underlying psychopathic personality disorder, which was identified both clinically and on personality testing.

Back in the community, he claimed that the original symptoms of psychosis had been invented, as these were a way for him to get diverted from prison into hospital. He was eventually discharged from the hostel to his own accommodation, where he re-established contact and formed a relationship with his drug-using peer group. He returned to his former, rather chaotic, lifestyle, which resulted in difficulties in engaging with the community mental health team. This led to further excessive drug use and social alienation, the latter particularly towards his care-givers, whose intentions he increasingly doubted, and they responded by becoming increasingly mistrustful of him. It was an essentially paranoid relationship. There were periods of very violent and threatening behaviour in the community, directed towards those close to him and community mental health workers. He was eventually readmitted into hospital, rising through the various levels of security and finally ending up in the original secure unit that had contained him previously.

His second admission was characterized by further episodes of manipulative and reactive violent behaviour. When aroused, he presented as extremely intimidating and hostile, alarming and frightening staff. He was also able to incite other patients to be physically aggressive towards the ward team, thus both corrupting the system and using other patients to express his violence vicariously. However, whereas previously the staff's reaction had been one of sympathy for someone suffering from a mental illness, their response now was much more negative and confrontational, much less permissive. The result was that the diagnosis, that is, the central problem, evolved (rather than an abrupt change) to that of primarily antisocial personality disorder, any illness being understood as emerging during periods of stress.

Over the following two years, he responded to a combination of factors within the system that led to increasing levels of trust, less violence, a gradual improvement in his ability to accept boundaries, as well as to reflect on his own personality and his tendencies to act out. He now expressed a desire to be contained emotionally and psychologically, while not wanting to be contained physically at a higher level of security. This, combined with a huge emphasis on relational aspects of his care, led to a gradual improvement in his ability to engage with one, two, and then more staff, just as a child moves from a dyadic relationship to a triangular one, involving both parents, and then to a more complex set of multiple relationships. Alongside this, staff feelings towards this individual changed over that period of time to such an extent that he was eventually viewed as being a helpful and even inspirational to other patients in many ways. This reached a point where, even though he was no longer legally detainable on the grounds of irresponsible or aggressive behaviour, he was still willing to remain in hospital, either informally or, even more significantly, on a compulsory order, but not submitting any request to be released by a Tribunal. During this period, he was able to forge relationships with members of staff who would care for him in the community, including at the hostel placement.

The above case demonstrates the importance of gut feelings in the assessment of a situation as well as risk management, on the background of a seemingly hopeless level of risk. The level of contact, support, and even medication was titrated against the level of neediness and dependency the patient felt when particularly under stress. In other words, some level of resonance had occurred between the feelings that he had inside himself and those the staff had about him. It was when these were in harmony that his level of risk was perceived as being low and relational security was seen as effective. He has continued much the same in the community, and remains outside hospital, now satisfactorily living in his own flat.

References

Cleckley, H. (1964). *The Mask of Sanity* (4th edn). St Louis: MO: Mosby.
Cope, R. (1993). A survey of forensic psychiatrists' views on psychopathic disorder. *Journal of Forensic Psychiatry*, 4(2): 215–235.
Freud, S. (1930a). *Civilization and Its Discontents. S.E.*, 21: 59–145. London: Hogarth.
Glover, E. (1960). *The Roots of Crime*. Thame: Imago.
Hale, R., & Dhar, R. (2008). Flying a kite—observations on dual and triple diagnosis. *Criminal Behaviour and Mental Health*, 18: 145–152.
Hale, R., & Hudson, L. (1999). Doctors in trouble. In: J. Firth-Cozens & R. L. Payne (Eds.), *Stress in Health Professionals*. Chichester, UK: Wiley.
Hare, R. (1991). *Manual of the Revised Psychopathy Checklist*. Toronto: Multi Health Systems.

Hinshelwood, R. D. (1999). The difficult patient. *British Journal of Psychiatry, 174*: 187–190.

Johnson-Laird, P. N., & Oatley, K. (1992). Basic emotions, rationality and folk theory. *Cognition and Emotion, 6*: 201–223.

Murphy, N. (2004). An investigation into how community mental health nurses assess the risk of violence from their clients. *Journal of Psychiatric and Mental Health Nursing, 11*(4): 407–413.

Slovic, P. Finucane, M., Peters, E., & MacGregor, D. (2002). Risk as analysis and risk as feelings: some thoughts about affect, reason, risk and rationality. *Risk Analysis, 24*(2): 1–12.

Symington, N. (1980). The response aroused by the psychopath. *International Review of Psychoanalysis, 7*: 291–298.

CHAPTER ELEVEN

Work discussion group for trainees working in forensic settings

Ruth Berkowitz

The context

The Work Discussion Group, the subject of this paper, is part of a two-year, psychodynamically orientated course for professionals working in forensic settings, such as prisons, special hospitals, medium secure units, and youth offending teams. This course was set up by Estela Welldon, originally, in 1990, as a one-year course at the Portman clinic, and then extended in 1993 to two years. Although it was at first called a course in forensic psychotherapy, it is now more a course for professionals from a variety of disciplines with the purpose of developing a psychodynamic approach to working with forensic patients. It is now called "Diploma in Forensic Psychotherapeutic Studies". However, the underlying philosophy remains the same:

> [they] must be properly trained in order to be able to respond adequately to the difficult predicaments of both private and public dimensions. They have to be equipped with insight into their own internal world and motivations, thus the need for personal therapy. It can be all too easy to respond unwittingly and automatically to unlawful situations: a "normal" reaction might be a very natural

reaction but can also amount to an abdication of professional responsibility. [Welldon, 1996, p. 181]

Applicants to the course are required to go through a selection process where their capacity for psychodynamic as well as academic work is assessed. The course consists of several components, apart from the Work Discussion Group: there are theoretical seminars consisting of general psychoanalytic theory, as well as psychoanalytically informed papers on forensic aspects. Each member of the course is required to see a patient in their particular setting for two years under supervision. Their work is assessed throughout the course, both in terms of feedback from staff members and written papers that are assigned and marked each term. They are also required, for the duration of the course, to be in once-weekly psychoanalytic psychotherapy. The group is, therefore, having an ongoing exposure to, and experience of, psychodynamic thinking.

The work discussion group to be described here offers an opportunity to the members of the group to begin to reflect on problems or difficulties that have arisen in their work settings. The emphasis is on reflection rather than action, and this may be more or less difficult for individuals, depending on their work setting, as well as their previous experience and exposure to psychodynamic work, both personally and professionally. Having said this, all of us who work in institutions are vulnerable to the dynamics that inevitably develop when individuals work together. It may be fair to say that working in a caring role may further add to the difficulties for a variety of reasons, which will be discussed. Perhaps, working in forensic settings may also compound the problem. A counsel of perfection would be the availability in any setting of a reflective space within the institution to consider difficulties and problems. Even approaching such a reflective space may be made difficult by a variety of pressures: patients who present as very disturbed or high risk, personnel who are disturbed, the need to account to management or government and meet performance targets, and lack of resources, both professional and financial. The aim of the work discussion group on this course is to introduce the idea that problems do not always have to be solved immediately by doing something, that there is real benefit in being able to think about them and to apply some of the principles of psychodynamic thinking to them.

It may be relevant to consider what, if any, action would be appropriate, that is, action based on thought rather than the reactive responses which may be more typical.

Theoretical background

Bolton and Zagier Roberts (1994) point out that those who work in the helping professions often experience failure in their work with damaged and deprived clients, which induces guilt and anxiety. They suggest that this reparative work with human beings arouses those very feelings that are like early life situations. The individual may have been drawn to their profession for these very reasons, and may, in their work, be dealing unconsciously with these situations. Main (1989) also suggests that there are deep and personal reasons for working in a field where the focus is alleviating the suffering in others. In addition, the main vehicle for work is the individual's own self, and they may wish to heal through their own goodness, which, when work goes well, is validating. However, when there is failure, it can be experienced as their own deficiency and may be difficult to bear.

Individuals may respond to these anxieties in a variety of ways. They may as Main (1989) points out, try to conceal them, becoming frantically good (hiding hatred), omnipotent, ambitious, angry, envious, blaming of others, forming alliances with others, or coalitions against others, including other staff, relatives, and patients. It may, as Hinshelwood (2001) points out, feel that all that is available are the two roles of health and illness. The staff may be, as he says, unrealistically helpful, and the patients unrealistically helpless.

While individuals may deal with anxieties in unhelpful ways, there are often dynamics that arise institutionally and, far from mitigating the individual problems, compound them. Menzies Lyth (1989), in her seminal paper, describes what she calls the social defence system. Its main characteristic is to facilitate the evasion of anxiety and does little to contribute to its true modification and reduction. This social defence system arises over time as a result of collusive interaction and, often, unconscious agreement between members of an institution about what form it should take. It becomes an aspect of external reality with which old and new members of the institution must come to terms. Hinshelwood (2001) describes institutions as potentially pathological containers, so explosive that they can explode and become disabled, or so rigid that there is no opportunity for real expression of what he calls the contents, and, thus, are then moulded to the containing space.

These problems may arise in any institution. The vulnerability of institutions whose main task is helping patients with personal difficulties is great, and may well increase with the greater disturbance in such patients. How much more vulnerable are the staff and the institutions where the focus is forensic patients? Norton (1986) describes how personality disordered forensic patients use strategies that tax the staff, who may react inappropriately by rejection or compliance with the patients' demands. Such patients, he says, want to short-circuit and undermine conventional boundaries.

All these authors highlight the importance of facing the anxiety-provoking experiences and developing a capacity to tolerate and deal with them more effectively. Adequate support should be given through supervision, appropriate training, and mutual respect for one another's views (Bateman, 1996). Hinshelwood (2001) outlines his views on how to mitigate and deal with the pathological responses of both individual and institution. He suggests that groups can offer a space where emotion can be tolerated and reflected on; this depends on a group which supports the capacities of reflection of all who are present, which, in turn, needs an atmosphere in which there is an effort to understand the emotional states of others. In such an atmosphere, there is the possibility for development and growth.

The work discussion group

This work discussion group, described here, differs in several important respects from the kinds of groups described above: the problems brought are not being discussed in the institutional context in which they have arisen; the individuals in the group are strangers to one another.

This has implications. There may be additional anxieties about revealing difficulties to strangers, although, on the other hand, there is an opportunity to discuss issues which would be difficult to confront in the individual's own work setting. The institutional dynamic is not *in vivo* in the group, but must be construed in a variety of ways from the individual's presentation and, to some extent, the responses of the group. None the less, the aims of the work discussion group are very close to those described above: to provide a safe environment in which individuals can own and explore their anxieties, and one in which there is the opportunity to develop a culture of reflection and understanding, rather than one of action. "What should we do?" is the question which is so characteristic of the experience of both patients and staff in forensic settings. The seminar leader is an experienced psychoanalyst or psychoanalytic psychotherapist with experience in forensic work.

Developing a culture in the work discussion group

Each member of the group presents in turn. All they are asked to do is to bring any problem that is preoccupying them which has arisen in their work setting. This request arouses huge anxieties, coming, as they usually do, from settings where problems have been mostly dealt with in the ways described above. Someone has to start, and understanding why a particular individual has volunteered may not be clear at the outset, but may become clearer over time.

The "culture" of the group is conveyed from the outset by the way in which the presentation is listened to by the seminar leader. The "way in which it is listened to" needs some elaboration. It is not unlike the way in which, from a psychoanalytic perspective, one might listen to a patient. Content is important, having a sense of the organization and its structure and the place of the presenter within the structure, the external objects. But as important, if not more important, is the way in which these external objects have been internalized, and, equally, the way in which the presenter expresses their experience of how, in turn, these "external objects" may have internalized the relationships and processes related to the problem under discussion.

The seminar leader pays close attention to the way in which a presentation is made, the mood, the tone, the language used, both verbal and non-verbal. Equally, the countertransference of the seminar leader is crucial, and the monitoring of one's own emotional responses becomes a vital clue. Just as when a patient brings their family, their social relationships, into an analytic relationship there is an attempt through this to construct the patient's experience, so, with the work difficulties (where largely personal relationships are excluded), one uses one's analytic self to conjure up the dynamics of the work setting.

Interventions are kept at a particular level, that is, confined to the work situation, and personal comments about the presenter are largely avoided. Very often, as with patients who have had little opportunity to give names to their emotional states, the comments might at first be simply the naming of emotions experienced. Mostly having worked in environments where anxiety is damped down and the us, "healthy staff without negative feelings", and the them, "sick patients with nasty feelings", is the currency, having their feelings recognized can come as a huge relief. It may not be a relief only to the current presenter, but also to those who are participating, who may begin to feel slightly freer to own their own difficult feelings.

It goes without saying that the participation of the members of the group in the discussion is crucial. There is usually a sense of awareness of a need for a shift in their thinking from that of their core discipline, whether it is medicine, social work, or nursing, where, generally, action is the way of dealing with difficulties, to a more psychodynamic approach. This can be experienced as painful, as with any change, and can be inhibiting for some who may then be reticent to offer comments. It matters, therefore, that everyone's views are responded to with interest and an attempt at understanding what it is they are trying to convey. It may, at times, be helpful to comment on the difficulty of making the transition from their former ways of thinking, which may be a suggestion that the presenter should do something or stop doing something. As the group progresses, and there is less anxiety and, perhaps, an increased capacity to respond, it is often possible to note the response of the group itself to a presentation. For example, the presenter may describe a terrifying situation and give no evidence of fear. The group members, in contrast, may express the fear. By pointing this out, the presenter may feel more able to own the fear himself or herself, rather than locating it in others.

As the group evolves and the cultural atmosphere begins to shift, it is more possible (given that this group consists initially of those unfamiliar with psychodynamic thinking) to make comments about such mechanisms as projection, projective identification, and splitting.

There is, as the group progresses through the two years, an increasing sense of a reflective space which is experienced as both the absolute time given to consider difficulties and also an increasing experience of a reflective space within the minds of others, initially that of the seminar leader, and, increasingly, of themselves and the other participants in the group.

The range of problems

The presenters bring a very wide range of problems, but what characterizes them is that their own capacity for being effective in their work is undermined, obscured, or eclipsed by the absence of appropriate time and thought in their setting.

A social worker is anxious and worried about the future of a looked-after child. She reports that the professionals in the case cannot be bothered to attend a professionals' meeting. The social worker, like the child, is not being appropriately "looked after". We are able to talk and think about the sense of helplessness throughout the family and professional systems. A psychologist has moved into a new setting with adolescents showing sexually concerning behaviours, both abused and abusers. He brought the problem of concern about his own public image now that he was working with this client group. We began to understand the shame he felt as a countertransference response to his clients, both abusers and abused. A nurse describes how she was landed with something very difficult, made a "boo-boo", and was shot down. No one in that team could own the sense of difficulty, near impossibility, of the case, and their own sense of impotence projected into the nurse turned them into omnipotent authorities. Newly qualified staff can often reach desperation without an opportunity to understand what is going on institutionally. Only weeks into her job, a probation assistant was hauled before the manager because her work was considered below par. She was overburdened with paperwork, and given no guidance at all about the content and structure of reports. In discussing the probation service, it became evident that it was near to breaking point with the demands on its resources. Managers, unable to face this and their own difficulties in meeting the unrealistic requirements, projected their own sense of inadequacy and, perhaps, fears of criticism into the probation assistant by demoralizing her. An art therapist was told, when working in a prison setting, that she should not have contact with a particular patient without an escort. However, making an arrangement for the escort proved difficult. In further discussing the patient, it became evident that the patient, like the therapist, felt that he could make little sense of his surroundings and did not understand what was going on.

Many of the problems are about inadequate supervision and management, stemming very often from supervisors and managers being overburdened themselves, or without adequate resources of personnel or staff. The consequences may be splits in the team, with the possibility of boundaries being breached, some staff full of rage and hatred for their seniors, at times feeling under threat of dismissal, and others too close and offered favours.

From time to time, a presenter will be very open about a personal problem: for example, being an immigrant to the country with all the associated anxieties and doubts. Work with certain patients in these circumstances can be undermined; for example, when the patients have a struggle with their own identity and have a sense of isolation and disconnection.

There are also those instances where the individual has been carrying fears and anxieties for years, feeling that no one would be able to understand or bear what they felt was the horror of it. Only as the group became a safer place were they able to describe the anxieties, in some cases, and terrors in others that they had been through and silently endured for years.

Two vignettes

A social worker, B, in a Young Offender's Team begins his presentation with a description of how isolated he feels in the team. He describes his situation, feeling that there is no one to whom he can talk about his work, and conveys a feeling of no one being interested in him. He then said he wanted to talk about a case that he couldn't really discuss at work. While he was at work, late one afternoon the week before, a request came in for a home visit to a young boy. The nurse who took the call usually went with a colleague, but that colleague was away. B volunteered to go with her. He conveyed a somewhat self-sacrificing attitude, doing work that was above and beyond the call of duty, but that he would do it even though he had more than enough work in his own case-load. His account became quite difficult to follow because he presented it at great speed and somewhat incoherently. What was possible to understand was that this case was not his responsibility, in fact it was out of his area, but he decided, without consultation, to go with a nurse to do the home visit. The boy was violent, had been caught threatening younger children with a gun, and had failed to attend his meetings at the YOT. He knew little about the case, although the nurse with whom he went had had some contact. The nurse usually relied on her co-worker for directions, and B described how neither of them could find the house where the boy lived. He went into great detail about the twists and turns they took in a built-up area of London, the hour getting later and later, yet they persevered, knowing that the boy was violent and that it was getting dark. Eventually, they found the house, where the boy was at home with his mother and younger brother. The boy was not keen to see them, yet they insisted that they go in, which they eventually managed to do. While they were talking to him in the kitchen, the father returned, and, seeing them, flew into a rage. He picked up a machete, shouting he was going to kill them, and they ran out of the house with the father in pursuit, although he gave up the chase. The opening words of the account gave a great deal of information about B. He was isolated, which meant he did not feel able to make contact with members of his team. He felt angry and hurt, and even, to some extent, humiliated. In his taking on work that was not within his remit, at one level he wanted to show them how hard he worked, and perhaps how courageous he was. The description of the journey and the rush of speech gave the sense of confusion experienced by B in his setting. As we continued to think about his difficulties, B's despair became more and more evident, and we were able to talk about how he had put himself at risk and that he might have felt that he could punish his colleagues by being seriously harmed or even murdered.

In the work discussion group, B seemed to feel relieved by being able to talk about this frightening experience, but also to allow himself to be more in touch with his own feelings of confusion and rage in his institution. His account elicited concern from the group that he should react in what might be seen as a foolhardy way, but also that he should put himself in such grave danger. It became clear, over a fairly long period of time, that the work was too taxing emotionally for B, and he decided to change his work setting.

A nurse described a case that she had had to deal with four years previously in a medium secure unit. She began by saying that she could not make sense of the material and was afraid that the group would find it difficult, too. This experience had stayed with her all these years and she had not ever been able to speak about it. She was unusually anxious and made several false starts. Slowly, she began to talk about a young man she had known for many years, "A lovely young man" who had made several suicide attempts. Other institutions had found it difficult to cope with him. When he was in a deep depression she could not get through to him at all. Through her contact with him, he only spoke about death, and she began to feel that she was immune to his words and that death had lost its meaning. On a particular Sunday when she was dealing with one patient in seclusion and another who was very demanding, the suicidal patient began making comments again about death. She said she felt that she and her colleague turned a deaf ear to him, having heard it so often before. Later that day, he hanged himself. It seemed as she talked that the whole institution had gone deaf to him. His threats of suicide had undermined their professional effectiveness; he would not be helped, that is, give up his suicidal wishes and actions. Not only this nurse, it seems, but also the whole institution could not bear or stay with his suicidality and what it meant. It only felt like an attack on them and their wish to help him. We were able to think about how patients like this can bring out murderous feelings, and that if they are not thought about and there is murder in the air, it may well be enacted. We returned to her feeling that no one would understand, which was perhaps how this young man had felt, that no one could understand his suicidality, or wanted to.

Discussion

The feedback from those participating in work discussions groups suggests that it comes to be a valued part of the course. From having found it anxiety provoking initially, they begin to look forward to having the opportunity to express their negative, sometimes confused and confusing, feelings as well as to having comments from the group. Although there are variations in the way in which presentations are prepared and given, many group members become freer as the course goes on, recognizing that there is information not only in the content of the presentation, but in the tone, the language used, and the slips made. They themselves might begin to comment on the group reaction as a source of understanding of the problem presented. Not only do the presentations become freer and less anxiety driven, but there is also a perceptible shift in the way in which they listen to one another. In addition, through having the experience of working with a patient, being in psychoanalytic psychotherapy, and having theoretical seminars, they begin to be able to apply their growing knowledge to the dynamics which are described.

From the point of view of the seminar leader, it is a role that requires a capacity to tolerate several difficult aspects. Some of the problems presented border on gross negligence or unethical behaviour of other staff members in their institutions. The negative impact on the functioning of the organization, on the staff members, and, of course, the patients, can be extremely painful. It may, at times, put a considerable strain on the capacity to understand, to reflect, and even to listen to what is being described. Then there are those group members who find the transition to a more psychodynamic way of approaching problems very difficult. They may cling to their old familiar ways of understanding and responding. For example, psychologists may hold on to a problem-solving approach, nurses may be inclined, or, from their daily work, need, to experience themselves as helpful. Allowing group members to proceed at their own pace while at the same time attempting to facilitate the move towards a more psychodynamic approach is a further strain. There is the added complication that while they increasingly value the opportunity for reflection, they may feel resentful that this hour and a half each week is not available to them in their work settings. Attempts to introduce the notion of a time for reflection in their own workplace, more often than not, ends in failure. Where there is confusion and deeply pathological dynamics, it may be extremely difficult to make sense of the experience.

While the aim of the work discussion group itself is to offer the time for reflection and the development of a growing understanding of a particular work-related problem, the overriding purpose of the group is to start a process of developing a more reflective capacity within the work setting itself. This is a tall order, but the experience of being in the work discussion group may provide a growing sense that, while their working environment may, at times, feel like mayhem, there is an alternative to becoming entirely caught up in it. It may just be possible to begin to be more of an observer, reflecting not only on the responses of others, but of themselves.

I have tried to convey that the work discussion group that deals with problems removed from their institutional context differs from a group within the institution. However, it may be that the effects of the former go beyond a capacity to reflect rather than act in situations of stress and pressure. Any action taken would, one hopes, be the result of attempts by the individual to understand. Such attempts imply that they may have some capacity to contain their own feelings, and, at times, those of others. Implicit in containment are the notions both of sustaining experience and of waiting. It may be that the value of dealing with problems in this way is communicated to other staff members, who begin themselves to be able to think rather than act immediately. Ideally, forums for discussing problems within the work setting might be established. This aim, although, in some cases, long term, is the most propitious outcome of the work discussion group presented here.

References

Bateman, A. (1996). Day hospital treatment for borderline patients. In: C. Cordess & M. Cox (Eds.), *Forensic Psychotherapy* (pp. 393–400). London: Jessica Kingsley.

Bolton, W., & Zagier Roberts, V. (1994). Asking for help: staff support and sensitivity groups re-viewed. In: A. Obholzer & V. Zagier Roberts (Eds.), *The Unconscious at Work: Indiviudal and Organizational Stress in the Human Services* (pp. 156–166). London: Routledge.

Hinshelwood, R. D. (2001). *Thinking About Institutions: Milieux and Madness.* London: Jessica Kingsley.

Main, T. (1989). *The Ailment and Other Psychoanalytic Essays.* London: Free Association Books.

Menzies Lyth, I. (1989). *The Dynamics of the Social*. London: Free Association Books.

Norton, K. (1996). The personality disordered forensic patient and the therapeutic community. In: C. Cordess & M. Cox (Eds.), *Forensic Psychotherapy* (pp. 401–422). London: Jessica Kingsley.

Welldon, E. (1996). The psychotherapist and the clinical tutor. In: C. Cordess & M. Cox (Eds.), *Forensic Psychotherapy: Crime, Psychodynamics and the Offender Patient* (pp. 177–187). London: Jessica Kingsley.

CHAPTER TWELVE

Valuing the splits and preventing violence

Oliver Dale, David Reiss, and Gabriel Kirtchuk

Introduction

Managing the risk of violence, be it directed toward others or the self, is a central function of an adult psychiatric service. Vital to this process is the risk assessment, which can be a difficult and lengthy process, requiring a methodical approach and space for reflection. It can be resource intensive and needs to be pitched sensitively to the individual situation.

It is clear that only through completing an appropriate risk assessment can a fitting management plan be developed. What we would like to focus on in this chapter is how the patient's relationship with clinicians can be used to provide important information which helps produce a more therapeutic, informed service, appropriate to the patient's needs.

The struggle to find meaning in violence

Those who commit the most serious violent acts often demonstrate a recurring pattern of incidents; as such, it is often a truism that a very good predictor of future behaviour is past behaviour. Actuarial and structured assessments place great importance on historical data and have provided much needed objectivity in identifying risky individuals. They are, however, very poor at helping us understand incidents, and often lead to a dry and rather wooden account of events. Limited time is spent on the now "taboo" activity of making sense of, and giving meaning to, violent acts, but not only is this a vital part of risk management, but also a key therapeutic goal, central to recovery.

It is tempting to dismiss violence as "mindless", but, although these acts may often involve little self-awareness, there is invariably rich symbolism. Such enactments tend to display a personal meaning that encapsulates, in a single moment, the patient's unspeakable and long-held dilemma. Deciphering this is usually left up to the psychotherapist, who will often struggle to draw out the themes. This is often devalued, but in order for us to better predict and prevent violence, we must offer a capacity for thought. How are we to predict the patient's risk if we do not understand it? How are we going to help the patient learn about their difficulties if we do not examine what it means for them? Somehow, we have to turn the mindless and unspeakable into words and thoughts that can be digested by all.

As the patient is often unable to make sense of his/her predicament we need to rely on the skills, understanding, and emotional experiences of those working with them instead. Often brushed aside and considered interference, these experiences represent vital data. For example, splitting and projective identification are not merely harmful products of the presentation, they are giving us a sense of the patient's inner world. By exploring the origin of these often disturbing and contradictory feelings, we can harness this information. Furthermore, a greater awareness of these dynamics will improve staff cohesiveness, as it validates the seemingly irreconcilable experiences that people may have.

Achieving this in any setting can be extremely difficult, but such work within a community team has its own particular challenges. Comparisons with fighting fires are common; responding to an endless series of crises with little space to think. This has not been helped by the fragmentation of services through the compartmentalization of care into highly specialized teams, so that it is

increasingly delivered across professional and structural boundaries. Although these developments do offer some advantages, they
rely on even better communication among staff, which is an aspect
of teamwork we are already struggling with. Consequently, it may
become even more difficult for a service to hold, in its collective
mind, a picture of the patient that includes not only a series of
facts but, more importantly, a complex and possibly contradictory
narrative.

The semi-structured approach that we outline here is able to
assist this process. It is flexible and accessible for all staff, offering
an innovative way to conduct a consultation with a team. It puts the
patient at the centre in a practical and acceptable way. By creating
a shared understanding of the whole range of experiences, the team
is able to make sense of the patient's contradictions and conflicts. In
doing so, the staff can start to formulate a narrative and think about
issues that the patient, at that time, cannot.

Basic principles

The approach described below is underpinned by an empirical
description of relationships from a psychoanalytic perspective. The
infant's experience of early parental relationships sets down a
template by which subsequent relationships are experienced.
Although we continue to learn throughout life, these early years are
our most formative, because it is through our first relationships that
we form a sense of ourselves. In addition to the genetic endowment, such first relationships are a fundamental part of the formation of our personality, as they give us a sense of the world around
us, who we are, and how we fit into it.

Object relations theory describes an interdependent development of a *sense of others* (object) and a *sense of self* (subject), which
initially are fragmentary, or part-objects (Klein, 1984). The fragile
and poorly defined self, set in a sea of ill-defined emotions and perceptions, is easily overwhelmed: hunger might feel like an absolute
and immediate threat and a delay in feeding might seem like an
attack. A responsive mother will act as an emotional mirror and,
over many interactions, will help the infant to both learn about their
feelings and sensations and discover how to respond to them

(Winnicott, 1967). For example, hunger is recognized as such, and a delay in satisfaction no longer results in outright hostility.

Such part-objects can be extremely contradictory and, consequently, the infant may experience intense feelings of love and hate. Gradually, the fragments integrate and the baby realizes the object of these feelings are one and the same. Klein (1984) described this as the transition from the paranoid–schizoid position to the depressive position. In a hypothetical perfect environment, the fragments are united and all the splits are integrated; however, as this does not exist, in reality we all rely on splitting to some extent, although this may only be revealed when we are under stress.

There are four important points to consider.

1.   These very first relationships influence all subsequent relationships. If an infant's experience is characterized by being criticized or treated with indifference, then they will have a tendency to expect those types of behaviours in the future. They will act accordingly, which encourages those around them to respond in a complementary way.

2.   A nurturing environment helps us develop a coherent sense of self and others. Adversity leaves a fragmented and contradictory self, and those around will have a similar dysfunctional image of that self/person.

3.   Childhood adversity may lead to an over-reliance on early coping mechanisms, resulting in a limited and stereotyped emotional repertoire populated with "good" and "bad" people (objects).

4.   These are not absolute states, with primitive defences *vs.* harmonious adjustment. The greater the anxiety, the more reliant we all become on such early patterns; consequently, mental health may be considered proportional to the degree to which we are able to tolerate anxiety (without cutting off).

How does this relate to the clinical setting?

The clinician has to deal with the above in every encounter. In a heightened state of anxiety, particularly when one is receiving care (in all its shapes and forms, including secure care/prison), a patient may only able to see (in the case we describe here) a critical and indifferent clinician. Despite this not being true and the presence of obvious evidence to the contrary, they will adopt behaviour that guards against the perceived attacks: for example, they might behave in a hostile manner and aggressively dismiss reasonable offers of support.

The less aroused the patient, the more of the real situation they are able to take in, and the more accepting of the help offered. Sometimes, just giving a patient a few minutes to calm down can make a big difference. They might then be able to acknowledge what happened and enter a more "depressive" state of accepting; the degree of the latter will depend on their ability to bear shame and mourn. However, we are all, to a greater or lesser extent, able to explain away such events through any number of defensive positions.

Providing care to very disturbed patients can be extremely bewildering for the clinician. We have all had the experience of thinking "where on earth did that come from?" It can be as if they are accusing you of someone else's misdeeds, and one might feel an urge even to say so. In the face of such outright and violent projection, it may be very difficult to keep a cool head. In this situation, we might interpret the patient's hostility as a sign that not only is there nothing that we can do, but also there is nothing we should do.

As well as feeling physically threatened, we might feel powerless and undermined in our professionalism. Depending on the healthcare professional's capacity to tolerate such "narcissistic" injury, this can be extremely uncomfortable. We have probably all, at some time, responded by having this sort of patient removed from the clinic. We may have justified this stance by describing their difficulties as "behavioural", someone who cannot be helped as they will not take responsibility for themselves or engage. In doing so, by criticizing them for behaving inappropriately, we confirm to the patient that their plight is to be treated with indifference.

In order to understand this interaction, we need to get away from whether it was right or wrong; it might well be that removing the patient was the correct approach, the distinction often comes down to how and why it was done. Often, most of the decision and action is taken unconsciously, with the clinician liable to identify themselves with the past in the present world of the patient. The patient's transference (they are indifferent to me) which the clinician observed as hostility, aroused in the clinician a corresponding countertransference (I am powerless to help) and he identified with this by expelling the patient.

For the care-giver to act in as therapeutic a manner as possible, they need to be attuned to this process. They should be able to interpret their own feelings of powerlessness and inadequacy as the patient's violent projection. In doing so, the clinician will remain in touch with the anxiety and need that the patient is trying to communicate: beneath all the bluster, they are trying to ask for help. The clinician needs to talk to that fragment of the patient's self and, one hopes, doing so will result in therapeutic boundaries being set in a caring and thoughtful way.

The broader service as a mirror and therapeutic agent

Let us suppose that, following their rather difficult meeting with the emergency clinician the night before, our patient then contacts their keyworker in the community mental health team (CMHT). The patient might be calmer, the anxiety lessened, and they might put across their need in a more acceptable manner. Proportional to the degree of disturbance, the patient's assessment of the night before will probably diverge from reality. A very different picture might be presented, one that corresponds to the patient being a victim of critical and indifferent carers. Such splitting is a defence that protects the patient from the unbearable (to them) loss attached to the depressive position. Although it protects and allows some stability, this is at the expense of reality and growth.

We rarely think of how the series of interactions, across different aspects of the service, affect the quality of care, but this is the experience of care that the patient has. The keyworker has a very different patient compared to last night, and there is a danger that the care will fragment. Will the clinician, verbally or not, side with the patient, reinforcing the victim status and impairing any learning?

How well clinicians come together and share their completely different experiences of the patient will have a massive bearing on the ability of a service to act therapeutically. Whether the team has the capacity to hold these disparate and contradictory aspects together, therefore preventing fragmentation, depends on many factors, some pertaining to the clinicians, some to the service and its structures.

In the introduction, we acknowledged some of the difficulties we face in sharing information among ourselves. It is the very nature of the modern acute service, with multiple fault lines, that allows for these fragmented parts of the patient to be expressed so clearly. It is interesting, therefore, that the greatest threat to integrated care is often a vital part of the task, that is, we need to help the patient pull these contradictory fragments together.

How can this affect risk management?

The concepts we have outlined above are fundamental to the assessment of risk of violence, whether to others or the self. Broadly speaking, there are two potential problems we need to consider.

The risk remains unseen

The emergency clinician is likely to have completed a risk assessment form. In doing so, a list of facts will have been collected and a relatively static picture of the risk obtained. There might be some attempt at connecting these factors with events going on in the patient's life, but this is often quite limited.

In our case, contact with the emergency clinician could have been a bewildering experience. The difficulties may have been determined as "just a personality disorder", and the contact terminated as the patient was "unwilling to engage meaningfully". If there is poor cohesion among the staff, concerns raised by the keyworker might be dismissed as "manipulation". Meanwhile, the keyworker may fail to grasp the severity of the disturbance and the threatening, violent aspect of the patient, considering the emergency clinician to be uncaring and irresponsible. With these entrenched views, there is a danger that the opportunity for a shared, more complete, understanding is limited and the risk is, thus, poorly grasped.

If the keyworker is isolated, through poor integration or inadequate supervision, the support they provide may become inappropriate, potentially placing themselves in a vulnerable situation. This dynamic is probably more common than we would like to admit. One striking example involved a restricted patient absenting himself without leave from a ward. Some weeks later, he was eventually spotted in the company of a member of staff. It transpired that they were having an illicit relationship, while the team member continued to work, turning up daily, even assisting in the search. Boundary violations to this degree are rare, but they are the culmination of countless, easily overlooked, more subtle and everyday examples.

If clinicians are able to integrate their views, they are better placed to appreciate what the patient's need is and how to meet it while maintaining appropriate boundaries. Our challenge is to keep to task in the face of the patient's inability to request help in a way that is likely to elicit appropriate and timely support. The clinician who breaks these boundaries often does so with good intentions, despite the obvious destructiveness which would be apparent to an observer, either within or outside of the team.

It is often said that different people pick up on different aspects of risk: for example, female staff may be more aware of the risk of sexual offences by male patients. Yet, as demonstrated by the example above, the reverse may also occur. Sometimes, the voice that signals the risk might be very small indeed, which can result in some staff overestimating and others underestimating it. Frequently, the true extent of any danger is only properly appreciated when the risk assessment is considered across multiple and completely different contacts with all staff who come into contact with the patient.

The risk can escalate

The second, interrelated, point is that the risk is dynamic and liable to fluctuate. It is quite obvious that by failing to act as a cohesive service, the quality of care is threatened. What is not so evident is that there is also the potential for an escalation in risk. This can manifest in a variety of ways, but it is related to the ability of the service to hold itself together in the face of looking after this patient in crisis. If the service fragments, then the patient remains more firmly in a state akin to the paranoid–schizoid position, further from the reality of the situation and the help they actually need.

On listening to forensic case reports, an often repeated feature is that the perpetrator has presented to different agencies, health, social, or police, asking for help prior to the index offence. One striking case involved a man requesting police assistance to move his possessions out of his home. Having been turned away, this individual went on to murder his ex-partner as he was collecting his belongings from their flat.

This is an extreme example, but we should consider that the patient has a need and is requesting help. The problem is, he or she is doing it in a way that is confusing and, therefore, unsuccessful. The confusion arises because the patient's mind and presentation is fragmented, leaving carers unsure about how to help, perhaps with a feeling of being manipulated. It is only through acknowledging the validity of these fragments that we can gain a fuller picture of the risk. In doing so, we offer a capacity for thinking that the patient is unable to contain within themselves, and, therefore, we develop the potential for reintegration and de-escalation. The concept of containment is about managing this process and pulling the splits together safely.

How can we improve our ability for integrated working?

Introducing interventions that encourage staff to work reflectively is very difficult. There are many approaches, and it is often the culture that makes the difference. Various structures have been employed in the past, for example, Balint groups, which are familiar to many and continue to play an important role in a modern service. Other approaches include staff-support, reflective practice, and community meetings, but even the team meeting and ward round are important in this respect. Some of the work described above is encompassed within these groups and, although the focus varies, all should encourage exploration and reflection.

Take-up of this sort of work is, however, quite ad hoc: in some quarters there may be steadfast resistance, often where the need is greatest. The reasons are often a mixture of personal and institutional. Some of the traditional groups mentioned above have drawbacks. There is a reliance on fairly stable populations to work within them: the process, thus, demands regular commitment.

Different professional groups can have very different languages and working lives, so they may tend to congregate among themselves.

Other criticism comes from the very subjectivity of this type of approach. Modern medicine holds objectivity as the gold standard. Consequently, there has been a lot more focus on the easier to measure aspects of risk, resulting in the development of actuarial assessments such as the Violence Risk Appraisal Guide (VRAG) (Quinsey, Harris, Rice, & Cormier, 1998; Webster, Harris, Rice, Cormier, & Quinsey, 1994). These instruments have indeed provided much needed objectivity to the process and do provide significant assistance to staff when used appropriately. The inner world, however, is often seen as inherently subjective, and, although clinical experience may be valued, "gut feeling" is sometimes denigrated.

The popularity of this sort of work is further undermined, because, to a greater or lesser degree, these groups tend to focus more on the clinician and less on the patient. Staff may feel extremely vulnerable in such circumstances. Working in the transference requires an ability to acknowledge powerful feelings that might appear to challenge our professionalism: the idea that we might act unconsciously can seemingly contradict the idea of a competent clinician. Given our very hierarchical workforce structure, with its accompanying emphasis on appraisal and apprenticeship, this can be too much to bear.

To answer some of these criticisms and to support staff with this process we have developed a semi-structured approach inspired by Benjamin's "Structural Analysis of Social Behavior" (SASB) model (Benjamin, 1996). With the patient placed right at the centre of the assessment, we consider the interpersonal dynamics manifested in the patient's contact with the service. In doing so, we can provide an accessible understanding of the patient's presentation. In conjunction with structured tools, a more complete understanding of the relevant static and dynamic risk factors is gained, and possible avenues for intervention become evident. While relying on the elucidation of subjective experiences, the method brings some empirically based objectivity to the process, encouraging the creation of a more complete and comprehensive narrative.

Working as a group, members of staff arrive at a formulation of the patient's difficulties. Through describing the dilemmas and the patient's adaptations to them, they are able to make some sense of their experience of the patient as she/he interacts with the service. Instead of being left with powerful feelings that threaten to isolate and fragment the care, staff members are able to make use of and validate these experiences. Contradictions that might have been left to fester can then be explained, fostering a shared understanding.

The tool

This approach was adapted and developed from Axis 2 of Operationalized Psychodynamic Diagnostics (OPD Task Force, 2001, 2008), a structured approach to psychodynamic assessment; the second axis focuses on the assessment of interpersonal dynamics. This part of the OPD assessment involves an assessment of the interpersonal interactions, which, when performed by a group, is referred to as "tuning", based on the SASB model. Our approach focuses on elucidation of the dynamics in this manner, and encourages those present to describe their interactions with the patient.

The SASB aims to provide an objective analysis of psychopathology in terms of interpersonal relationships. It builds on earlier work that can be traced back to 1938, when Murray (1938) produced a list of fundamental human needs using factor analysis. Building on Murray's work, Leary (1957) arranged a selection of Murray's needs around horizontal and vertical axes to form a circle. The interactions described by the interpersonal circle focus in two directions, the other or active, and on the self or reactive (Benjamin, 1996). The *active* indicates how the self perceives the acting or attitudes of the other, the *reactive* is how the self responds to these perceptions. There are, therefore, two layers to the interpersonal circle: the "active layer" (Figure 1) and the "reactive layer" (see Figure 2). The two axes on the active circle represent continua: the horizontal axis ranges from love/idealize to hate/destroy; the vertical axis spans the range between control and allowing independence.

For the reactive circle, the vertical polarities range between assert and submit, with the horizontal axis having recoil on the left, extending to reactive idealization on the right (Figure 2). An example of an active process causing a reactive response is where a

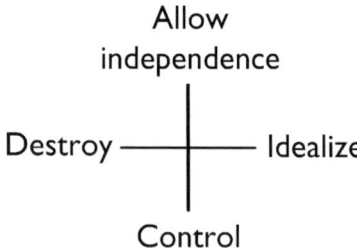

Figure 1.   The active layer of the interpersonal circle.

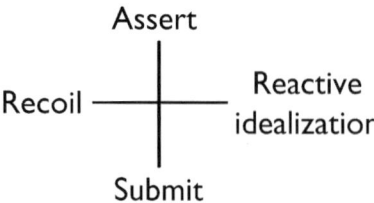

Figure 2.   The reactive layer of the interpersonal circle.

person who is perceived as controlling may lead to a submissive response in someone else.

If you consider a relationship between two people, both have an experience of each other, and both have an experience of themselves in response to the other. There are, therefore, four different perspectives. There is a perception of the self for each of the people in the interaction, a description of which would be preceded by "I" statements, and there are also two corresponding perceptions of the other, which might be preceded by "you", "he", "she", "them", or "they" statements. These perspectives allow for a variety of possible interactions and further points are, therefore, added around the circle to describe the interactions in more detail (Figure 3).

The OPD Task Force (2001, 2008) "opened up" these circles and presented them as a list, forming a type of menu which healthcare professionals can use to describe the observed, dysfunctional, repeated interactions within each of the four perspectives. Not only does this give the ingredients for a formulation, it also illustrates the dynamic nature of the relationships. Seemingly minor interactions can then be described in a context that may sometimes significantly alter their meaning.

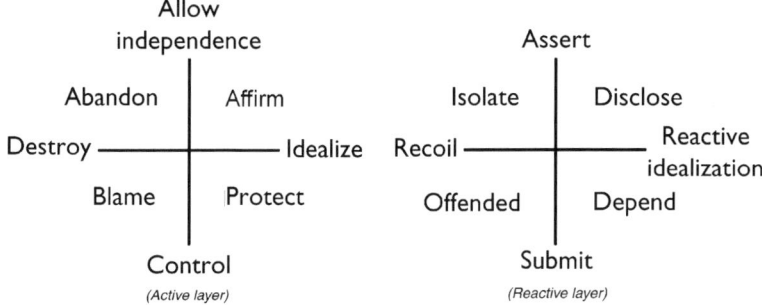

Figure 3. The four perspectives of a personal relationship and the possible interactions arising therefrom.

Working in this way offers a number of advantages:

- it serves as a prompt to consider the various perspectives of a relationship, encouraging the clinician to consider each view;
- it supports the forming of hypotheses about an individual's states of mind;
- it validates feelings that may be deemed unprofessional, nonsensical, or unpopular, which are vital data in understanding the presentation;
- it allows for simple representation of the repeating patterns of behaviour which are at the heart of the presentation and risk;
- it is accessible to a wide range of staff and may be incorporated into most different types of clinical practice;
- it can be used on a consultation basis.

We practised and developed this approach, working in a small group. Meeting weekly, we presented cases, both from general psychiatry and forensic services, explored the four perspectives, and made formulations. The presentations involved a very brief psychiatric history, focusing on childhood, family life, previous incidents, and also the current feelings of both the staff and the patient towards each other. The recollection of the patient's "I" and "you/he/she/they" statements, as well as similar disclosure by staff is encouraged, emphasizing perceptions and feelings.

In some cases, we had the opportunity of working directly with clinical teams, but at other times the group provided a consultative service. We have built up a considerable amount of experience, with a large number of cases being assessed. Below, we describe two fictional clinical pictures, based on cases we have assessed and treated over a prolonged period of time and in different institutions.

Risk unseen

Steven was a fifty-two-year-old Scottish man who was referred to the outpatient clinic by his GP, who reported that he had depression. He had previously been seen in the clinic on several occasions over the years by a number of clinicians. He usually seemed to engage well and was relatively settled. The doctor he saw often continued to offer appointments because the patient said they were helpful, as they gave him "someone to talk to"; however, the clinician was not sure what he was offering. The patient often spoke of his difficulty tolerating injustice around him, and linked this to childhood adversity. His had been a violent upbringing; his alcohol-dependent father would regularly beat his mother and the patient. When Steven was aged fourteen, his mother killed his father. Although she was eventually cleared of manslaughter on the grounds of self-defence, Steven expressed doubt and confusion around his father's death.

At the age of fourteen, Steven was involved in an escalating pattern of crime. At sixteen he was sent to a Borstal, which he described as having a brutal regime. While there, he was subjected to physical and sexual abuse. Following his release, he continued to engage in criminal activity and violence. At the age of twenty, he was sentenced to six years for grievous bodily harm. Following his release, he seems to have managed to avoid further trouble with the police.

As time went by, Steven disclosed more and more about his violent past. He explained how he rejected this side of him, yet sometimes had to step in to protect the vulnerable. He espoused a particularly brutal form of justice, but often described how he had been tormented by having this role foisted on him, due to his large stature. He also described assaulting an accident and emergency department doctor who was treating him for an injury when he caused some pain in the process. He justified this by saying he had warned the doctor once before.

The treating psychiatrist was due to change his post, which Steven was aware of, and during their final appointment, Steven appeared to be very disturbed. He spoke of his fears about his new doctor, would he be kind like the current one, or would he be brutal, rigid, and uncaring. He described in graphic detail how he would violently respond to an imaginary doctor who was unjust to him. In the midst of this fantasy, he "confessed" to killing his father and how his mother had taken the blame for him. He recounted in detail the "premeditated murder".

The psychiatrist was stunned by this account, and carried on with the appointment with the confession fading into the background. They ended in amicable terms, bidding each other good luck, with the patient finally warning the doctor to take care as some of his patients might be dangerous. The confession was initially dismissed, but it was only on mulling it over and following the psychiatrist approaching his supervisor that it was taken further. With some ambivalence, due to a fear for his own safety and also a sense of betrayal, a statement to the police was made.

Assessment and formulation

The doctor concerned felt very troubled by this episode, and brought the case to the group for consideration. It was felt that the patient saw others starkly: either they were *intimidating and attacking* him or he perceived them as *attending to and caring for him in every way*. Subsequently, the patient responded by either *supporting* others or by *intimidating and attacking* them (such as with the accident and emergency department doctor when Steven perceived he might experience some physical pain).

Others found the patient as either a *domineering* or *attacking* figure, or someone *caring* who was *admiring* of the doctor. The doctor experienced himself as *attending and caring for the patient in every way* (but could not understand how), and at the same time *intimidating and attacking* him by informing the police of the reported homicide. He also reported having a fantasy of being protected by the patient in the community. It is probably because of this sense of protection that he felt that his disclosure to the police was an attack on the patient.

The split between the attacking and helpful aspects in both the patient and the doctor was quite striking. It was only at the very end of their contact that the doctor became aware of how "close" they had become. It was in "touching on" the patient's painful vulnerability to perceived abandonment that the psychiatrist became dangerously exposed to the patient's psychological attack. The group considered that the doctor's lack of awareness of the danger during their contact, especially during the last meeting, showed how he was almost incapacitated in his ability to act professionally, for example, to make an appropriate risk assessment. At a different level, one can consider the disclosure of the crime, whether or not it was accurate, as an attempt by Steven to regain control of the situation by killing off the doctor/father, removing the possibility of feeling being rejected by yet another significant figure and becoming a victim once again.

The splits were so stark and precipitous that holding both sides in mind was extremely difficult. On reviewing his notes, the absence of a risk assessment or forensic history seemed quite telling. Due to the fragility of the status quo, it seems that this lack of awareness might also serve a protective function, but at the cost of the risk being overlooked and the patient's needs being missed.

This balancing act allowed the patient to idealize the doctor, and left the doctor with a feeling of having helped but not sure how. Until the very end of the relationship the risk remained unspoken. With a strong wish to "protect" the patient, it was only on speaking with the rest of the team that the helpful and therapeutic aspects of making a police statement became apparent, yet there remained much ambivalence.

The doctor found this formulation very helpful in coming to an understanding of what had happened. Acknowledging the ambivalence was an important part of this process. The treating team were informed of the assessment and a thorough forensic assessment was made.

Escalation through rejection and neglect

Jane was a twenty-one-year-old Afro-Caribbean woman who had been in care since the age of six. Her father never had any contact with her, and she was raised initially by her mother, who was dependent on illicit substances. She was fostered by her grandmother and, at the age of six, was taken into the care of social services as the grandmother was unable to cope with her. There followed countless further placements, which rarely lasted more than six months, often breaking down because of Jane's difficult behaviour.

During these years, Jane was occasionally physically and sexually abused at the hands of some of her carers. She was not able to sustain any stable period of education and, by early adolescence, Jane was engaged in drug-taking behaviour and petty crime. She frequently placed herself in vulnerable situations, particularly with older men. At the age of sixteen, she had her first psychiatric admission, exhibiting symptoms of mania. Following this there were other admissions, with an increasingly psychotic flavour. Even when well, she posed major challenges to the staff, characterized by emotionally unstable and borderline traits.

Staff often found Jane to be demanding and abusive, as she accused them of not caring and winding her up. At times, she complained they never gave her any attention, and on other occasions she reported that she felt they wanted to lock her up and never let her out. There was a sense that nothing could be done for her and staff often felt confused, afraid, and resentful. Over the course of a few weeks, there were a number of escalating incidents, which followed the sudden departure of a care co-ordinator, with only a few hours' notice given over the telephone. Jane's behaviour included an assault on a member of staff, who initially did not report it as she considered it mild, even though it had resulted in painful bruising.

During a ward round, it was thought that things were settling. The patient was not available for review and no changes were made. The following day, there was the chance disclosure by another member of staff that she had discovered the patient was carrying a knife. At this stage the patient was informal (the previous treatment order having earlier lapsed unnoticed while she was on a locked ward). The responsible medical officer (RMO) assessed her, found her to be psychotic, and, due to the escalating pattern of risk, placed her on another treatment order (section 3 of the Mental Health Act 1983).

Several hours following her detention, the patient was transferred to another unit after she volunteered to make space for a new admission. This was without wider consultation, and there followed a rift between the ward staff and the medical team. Staff justified their actions, saying the patient wanted to move, and found it difficult to acknowledge their own, understandable, relief from the respite.

Assessment and formulation

The patient felt the staff were *domineering and overwhelming her* with their demands, and that they were either *accusing* or they *ignored* her. Subsequently, she felt that she had to *attend to and care for the staff in every way* and became over-helpful (for example, by volunteering to move ward). If that failed she would tend to *cut off contact* with them by taking leave.

In turn, the staff felt that she was *draining* their resources by *domineering and overwhelming them* with her demands, which at times escalated to *intimidating and attacking them*, for example, with the knife. In response, they felt they *allowed her too much independence* (by agreeing to her suggestion that she should move ward) and often found themselves with a sense of *rejecting and excluding her*, thereby repeating the story of her life.

The failure to report incidents and even the accidental lapse of her section seemed to make some sense in this light. The somewhat insensitive way in which her care co-ordinator broke the news of departure only served to heighten an already sensitive situation.

The isolation of the patient and her consequent neglect by the staff seemed to confirm this rejection, but it also served as a temporary (but dysfunctional) solution in that it allowed for some space to diffuse tensions and avoid further conflict. Throughout her life, this tension between locking her up and letting her free was evident. When the RMO re-detained her, he altered this precarious balance without fully considering the full impact. The staff and patient, therefore, colluded unconsciously to redress this.

Following presentation at the group, the psychiatrist felt more confident to request the patient's return to the unit in the face of considerable resistance. He also found the exploration of the risks and benefits of the isolation very helpful, and was able to understand the ward staff's predicament in a more sensitive light. Following her transfer, a more satisfactory reporting of incidents and a greater sensitivity about what the patient found distressing was noticeable. With time, the patient began to settle and engage. Leave was reinitiated and she was successfully discharged to a hostel.

Summary

We believe these cases demonstrate how risk can easily become overlooked, and it is this aspect which is particularly pertinent to adverse incidents. Keeping alert and sensitive to the indicators of risk is a challenge we face daily. Although major developments have been made, the meaning behind incidents tends to be side-lined and formal assessment is often lacking.

The above cases also illustrate how much of a burden it can be to manage risk and care for patients. Not only can it affect individual staff, causing significant confusion and anxiety, but it can also cause conflict. Through exploring these presentations, we can create an understanding that not only allows us to improve the quality of care, but it can also encourage staff development and maintain morale.

We have outlined here an accessible and empirically based method that overcomes some of the barriers more traditional approaches have encountered. In order to prevent further incidents and promote recovery, a team-based approach to exploring interpersonal relationship has the potential to be an extremely important part of the assessment and management of psychiatric patients.

References

Benjamin, L. S. (1996). *Interpersonal Diagnosis and Treatment of Personality Disorders*. New York: Guilford Press.

Klein, M. (1984). *The Psycho-analysis of Children*, R. Money-Kyrle (Ed.), A. Strachey (Trans.), *The Writings of Melanie Klein* (Vol. 2). New York: Free Press.

Leary, T. (1957). *Interpersonal Diagnosis of Personality: A Functional Theory and Methodology for Personality Evaluation*. New York: Ronald Press.

Murray, H. A. (1938). *Explorations in Personality*. New York: Oxford University Press.

OPD Task Force (Eds.) (2001). *Operationalized Psychodynamic Diagnostics: Foundations and Manual*. Seattle, WA: Hogrefe & Huber.

OPD Task Force (Eds.) (2008). *Operationalized Psychodynamic Diagnosis OPD-2: Manual of Diagnosis and Treatment Planning*. Cambridge, MA: Hogrefe & Huber.

Quinsey, V. L. E., Harris, G. T., Rice, M. E., & Cormier, C. A. (1998). *Violent Offenders: Appraising and Managing Risk* (1st edn). Washington, DC: American Psychological Association.

Webster, C. D., Harris, G. T., Rice, M. E., Cormier, C., & Quinsey, V. L. (1994). *The Violence Prediction Scheme: Assessing Dangerousness in High Risk Men* (1st edn). Toronto: University of Toronto.

Winnicott, D. W. (1967). Mirror-role of the mother and family in child development. In: P. Lomas (Ed.), *The Predicament of the Family: A Psycho-Analytical Symposium* (pp. 26–33). London: Hogarth.

CHAPTER THIRTEEN

The healthy and the unhealthy organization: how can we help teams to remain effective?

Phil Stokoe

Introduction

I n this chapter, I shall describe the factors that I believe are essential to the healthy functioning of an organization, applying psychoanalytic ideas to clinical work, teams, organizations and culture.

I shall also describe the sorts of things that inhibit healthy functioning, particularly in forensic and mental health organizations, and describe some interventions that can be used to help organizations in trouble, including:

- consultancy to management;
- reflective practice groups and staff support groups;
- clinical consultancy to teams;
- education.

Healthy organization

What I am about to do is to create a myth, the idea of a healthy organization. In a way, I am being a bit provocative, but I hope that it is a useful provocation in two senses: first, that it makes us all think carefully about our own organizations, and second, that it offers a model that helps us to analyse organizations methodically.

I describe four factors that I think are essential in creating a "healthy" organization. There are three factors which I think are common to all organizations, from industry to the helping services, and there is a further factor which marks the difference between the management of the helping professions and management of industrial or commercial enterprises, as shown in the summary below.

Four factors for a healthy organization

• Clarity about the primary task (what we are all here to do).
• Clarity about shared principles (how we set about the primary task).
• Clarity about the different layers in the hierarchy: specifically, what decision-making is delegated to each level and with what authority.
• The factor that is specific to our work in the helping professions is the provision of a "container": this requires attention to something that does not arise in business, the management of "good practice". In industry, for example, it does not matter how the workforce treat the raw material on the way to producing a dustbin; in our work, it matters very much indeed how we treat our "raw material", because we are working with people, not lumps of plastic and metal.

Then I try to show that the healthy organization can be thought of as being like an organism in which there is a constant flow between "mind" and "body". Information is absorbed and authority is delegated in the service of maintaining a contact with "reality", which requires a "state of mind" or a mental predisposition of "enquiry". You could say this is the organizational equivalent to the depressive position, as described by Melanie Klein. Klein described two states of mind that characterize both early development and our daily progress through life. The earliest stage, which she called the paranoid–schizoid position, is characterized by a sense of certainty; the world is perceived as sharply delineated: either right or wrong, black or white; there are no shades of grey, no complexity, and, therefore, no ambiguity or ambivalence. This whole state of mind is preserved in the service of one's survival, which is all that matters. Later, as a result of the infant being able to face reality because he feels there is a carer who supports him, he can recognize that life is, indeed, complex and that he needs help; in this state of mind what matters is the survival of the helper; the baby develops concern for others and, therefore, the capacity to form loving relationships. At the same time, the mind is no longer characterized by certainty, but by curiosity and a desire to discover, to enquire.

The four factors

I should begin by saying that my way of thinking about organizations is profoundly influenced by the method that was created by the Tavistock Institute of Human Relations, often referred to as the "Group Relations" approach. This model has arisen as a result of consulting to organizations, and one of the working concepts that I will not be referring to in this chapter until I get to the point about what happens next, is the "Organization in Mind", a vital means of understanding how an actual organization is functioning, which has been written about in a very helpful way recently by Armstrong (2005). I mention this now because the underlying principle is that organizations have an unconscious, and that the individuals who work in the organization become part of that unconscious *without knowing it*. They express ideas, feelings, and beliefs that represent the unconscious preoccupations of the system, while believing that these are entirely rational phenomena generated entirely by their conscious mind in a completely objective way. This way of thinking is based on the central hypothesis that organizations, because they are created by people, will be a reflection of the individual human mind.

Primary task

One of the earliest concepts developed by the group relations' thinkers was that of primary task. This is variously defined by different writers but is essentially the *raison d'être* of the organization;

this is what it is here to do, it is what gives its existence meaning, and is its means of survival. One of the things that you can do in consulting to an organization is to ask people what they think the primary task of their organization is; the answers will often provide information about what is going wrong! However, what I want to do is to apply the lessons we have learnt from that sort of enquiry and set up a principle: if the primary task is explicit (and I mean written down and available for all to see) *and* if it is constantly being monitored for relevance (I will define this later), then it will provide an important benchmark for good decision making.

It is not always easy to know what the primary task is: for example, helping professions often appear to be carrying out several tasks at the same time. Turquet (1951), in his famous paper about leadership in organizations, shows how to test for the true primary task by taking things to an extreme. He gives the example of a teaching hospital and asks which is the primary task, teaching or healing? Then he gives the example: a patient starts to haemorrhage during an operation, what does the consultant do? If the primary task is to teach, he ought to step back and say, "Ideas anyone?" Clearly, then, the primary task of the teaching hospital is to heal; teaching is a subsidiary task. Now, what is most pertinent to our enterprise at this time is that Turquet deduces the primary task by creating a context of decision making; I am saying that clarity about primary task will facilitate decision making (and I shall describe the importance of decision making later).

Shared principles.

I put "shared principles" next among the four factors because they provide even more benchmarks for good decision making. If the primary task tells us what we are doing, then the shared principles tell us how we set about doing that. They are partly an ethical statement, partly a statement of efficiency, and partly a statement of policy or structure. For example, we might agree that we do not bully in this organization, and we might agree that we do not waste money, and we might agree that we respect the decision-making functions reflected in the hierarchy, or that we provide equal opportunities in our recruitment procedures. In other words, the shared principles provide the parameters for our work. This means that they are the detail that will hold the organization in contact with reality, for example, the reality of finance and the reality or rationing or of limited resources. In this way, we can use the same formula that we did for the primary task, which is that if the shared principles are explicit (and I mean written down and available for all to see) *and* if they are constantly being monitored for relevance (I will define this later), then they will provide important benchmarks for good decision making.

Decision-making hierarchy

The reason why I use the model of an organism (actually a human being) for the understanding of an organization is that organizations are created in order to carry out human functions more efficiently. They are our attempts to create something in our own image, and they will only function well if they have built into them those aspects that make us function well. In this respect, the capacity to make good decisions, based in reality and with an ability to check out the efficiency of those decisions, is crucial to the survival both of the individual and of the organization. So, what do we know about decision making?

- Decisions are responses to problems.
- Good decision-making requires good information.
- Decisions are (one hopes, temporary) acts of omnipotence.
- Very closely linked to the above, decisions are actions.

It is my contention that it follows that efficient decision making cannot be carried out by a group; it must be done by an individual— democracy does not work in an organization. (Actually, it does not work for a country in terms of day-to-day decision making; it works by appointing individuals who will carry out the decision-making functions on our behalf. The next election will be the point at which those individuals are called to account for their performance as decision makers on our behalf.) In a healthy organization, the delegation of decision-making functions is clear and explicit. These functions reflect the attempt to create the best structure to achieve the primary task according to the shared principles. Jaques (1989) did much very helpful work in studying the hierarchies of organizations, discovering, for example, that it is possible to clarify the difference between levels in a hierarchy by identifying the longest time scale that any decision maker is operating to.

Very often, organizations "solve" a problem by creating a layer of management with the sole responsibility of ensuring that such problems will not happen again. Social Service departments are very good at doing this. The problem is that such posts actually do not carry any decision-making function not carried by those either apparently above or apparently below on the "line management scale". You can check this out for yourself by asking the question, "What is the limit of your decision-making function?", then, "Where do you go to get that decision?", and, finally, "Is this your line-manager?" Often it is not, in which case we are left with the question, what function does the line manager serve if he cannot make decisions that you cannot make? Sometimes, there is some-one who is apparently senior to you, though not your line manager, who similarly does not carry any decision-making function not carried either by you or your manager, which leaves us with the same question, what function does this person serve? Of course, the answer is usually that it is a buffer; this is someone whose respon-sibility is to make sure that some particular sort of incident does not happen. There *is* a function that can be set up in this "intermediate" arena that makes sense, and that is a co-ordinator post, someone whose job is to bring together others on a particular hierarchical plane, a genuine *primus inter pares*.

There is a problem that occurs in the reverse direction, that is, when there is not a proper decision-making process and staff are left with the need to make a decision and no authority to do so; under these circumstances, they will turn to what I call personal authority.

So, where does all this leave us on our quest to discover the "healthy organization"? It seems to me that we conclude that it is essential that the organization is arranged in a hierarchical manner to serve the achievement of the primary task; that everyone should know who has the decision-making function for what, and every-one should know the limits of their own decision making. In this way, we can produce another formula: the point at which I cannot make a decision, I have a *duty* to advise. Why do I say that? I hear you ask. Well, it is straightforward, really: best decisions require best information, I think we would agree. If you are a manager, you cannot know about the impact the work is having on your team unless they tell you. You need to know about this because your decisions must be having an impact, or else they are not real decisions (I shall be discussing this notion of "impact" later). The thing that created the need for a decision was a problem, but how did you know there was a problem? Only because you have been told by your subordinates.

I ought to say that, when this system works, it often looks as if a group is making a decision. The way that I understand this is through Bion's concept of the work group (Bion, 1961). When a group is in that state of mind, the members feel able to participate. I think that a group faced with a task of making a decision about something is actually faced with two tasks: to thrash out the pros and cons, and then to decide among them which way to go. This is often too much, and it creates a "basic assumption mode" (Bion, 1961) which has the tell-tale feature that there are some individuals who are clearly unable to contribute. On the other hand, when the group is told that it will not be making the decision, but that the manager will, there is only one task and that is to influence the manager as best one can. The manager's task is to keep the group on task. What an external observer will see is a group functioning as a work group with everyone free to contribute so that the discussion gradually makes the decision obvious; this gives the illusion that the group has made the decision. It is one of life's little tragedies that managers often do not understand that really engaging their workforce in discussion about the trickier issues actually makes the job of management easier. It is as if managers believe that the workers cannot face reality and only they (the management) can.

Management of practice: the container

Up to this point, I have been describing factors that I believe to be essential to good function in an organization. I need now to describe something that is particular to the helping professions, but is not necessary for industry and commerce. I think that this distinction is something that the successive governments following Mrs Thatcher have utterly failed to understand. This failure lies behind the dreadful state of our public services today—the NHS, social services, and education. The trouble is that, as I embark on this section, I realize that I am referring to an idea that I have not yet described, the mind of the organization. On the other hand, this seems to be the right place to describe the fourth factor. What I propose is that I describe the essence of this fourth factor here, and then talk about mind.

The point is that, thinking in open systems terms, it does not matter in industry, say, how you treat the raw material during the processing part as long as you produce your output in the most financially efficient way that you can. (In its simplest definition, the model of an open system relates the site of work to the context in which the work is taking place (essentially the environment). Thus, we would think about an "input" from the environment into the workplace, then some work happens that can be said to transform the "input", and, finally, the product of the transformation is returned to the environment in the form of "output".) In other words, you can either talk to pieces of steel in an attempt to get them to form the shape of the dustbin you want to make, or you can hit them with an industrial hammer; the only concern would be efficiency; there will not be crowds of people with placards accusing you of mistreating steel. But it *does* matter what we do with the raw material in the helping services because the raw material is people.

Now, you may say that the way that the raw material is to be treated will be enshrined in the "shared principles", which is true; however, I think that, although these will indeed reflect the ethical code of the professions involved, there is more going on than parameters here. You might say that we are talking about the personality, or the soul, of the organization; indeed, I think that Armstrong is describing exactly this in his recent work (Armstrong, 2005). I want to illustrate what I mean by a little vignette. One of the best managers I ever worked for was the Director of a Youth Treatment Centre, where I had my first experience as a manager. This place was run directly by the government for the treatment, in secure conditions, of the most dangerous and disturbed adolescents in the country. We had a finance officer who was a fully paid-up civil servant; in other words, he had status, presence, and a sense that the money we were spending was his own. I had made a case in a management meeting for spending a significant amount of money refurbishing my treatment unit, on the grounds that this was good clinical practice. The finance officer had said that there was no money in whatever budget was used for these purposes, and I, feeling very intimidated by him, was about to give up, when the Director said that he thought that I had made an important case, that the clinical argument clearly took precedence, and that he had confidence in the finance officer's ability to do his job, which meant finding a way to raise the money for the project. To my amazement, the finance officer accepted this and did, indeed, obtain the money. Now, one of the things about this Director was that he was very clear that, although he was the boss, he did not know as much as his junior managers about the business of treatment techniques. What he did know was how to make a judgement about what to do in the context of advice, and that he was very clear that the main reason for our existence was to find the best treatments we could for these very difficult adolescents. In other words, he saw that the heart of the enterprise was clinical, and that the management of structure and protocol ought to support the clinical enterprise.

I want to make a distinction, therefore, between the management of "process" and the management of "practice". The former is the management of procedures and of hierarchies and of structures, in fact, everything that my previous three factors have been referring to. The latter is the management of clinical practice, meaning the business of designing clinical services to meet perceived needs. It is my contention that, in the helping services, the management of practice *must* take the lead over the management of process, which ought to support it. Now, of course, I am not saying that all clinical wishes ought to be given support, because this flies in the face of reality. In fact, it is this business of the role of "reality" that means I must step out of the description of the fourth factor briefly. Before I do that, I want to say something about my proposal for the realization of the management of practice: I call it the provision of a container. Now, I am not claiming that this is a new idea, as many people have referred to the provision of a container in designing a treatment setting, but I want to be precise about how I think of this concept. Of course, I am drawing here upon Bion's idea of "container–contained" (Bion, 1962a), which already suggests something about the organization having an equivalent to a "mind", and I need to turn to that before developing the organizational container.

The living organization

Human beings have designed organizations to carry out functions on behalf of others. This means that we have designed them to be, as it were, superhuman: to achieve what we cannot do on our own. Indeed, certain forms of mysticism set up rituals in which a group becomes ecstatic so that the spiritual leader can channel that ecstatic energy through himself to make him more powerful (but that is a whole other book). I think it is clear that groups do have the potential to achieve more than anyone can achieve on his or her own. The only problem is the unconscious processes set up by the creation of the group. Organizations, obviously, suffer the same fate. For now, it is sufficient to say that the model for an organization is a human being. Therefore, we shall be studying the way that the organizational mind works as well as how its body links to the mind in the service of the task for which it was created.

State of mind

Bion has shown us how we can think about group states of mind (Bion, 1961). He demonstrated that the group acts to avoid anxiety and that this is a paradox, because anxiety is the result of being confronted with a task. It follows that for a group or an organization to function well, it must *expect* anxiety and it needs to set up a system to "process" this anxiety. In simple terms, such a process will turn anxiety into meaningful data. It is the organizational equivalent of alpha-function, a term used by Bion for a process that we might call thinking (Bion, 1962b). In my view, psychoanalysis has demonstrated that the thing that makes us human (i.e., different from other species), which lies behind the development of both an "inner world" and consciousness, is the genetic programme that Freud and Klein called the "epistemophilic instinct" (Freud, 1916–1917). I am afraid that I tend to use ordinary English words whenever I can, and I think what we are describing here is curiosity and interest. Having said that, I think that this "instinct" takes a particular and central form in the human mind; it appears to act like a computer programme that requires us constantly to explain to ourselves what is happening to us. Of course, we can only do this using models that we already know. However, a capacity to remain open and interested means that we are able to "learn from experience", which means to modify previous "explanations" as a result of receiving a new and different view. The explanations that we create form a set of unconscious beliefs which build into the conscious mind. The healthy human being is one who maintains curiosity, interest, and an open mind.

For an organization to function in a healthy way, this needs to be built into the fabric. In other words, there needs to be a basic establishment of a *culture of enquiry*. Without this, the system will become seriously dysfunctional. Now, just as with individuals, even where such a system has been established initially, it can be switched off. Indeed, the prevalence of a paranoid–schizoid or fundamentalist state of mind will tend towards certainty as preferable to discovery, which brings us to the development of open systems theory and the relevance of feedback loops. For a long time it was believed that scientific experiments could only take place in closed systems, such as a test tube: an environment in which the only items involved were known about and, therefore, the variability was under the control of the experimenter. The need for better and better mechanisms for accurately firing big guns led to the study of feedback loops. This led scientists to realize that you can observe and experiment on systems that are open because you can take into account the effect on the environment of those systems and the effect of the environment on them. This opened a whole new science, which has led us to be aware of ecology (again, I am in danger of a digression). What I want to abstract from this is the concept of the feedback loop and the way that it is so important to the particular open system that we call an organization. Just as the plant needs to be able to connect to the surrounding environment, so the organization needs to connect not only to its environment, but also to its own internal processes. A healthy system is one in which there is a flow, like that of blood, in which there is a delivery downwards and a reception upwards. The delivery is of delegated responsibility and the reception is of information. To put it another way, anxiety is passed up the system (so that it can be processed by the "mind" of the organization) and authority to act is passed down the system. The "ground floor" provides the most sensitive sensory system, providing information about the interface with the work or with the environment. This contact provides both conscious and unconscious information. Crudely speaking, the worker can make observations about the work, but will also be unconsciously affected by it. The conscious observations can be passed up in the form of reports and the unconscious information will be experienced as some form of emotional experience, usually connected with anxiety. This is often the most important form of feedback and requires a system for turning it into meaningful data.

Team as container

To come back to the issue of containment that I left to give a quick view of what I mean by the "mind" of an organization, I need just to say something briefly about this function. As I said earlier, I am drawing on Bion's model of container–contained (Bion, 1962a). This is not a static arrangement like an object held in a glass. It is a dynamic arrangement in which the contained is in active intercourse with the container. The container itself is in an active internal intercourse that serves to transform the raw, emotional communication from the contained into meaningful information that can be understood and fed back to the contained in a palatable fashion. The key here is that the container is able to absorb emotional and psychological communications without retaliating, and has a capacity within itself (internally) to turn the emotional content into meaningful information. Bion, describing the relationship between mother and baby as container–contained, described the mother's capacity to make this transformation as "alpha-function" (Bion, 1962a); another way to describe it is "thinking". This leads us to ask the obvious question: what, in an organization, equates to thinking in an individual? The answer to that is thoughtful, open communication between all parts of the system, which is then acting as if it were a "container". Finally, it is important to recognize what makes up a container. It is the physical environment in which the work is carried out, the administrative systems that process information, the supportive systems that maintain the environment, the rules that provide socio-emotional boundaries for the activity and, most importantly, the staff team.

What can get in the way of healthy function?

I am turning now to the specific client groups that we are discussing in this book, those with complex and challenging mental health problems and particularly those from a forensic population. Nevertheless, the first thing to be said applies to all human service organizations. The thing that gets in the way of the organization working well is people, both workers and clients, although the particular character of any organization will be a reflection of the client group.

What do I mean by saying that the people get in the way? It is an often repeated joke to say that this school/hospital/social work unit would work beautifully if it was not for the pupils/patients/clients. The moment you get a group together and confront them with a task, anxiety arises (as Bion (1961) pointed out). It is equally true to say that patients or clients only enter a "therapeutic" system with anxiety. When the anxiety of the client group meets the anxiety in the staff group, there is room for either a very interesting exchange or an investment in setting up systems to avoid this sort of encounter. Unfortunately, the latter option appears to be the option of choice. Hence, the term coined by Jaques when he first described this phenomenon (1951), "Social systems as a defence against anxiety" (this phenomenon is best described by Jaques' colleague, Menzies Lyth, in her seminal paper (1988)).

The processes that can obstruct healthy functioning in an organization, not surprisingly, are versions of those that obstruct healthy function in the individual. If we take each of the elements in turn, we can describe these sorts of defensive arrangements.

The physical environment

Often, the clients attack the environment, typically by dropping litter, cigarette ash, or drinks, sometimes by writing on the walls or furniture. The organization that recognizes this as a communication addresses it, but the organization that cannot do this either produces more and more stringent rules to "control the behaviour", or gives up in a rather hopeless, depressed way and leaves the environment to collapse. A supervisee of mine, who was providing consultation to a hostel working with very challenging long-term mentally ill patients, discovered that, although she arrived in good time for the consultation, she could not get in. This turned out to be because the front door bell did not work. Not only did the staff know about it, they seemed incapable of addressing it. Several weeks went by, with the consultant forced to bang on the door to be let in, before the bell was mended. Of course, that only happened after she was able to help the team to understand the meaning of this sabotage.

Administrative structures

Under this heading, I want to gather not only the bureaucracy of the recording system, but also the people who record the data, the means by which records are shared, and the methods by which one layer in the system communicates with another. When it is functioning properly, this is an important feedback loop. However, as with the physical environment, the message may be too "emotional" for the team to pick up and handle. It is often the case that the secretaries in a psychological therapies unit hold a central place. The question to ask is: what does the specific nature of this place tell you about the way the system is functioning? A typical example is the way that secretaries might start to complain about the way they are treated by the clinical staff. A cursory glance might produce a decision to require clinicians to act in a more sensitive way. While this is not inappropriate, it seems clear that the feelings, the beliefs about the feelings, as well as the consequent solution, are accepted without any attempt to understand what, if anything, might lie behind this. In the example I am thinking about, when it was suggested to the clinicians that one of them ought to take time to meet with the secretaries to think about the problem, it became clear that there was massive resistance to doing so. My interpretation was that it served some purpose to leave this tension between administration and clinician. A meeting did occur, and it was found that the feelings of intrusion and demand that the secretaries were lodging with the clinicians reflected exactly the experience that the trainee clinicians were having but not speaking about. Further investigation revealed that there had been a significant increase in borderline personality disorder patients recently. These less experienced clinicians were feeling very intimidated by them, but, equally, because they were training, they felt they could not complain. This was an important discovery, because the feelings that the clinicians were avoiding gave real information about the state of mind of the patients: their powerful neediness that was also very demanding and controlling.

Supportive systems

Here, I am referring to those roles and structures designed to keep the show on the road, which includes cleaners, cooks, receptionists, and porters. For example, I remember that when I was newly appointed manager of an assessment centre for adolescents, I began to meet once a week with the domestics, giving them an opportunity to talk about their work, their frustrations, and so on. They quickly became quite worked up as a group, and it seemed as if there was a big problem between a couple of the domestics, who also worked as assistant cooks, and the head cook. There were disputes as to whether the cook stuck to the agreed menu. The assistants were complaining that she was no good, she kept changing the menu, she could not cook anyway, and had only been made a cook because nobody else wanted the job. The head cook was, in turn, angry with them for undermining her. At first, it seemed as if this was a personal, or group, issue, not in the least connected to the clients. However, by spending some time trying to explore the issue, it became clear that what was being experienced was a massive attack on the whole group from the adolescent residents. Not surprisingly, these adolescents, brought into care because they were not being properly looked after at home, were expressing all of their feelings about nourishment by attacking that provided by the institution. Of course, the problem for the domestic staff was that nobody had warned them this might happen; they were struggling to make sense of their food being rejected and they found an explanation in an unresolved group issue. The key to all of this lay in examining why it was that nobody had wanted the job of cook when the current cook had finally taken it on. It was because there was no pleasure in having your food constantly rejected. Once it was possible to see that the problem pre-dated the apparent explanation, the group were able to think about what was really going on. The issue could then be taken up by the team with the

adolescents, who eventually no longer needed to express their feelings in this destructive way.

Rules

These are often the most important elements of a therapeutic
container. It is a mistake to think that the rules have to be some sort
of "final word"; they are really there to enable encounters to take
place. A "not here but there" or "not then but now" rule allows for
something to be acted out and yet thought about. In other words,
the technique is, in the first place, to reinforce the rule and immediately to explore the reason why it was breached. Things go wrong
when the rules become the most important part of an encounter.
When Richard Balbernie turned the Cotswolds Approved School
into the Cotswolds Therapeutic Community, he revealed something
important (Wills, 1971). He told the staff, whom he had inherited
along with the establishment, that he was going to reduce the rules,
get rid of the regimentation and replace it all with discussion. They
told him that he was mad, and that there would be riots. They were
right. Before he arrived, the approved school had a good reputa-
tion, there was never any trouble, nothing to set off an enquiry,
everything was peaceful and ordered. Of course, it was also true
that the place did not stop any of its inmates from reoffending.
Balbernie's changes revealed that the system had been so peaceful
because it was held together by bullying. The older boys were able
to live a quite privileged life as long as everything was calm, so it
was in their interests to keep the younger boys in line. Of course,
the younger boys did not complain about this, not only because
they were frightened, but also because they knew that they would
be in the position of the older boys in due course. The point is that
the anxiety that the staff expressed when Balbernie threatened to
remove the rules, that everything would become violently out of
control, was the reason that the system had created such a rigid,
rule-bound structure in the first place. The cost was that no real
work ever happened because there were never any real encounters
between staff and residents.

Staff

This is the part of the container that is most vulnerable to the setting
up of defensive processes. It is not only the most sensitive receptor

of emotional communication, it is also the mechanism by which the group equivalent of thinking can take place. You will remember that I said this was free communication. The thing about organizations is that they need to be thoughtfully created, which means that important processes have to be part of the structure. In the case of the process that Bion called alpha-function and I am calling thinking, a structure is also required. In other words, it is vital for the healthy team that something like a clinical discussion or a reflective practice meeting is fixed in the timetable and that attendance is obligatory. Even then the general facts about groups will apply, that is, there will be pressure to avoid anxiety by some sort of defensive process like Bion's basic assumption states (1961).

I want to make a final statement here. If you think that a healthy organization is free from these processes, you are very much mistaken. The fact is that struggling with the impact of projections and anxiety *is* the work. Clients or patients will communicate the most important messages unconsciously and through an emotional language. These communications will be received unconsciously, as Freud pointed out, "It is a very remarkable thing that the unconscious of one human being can react upon that of another, without passing through the conscious" (Freud, 1915, p. 198), which means that the recipient is often the last person to recognize what has happened. However, his or her colleagues will, even if their first explanation for this attaches to the personality of the staff member rather than a guess about the true origin in the patient group. This is why thinking in the context of teamwork requires more than one person; the "other" is required to point out what the subject does not notice.

*What interventions might be brought
to bear to enable healthy function?*

I cannot provide a complete summary of all the interventions that might be brought to bear in the attempt to help an organization or team with a problem. What I shall do is to describe how I would approach a referral. This approach represents the protocol that has been set up at the Tavistock Centre in the Adult Department by a team that I used to run called the Short Course Intervention Team.

This clumsy name reflects two things, my own problem finding titles for things and the more specific difficulty of capturing the philosophy that lies behind the intervention itself. I shall try to capture something of that and then describe the process of dealing with a referral.

When I was twenty-seven, I was promoted to be the manager of one of the treatment units in the Youth Treatment Centre that I described earlier. I was the youngest member of staff on site and younger than all of my own staff team. This led to the most awful couple of years of my professional life. I used to shake on the way to work, feeling overwhelmed with anxiety about what would be waiting for me when I got there. I would also feel terribly guilty if something had happened, if, for example, one of the adolescents had been acting out. Eventually, I trained in Organisational Consultancy at the Tavistock Centre, and suddenly I felt as if I could see. I discovered that these awful feelings were not simply mine and my responsibility to deal with (I used to feel I had to keep them hidden from my team, for instance). Actually, they were feelings that were projected into me by the clients and by the staff. Best of all, I discovered that they had a meaning and that, if I could only talk about them with the team, we might be able to understand it. Almost overnight, that which had been a source of great unhappiness and self-doubt became the opposite; it became the source of excitement because these were all clues to understanding at a really deep level. This experience made me want to share the model that enabled that to happen.

Over the many years between qualifying as an organizational consultant until I came to work at the Tavistock Clinic, I had a very frequent experience. Someone from a team would contact me to ask for consultation and I would discover that they were unable to use the consultation because they did not have a shared language or a shared model for understanding their work. The combination of these experiences led me to create the intervention: a combination of teaching a model for the understanding of the emotional and psychological development of the human mind, and how that connects with group dynamics and organizational processes. It is unapologetic didactic teaching of a model that the team member will understand at the end of the process, although they are free either to accept or reject it. The trick lies in the fact that this teaching session is followed after a break by a mini group relations session. The task of this meeting is simply to link what the members are learning to their work and to their current experience in this group. The tutor/consultant (as we call ourselves) points out to the group what is going on that they are not aware of. Thus, they have a direct experience of how the model may be applied to them as a team.

In addition, we have some basic principles, which I have summarized below.

The model

- We believe that there really *is* a model that helps to turn what appears to be difficulty into *information*, so we present that model unapologetically and clearly, while conveying that the students are free to take it or leave it.

Learning

- We believe that the student's learning is the responsibility of the tutor/consultant, who is free to alter the focus of the session according to what is going on in the room . . .
- Therefore, we provide handouts that summarize the content, so students do not have to take notes.
- We speak plain English: I believe that, although jargon is a useful shorthand among professionals, if it is used in teaching sessions, it is probably because you do not understand what you are talking about (or what your task is).
- We encourage questions and challenges during the lectures.
- We believe that the process will reveal the unconscious preoccupations of the group. Part of what we are doing is to help the team to discover organizational factors getting in the way of the work.

Flexibility: each group accessing this intervention has specific requirements

- Therefore, the syllabus includes "bolt-on units" to meet those particular needs.

- Although it is usually a ten-week intervention, we can alter this if necessary (we have run the intervention in the form of a series of one-day workshops).
- We apply our model from the first contact, so we begin by trying to understand why this organization has come to us.

This is often the intervention of choice for many of the teams and organizations that we are invited to help. The reason for this is that, although they are dealing with some of the most challenging and difficult client groups, the workers are often young, inexperienced, and untrained. Essentially, they are struggling to survive without any access to the most important tools for survival.

The process that leads to a decision about an intervention often begins with someone from the distressed team calling to ask for help. From my point of view, the moment I start this initial conversation (usually a telephone call), I have started the consultation. This means that I listen to what is being described and what is being requested, but I take it as axiomatic that the main problem is hidden, so I am also listening for what is not being spoken about. I observe my own emotional response to the referrer and assume that this will be relevant to understanding the problem. I do all of this, but I do not assume yet that I can work out what is really going on. The next thing is to find out who is able to authorize the work, and I arrange a meeting. I have learnt from bitter experience that it is absolutely essential to establish exactly who has the delegated authority to make a contract—who holds the purse strings?

So, my next step is to arrange a meeting with the management group. I let them decide who should be there as long as the person with the authority is one of them. Clearly, whom they invite to the meeting will be further information for me. There are two reasons why I meet with the management first: the first is that a successful intervention with the team will almost certainly lead to a demand for change (in my experience at the end of the intervention, over 80% of the teams decide that they have to create a structure that assures a place for thinking), thus, management need to be signed up to this in advance. Second, it often becomes clear that the management group themselves need some sort of intervention, in which case it is better to start with them.

After meeting with the management and hearing their view of what the intervention should address, I meet with the team itself and go through the same piece of work, identifying the problem and getting them to sign up to it. Only after all of this do I go away to think, ideally in a meeting with colleagues who have not been part of this process, about the best intervention. I write up a proposal that I bring to the management and then to the team. The last point, however, and this is, in many ways, the most important, I do not start the work until there is a signed contract that names the task of the intervention. I need to be authorized in order to act; the contract is my authorization. The following is a list of some of the interventions that I might offer.

Consultancy to management: This can take the form of a full consultation to the management team or the Board of Directors, or it might be a role consultation for the manager of the system that seems to be in trouble.

Reflective practice groups: These are essentially opportunities for staff to come to speak about their experience of their work, bringing examples. The aim of the meeting is to think about the unconscious factors that are affecting the team and apply them as information about the work. In my view, the reflective practice group has taken the place of what used to be called the staff support group, or the staff sensitivity group, although some may argue that the staff support group has a wider brief, that is, to consider the organizational issue that impinges on the team. In my view, you deal with these things in a reflective practice group as well. The important thing is to make a contract that makes it absolutely clear what the task of the group is. I find that I need to write into the contract something about the principles that I bring to the work and that will guide the way I intend to conduct the group. There are two main principles:

1. I hold it as a fact that we are all professionals who come to work in order to do a good, professional job. However, it is axiomatic in this sort of work that, if we are any good at the job, we will get caught up in it. This will often be expressed as behaviour or attitudes that appear to be unprofessional. It is,

therefore, the purpose of the group to notice how we become caught up and to address that from the point of view of understanding what this tells us about the work. It is not an investigation into the personality of the individual member of staff.

2. Whatever comes into this group is confidential to the group, but, if there is anything that gives me cause for concern about the work and the group seems unable or unwilling to take it up properly, I shall feel free to take my concerns to the management, because I am accountable to the management for this work.

You may notice that principle number one is absolutely vital to this process because we are such complex creatures that any behaviour, particularly behaviour that causes concern to our colleagues, will always seem to be explicable in terms of our own personality. Therefore, if we begin with an exploration of the personal, we will always appear to find the cause there. However, beginning with the exploration of which aspects of the work might explain what is happening here means that either we find that explanation, which is good, or we do not, which means we have proved that it really is about the individual. At which point the issue becomes a management one, to be addressed outside the group.

Clinical consultancy to teams: Clinical consultation is a focused intervention in which the individual members of the team bring their clinical work for an in depth discussion It is a form of supervision. Work discussion (or work based discussion): This is another term for clinical consultancy except that it is part of the tradition for trainings that feature in the Tavistock and similar institutions. As part of their course, students are provided with a seminar to which they bring examples of their work for discussion by the seminar group, under the leadership of a member of the teaching staff. This approach has been taken out into the field, although it is still usually part of a larger training intervention.

Education: I think that whatever intervention we make, we need to be aware that there is always a need for some sort of training. For example, supervision, particularly in the beginning, involves teaching by using the presentation to provide an opportunity to give a name to a process and then link that to theory.

Conclusion

I have tried to offer a model for thinking about organizations and about what can go wrong with one. My belief is that organizations are constantly trying to manage unconscious processes in the same way as we are individually. There is a generic tendency to avoid anxiety, which is often accompanied by organizational structures that serve to keep anxiety at bay. Anxiety is the emotional accompaniment to the unconscious transfer of information from client to team. If this anxiety is responded to by a mechanism that shields the system from knowing about it, the information that is carried within this "wave" of anxiety will be lost to conscious thought. It will become part of the material for a different kind of attention, the attention to the team and its members and their personal problems. In other words, the "information" will be lodged in the system and will be experienced as if it originates therein. This is dangerous, both to the team and the individuals. The alternative is to recognize that this emotional exchange is inevitable as long as we are working, therefore, it is in the best interests of all concerned to create a space designed to identify these pieces of information and translate them into meaningful data.

References

Armstrong, D. (2005). *Organization in the Mind*. London: Karnac.

Bion, W. R. (1961). *Experiences in Groups*. London: Tavistock.

Bion, W. R. (1962a). *Learning from Experience*. London: Karnac.

Bion, W. R. (1962b). The psycho-analytic study of thinking. *International Journal of Psychoanalysis, 43*: 306–310.

Freud, S. (1915e). The unconscious. *S.E., 14*: 159–204. London: Hogarth.

Freud, S. (1916–1917). *Introductory Lectures on Psycho-Analysis. S.E., 15–16*. London: Hogarth.

Jaques, E. (1989). *Requisite Organization*. Arlington, VA: Cason Hall.

Menzies Lyth, I. (1988). The functioning of social systems as a defence against anxiety. In: *Containing Anxiety in Institutions* (pp. 43–85). London: Free Association Books.

Turquet, P. (1951). Leadership, the individual and the group. In: D. Colman & M. H. Geller, (Eds.), *Group Relations Reader 2* (pp. 71–87). Springfield, MA: A. K. Rice Institute, 1985.

Wills, W. D. (1971). *Spare the Child*. London: Penguin.

INDEX